INTENSIVE PSYCHOTHERAPY
OF ALCOHOLISM

INTENSIVE PSYCHOTHERAPY OF ALCOHOLISM

By

GARY G. FORREST, Ed.D., Ph.D.

Clinical Psychologist
Executive Director, Psychotherapy Associates, P.C., and
The Institute For Addictive Behavioral Change
Colorado Springs, Colorado

JASON ARONSON INC.
Northvale, New Jersey
London

1997 printing

THE MASTER WORK SERIES

First softcover edition 1994

ISBN: 1-56821-360-3
Library of Congress Catalog Card Number: 94-77918

Manufactured in the United States of America. Jason Aronson Inc. offers books and cassettes. For information and catalog write to Jason Aronson Inc., 230 Livingston Street, Northvale, New Jersey 07647.

TO VICTOR, ELLEN, AND VIC

PREFACE

Alcohol addiction and alcohol abuse cause major social, health, psychological, economic, family, and legal problems in the United States. Many behavioral scientists believe that alcoholism is the number one American health problem.

It is estimated that there are over eleven million alcoholics in this country. One out of every ten adults in this country has a serious drinking problem. Approximately three million adolescents have received professional treatment for alcoholism or alcohol abuse, and American teenagers typically begin to drink between the ages of thirteen and fourteen. Twenty-five percent of adolescents in grades seven through twelve drink alcoholic beverages on a weekly basis. Thousands of Americans are killed each year in automobile accidents by intoxicated drivers. Alcohol abuse costs industry over forty-five billion dollars each year! Thirty percent of our hospital beds are occupied by individuals who are being treated for alcoholism or various medical complications that have been caused by drinking and intoxication. Marital and family problems, job loss and vocational problems, sexual dysfunction and deviation, depression, stress, incest, child abuse, and violence are consistently facilitated by alcoholism or alcohol abuse.

Traditionally, alcoholics and alcohol abusers have been reluctant to enter psychotherapy and seek out professional treatments for their drinking disorders. Psychotherapists have been reluctant to treat alcoholics, and many clinicians have refused to attempt therapy with these individuals. The general public has long believed that alcoholics are "weak-willed," evil, or immoral and incapable of remaining sober. Unfortunately, many psychotherapists and health service providers continue to believe that alcoholics and problem drinkers rarely evidence constructive growth and behavioral change as a function of psychotherapy and psychological treatments.

Many of the old beliefs, dogmas, and stigmas associated with alcoholism and alcoholism treatment have changed significantly during the last decade. Indeed, the zeitgeist has been right for numerous constructive changes within the alcoholism field for several years. Behavioral scientists have begun to recognize the intricate relationships and associations between alcoholism and a plethora of health, social, psychological, economic, and legal processes. Millions of federal and state dollars have been allocated for alcohol and drug abuse research. Graduate schools and medical schools are beginning to include formal courses and instruction in the areas of alcoholism and addiction. Addiction treatment programs are becoming an integrated component of the mental health center, hospital, military, and private psychotherapy practice health service delivery systems.

Several hundred thousand alcoholics and alcohol abusers seek out psychotherapy and other professional treatments each year in the United States. These individuals are frequently "nudged" or forced into treatment by a social system that has become increasingly intolerant of their various alcohol-facilitated inappropriate or deviant behaviors. More alcoholics are self-motivated to enter psychotherapy. Community and media alcohol education and awareness efforts consistently tell these individuals and their families that recovery and effective treatments are possible. Certainly, the "public" alcoholism recoveries of our former First Lady, Betty Ford, and Billy Carter, as well as several famous celebrities and athletes, have made it easier for the average person to (1) admit and accept the reality of manifesting a serious drinking problem, and (2) seek out professional help for such a problem. As thousands of alcoholics recover each year, our collective societal systems of denial, ignorance, stigma, and irrational beliefs undergo a slow but systematically adaptive, constructive, and enlightened evolution.

Psychotherapists are becoming progressively more cognizant of these same realities. Increasing numbers of psychologists, psychiatrists, family and marital therapists, social workers, school counselors, rehabilitation counselors, and pastoral counselors are attempting to do psychotherapy with alcoholics and problem drinkers. Most clinicians have very little formal clinical training, education, and supervision in the areas of alcoholism and addiction psychotherapy. Many therapists do attempt to gain expertise in alcoholism psychotherapy by attending educational seminars and workshops that provide didactic and experiential training in this area. Unfortunately, some therapists and counselors continue to use the trial-and-error approach to learning how to do effective alcoholism psychotherapy.

This book is written for all therapists and health service providers that are involved in the psychotherapy and rehabilitation of alcoholics and alcohol abusers. Psychiatrists, psychologists, physicians, social workers, alcoholism counselors, nurses, rehabilitation counselors, counselor educators, and all health educators will find this text extremely useful in their clinical and academic work with alcoholic patients, as well as students. This book is an excellent resource for supervising psychotherapists and advanced clinicians. Indeed, the book represents a major contribution to the alcoholism treatment literature. The focus of this work is the intensive psychotherapy of primary alcoholism.

The basic psychopathology of alcoholism and addiction is explained in Chapter One. The aetiological and characterological dimensions of narcissism, anxiety, orality, depression and dependence, avoidance defenses, sadomasochism, paranoia, rage, acting-out, guilt and obsession, and compulsion in primary alcoholism are systematically explored. Differential diagnosis of drinking disorders, alcoholisms, and the diagnostic process in intensive alcoholism psychotherapy are considered in Chapter Two. The alcohol-related DSM–II and DSM–III categories are also delineated in this chapter. Chapter Three addresses the basic components of the early stages of intensive alcoholism psychotherapy: structural dimensions of treatment, establishing a working and productive therapeutic alliance, genetic reconstruction work, initiating an addiction focus, confrontation techniques, patient commitment to abstinence and the treatment process, and the use of therapeutic self-help adjuncts. Chapter Four delineates the basic components of the middle stages of intensive alcoholism psychotherapy: insight, interpretation and self-awareness, resistance, transference and countertransference dynamics, initiating a

here-and-now treatment orientation, cognitive-behavioral intervention strategies, sexual counseling and sex therapy, intensive
confrontation techniques, maintaining an addiction focus, and
relapse and massive regression. Chapter Five explores the basic
components of the later stages of intensive alcoholism psychotherapy: synthesis and working through, projective identification
and identity consolidation, dream work, termination, and ancillary treatment issues. The final chapter considers the vicissitudes
of alcoholism recovery: treatment outcome and effectiveness, abstinence and beyond, responsibility and life style changes, love and
intimacy, work, social concern, and fully-functioning and potential self-actualization.

There are a multiplicity of treatments available for alcoholism
and substance abuse. Professional health service providers use
individual, group, family, conjoint, and somatic therapies in their
treatment efforts with alcoholics. Different *schools* of psychotherapy utilize relatively different therapeutic approaches and techniques. The nonprofessional or self-help treatments for alcohol
addiction include Alcoholics Anonymous and the AA community,
exercise and nutrition, positive addictions, and religion.

All primary alcoholics and many alcohol abusers need intensive individual alcoholism psychotherapy. Moreover, these individuals usually receive various forms of individual counseling
and therapy as a part of the various alcoholism treatment programs that they enter. Unfortunately, most alcoholics and alcohol
abusers never receive effective intensive psychotherapy. Alcoholics do not receive intensive individual psychotherapy because
most alcoholism therapists and counselors are not trained and
experienced in the use of this particular treatment modality. This
book provides systematic and comprehensive clinical training in
the use of intensive alcoholism psychotherapy. The various therapist skills and techniques that are needed to do effective intensive
individual psychotherapy with primary alcoholics are thoroughly
examined throughout this book.

Most alcoholics receive some form of supportive and superficial individual counseling for a number of other pragmatic reasons.
The patient's spouse or family refuse to enter treatment; hundreds
of thousands of primary alcoholics simply do not have a spouse or

family; the patient refuses to participate in other treatments and alcoholism treatment programs; and psychotherapists tend to be limited in the number of professional therapy alternatives that they can provide. This book provides a very effective and pragmatic solution to these various dilemmas: intensive alcoholism psychotherapy.

Many people have contributed to this book. I must thank my wife, Sandra, and our children, Sarah Ellen and Allison Giustina, for their love, patience, support, and encouragement. Living with a writer can be difficult, and they have simply made this process much easier and less painful for all. My colleagues and friends at Psychotherapy Associates, P.C., and The Institute for Addictive Behavioral Change, David A. Sena, Ph.D., Lawrence E. Wellman, Ed.D., and Barbara Martin, ACSW, LSWII, have been very encouraging, helpful, and supportive. A great deal of appreciation must also go to my typist, Mrs. Dorothy Allen, who has done a superb job of interpreting, translating, and typing a difficult manuscript!

Finally, I must again communicate a special thanks to the many patients that I have worked with in therapy over the last fifteen years. We have taught each other a great deal. They have taught me about alcoholism, recovery, and life. More importantly, our work and experiences have taught me how to do effective intensive alcoholism psychotherapy. These experiences in alcoholism therapy have enabled me to help several hundred alcoholics recover. Hopefully, several of the ideas and concepts in this book will eventually prove heuristic.

CONTENTS

INTENSIVE PSYCHOTHERAPY
OF ALCOHOLISM

Chapter I

THE PSYCHOPATHOLOGY OF ALCOHOLISM

INTRODUCTION

It is impossible to do effective psychotherapy with alcoholics in the absence of a sensitive understanding of the global psychopathology of alcoholism and chemical dependency. The psychotherapist needs to be consistently involved in psychotherapy with alcoholics for several years in order to develop a keen awareness of the behavioral, cognitive, affective, and life-style pathology of this clinical population.

Every alcoholic or alcohol abuser (Forrest, 1978, 1982) is a relatively unique human being. The psychopathology of alcoholism does not always generalize to include a specific symptom structure that applies to each alcoholic. It is important for the psychotherapist to recognize that his or her alcoholic patients manifest a wide range of individual differences. The basic common denominator in alcoholism is simply the inability to drink responsibly (Zimberg, 1982). Alcoholics are unable to control their drinking. Beyond this point of commonality, some alcoholics are continuous drinkers, while others are sporadic binge drinkers. Some alcoholics drink only vodka, while others drink wine or beer. Many alcoholics appear to be behaviorally passive and dependent. Others are assertive, aggressive, and overtly sociopathic. In short, alcoholics manifest relatively different behavioral, cognitive, affective, and life-style symptom structures.

Alcoholism is a disorder of paradoxes (Forrest, 1983b). The psychopathology of alcoholism involves many chameleon-like dimensions. The alcoholic can appear to be passive, inadequate, and depressive one minute, and angry, manic, and perhaps even dangerous the next. Alcoholics are unable to control their lives, and yet they manifest an uncanny ability to control and manipulate everyone around them. The paradoxical dimension of the alcoholic adjustment style includes the capacity to manifest any or all forms of the psychopathology elucidated in this chapter. A few alcoholics do not overtly display the varieties of pathology that are discussed throughout this chapter. However, once engaged in the process of intensive psychotherapy, most alcoholics do evidence a basic core of psychopathological behaviors, cognitions, and affects. This constellation of pathology forms the content of this chapter.

The psychopathology of alcoholism is also progressive. Alcohol abusers and incipient alcoholics are generally less psychologically conflicted and less disturbed than chronic alcoholics. The developmental process of alcoholism encompasses increasing affective disturbance, family disturbance, progressive medical complications, and acting out and social deviance. Alcohol abuse and alcoholism eventually cause (Forrest, 1983a) sexual dysfunction and even sexual deviation.

Alcohol addiction, per se, also occurs in a progressive fashion. In general, experimentation with drinking and alcohol leads to alcohol abuse that eventually precipitates alcohol addiction. This paradigm describes the drinking history of most alcoholics. Alcoholics do not become tissue addicted within a matter of days or weeks. Most alcoholics become addicted to alcohol following several months or years of drinking. Women alcoholics and adolescent alcoholics (Forrest, 1983b) do tend to develop alcohol addiction more quickly than the adult male alcoholic. Alcohol dependence results in a physiological imperative to drink. The addicted person experiences acute anxiety, agitation, possible hallucinations and delusions, disorganization, and changes in pulse, respiration, coordination, blood pressure, and other basic vital signs following the abrupt cessation of alcohol ingestion. Alcoholics drink in order to deter the experience of delirium tremens, otherwise known as "DTs" or "the shakes." The withdrawal process actually begins when the alcoholic sleeps or is unable to ingest alcohol over a period of several hours.

Psychological dependence accompanies the process of physical dependence. The alcoholic is psychologically dependent upon alcohol and drinking prior to the establishment of tissue dependence. Psychological dependence entails relief drinking, drinking in order to experience anxiety reduction or euphoria, and drinking in order to feel powerful or adequately masculine or feminine. Indeed, psychological dependence upon alcohol is a precursor to the development of physical dependence.

Clinicians and psychopathologists (Fenichel, 1945; Cameron, 1963; Blane, 1968; Forrest, 1978; Fann, Karacan, et al., 1980; Forrest, 1983b) have written a great deal about the emotional conflicts and psychopathology of the alcoholic. Unfortunately, most of the clinical and research literature that addresses the psychopathology of alcoholism is truncated, fragmented, and lacking in depth. The specific aetiology of alcoholism remains unknown.

In spite of the paradoxical and sometimes conflicting dimensions of alcoholism, it is possible to delineate the basic psychopathology of this disorder. This chapter elucidates (1) the aetiological factors in alcoholism, and (2) the intrapersonal and interpersonal psychopathology of alcoholism.

AETIOLOGICAL FACTORS IN ALCOHOLISM

There are several (Gottheil, Druley, Skoloda, and Waxman, 1983) aetiological theories of alcohol addiction. In reality, the specific cause or causes of alcoholism are not known. Several types of alcoholism have also been delineated in the clinical and research literature (Knauert, 1979; 1982; Pattison, 1980, 1983). Psychotherapists need to be familiar with the various models and theories of alcohol addiction. Therapists also need to be cognizant of the many limitations that are basic to current theories of addiction. The psychotherapist's beliefs and knowledge associated with the aetiological theories of alcoholism shape and determine his or her style of therapy and use of particular treatment interventions with alcoholic patients.

Alcoholism is a multivariantly determined disorder. Thus, biologic and physiological variables in combination with psychological, sociocultural, familial, and situational factors contribute to the development of alcoholism. Historically, alcoholism researchers and therapists have failed to (1) adequately understand the role of multiple causality in the aetiology of alcohol addiction, and

(2) realize that there are several types or forms of alcoholism.

There are many biologic and genetic theories of alcoholism. Yet, biological science (Goodwin, 1983) has not demonstrated the precise role of heredity in the aetiology of alcoholism. Jellinek (1945) investigated a sample of 4,000 alcoholics and found that 52 percent of the group had at least one alcoholic parent. This researcher (Jellinek, 1945) concluded that alcoholism is determined by hereditary influence vis-à-vis constitutional instability to the social risks of inebriation. Family and twin studies (Winokur, Reik, and Rimmer, 1970; Schuckit et al., 1972; Cadoret, Cain, and Grove, 1980) consistently indicate that one-half of the male first-degree relatives of alcoholics develop alcoholism. Nearly one-half of the female first-degree (parents, children, siblings) relatives of alcoholics have a history of depressive disorders.

It has also been theorized that alcoholism is caused by an endocrine disorder (Smith, 1950, 1951). This model asserts that alcoholism is caused by a pituitary deficiency, which results in secondary adrenal-cortex exhaustion. Scientific research has not validated the endocrine theory of alcohol addiction.

Williams (1951) proposed a genetotrophic theory of alcoholism. This model asserts that an inherited defect in metabolism results in nutritional deficiency that causes an abnormal craving for alcohol. Research evidence does not substantiate the validity of this theory.

The "allergy" theory of alcoholism maintains that a particular body chemistry results in a loss of control over drinking once the allergic person ingests alcohol. Human beings manifest various degrees of physiologic and psychological sensitivity to the ingestion of ethanol. However, the allergy theory is not widely accepted by clinicians, and research data do not support this model. It has been found (Fenna, Mix, Schaefer, and Gilbert, 1971) that Eskimos and Indians do require longer periods of time to clear alcohol from the blood than Caucasians. Thus, research evidence suggests that there are racial differences in sensitivity and response to ethanol.

Recent research (Shoemaker, 1982) suggests that alcoholism may be facilitated or caused by brain chemistry and central nervous system factors. The roles of brain chemistry and the neurotransmitters in the aetiology of alcoholism are not clearly understood. However, this area of scientific investigation is exciting and may represent the focal point of future alcoholism research. It is known that alcohol has a profound effect on the neurotransmitters. Alcohol causes a very rapid turnover of CNS norepinephrine. Alcohol also has a toxic effect upon the brain and can result in cerebral atrophy.

The biologic and genetic theories of alcohol addiction are directly or tangentially associated with the "disease" concept. The disease concept of alcoholism simply suggests that alcohol addiction is a disease. The American Medical Association defined alcoholism as a "disease" over twenty years ago. Alcoholics Anonymous has been a major social and organizational proponent of the disease concept of alcoholism for over forty years. The National Council on Alcoholism recognizes alcoholism as a disease. According to the disease model of alcoholism (Edwards, 1970), when the predisposed person comes into contact with alcohol, he or she activates a disease process that ultimately includes the various symptoms and characteristics specific to the diagnosis of chronic alcoholism. As a disease, alcoholism is congruous with leukemia, cancer, diabetes, and other recognized physiological disease processes. Many alcoholism researchers (Armor, Polich, and Stambul, 1978; Emrick, 1983) reject the disease concept of alcoholism. Indeed, the disease model of alcoholism has generated a great deal of heated controversy and debate among alcoholism treatment personnel and the lay community.

Psychological theories of alcoholism are also divergent in scope and content. Psychoanalytically-oriented theories of alcoholism (Menninger, 1938; Fenichel, 1945; Blum and Blum, 1967; Forrest, 1983b) stress the importance of intrapersonnel processes in the development of this disorder. Thus, oral fixation, self-destructive trends, sexual conflicts, and early childhood experiences are basic to analytically-oriented explanations of alcoholism. It is important to point out that the psychoanalysts have not been active in the treatment of alcoholism and substance abuse.

Personality theorists (Blane, 1968) have attempted to identify the "alcoholic personality." These efforts have failed. There is no basic or singular personality type that is associated with alcoholism.

However, there are several personality and behavioral traits or characteristics (Forrest, 1980) that alcoholics manifest. These behavioral and personality traits include poor impulse control, low frustration tolerance, sexual and identity problems, irresponsibility, depression, anxiety, immaturity, inferiority, grandiosity, dependency, and manipulation.

The relief theory of alcoholism is based upon the clinical observation that many alcoholics experience significant psychological relief following the ingestion of alcohol (Milt, 1969). This theory of alcoholism is based upon learning theory. The alcoholic experiences stress, anxiety, fear, or other powerful negative affects, and then ingests ethanol. Drinking results in relief or anxiety reduction. This process is repeated, learned, overlearned, and eventually becomes a physiologically determined response. Alcohol ingestion (Yost and Mines, 1984) does result in stress and tension reduction. Drinking also creates feelings of well-being and euphoria.

Applied social learning theories (Wellman and Evans, 1978) of alcoholism assume that (1) all voluntary behavior is learned, (2) since behavior is learned, it can also be "unlearned" or extinguished, and (3) the primary problem is the maladaptive (alcoholic) behavior. Learning, conditioning, and reinforcement are key ingredients in the aetiology of alcohol abuse and alcohol addiction. Social learning theories also suggests that poor social skills and faulty learning, in combination with drinking in order to extinguish feelings of anxiety, contribute to the development of patterns of alcohol abuse.

A recent (Forrest, 1983b) psychological theory of primary alcoholism indicates that consistent early life narcissistic injury is a primary aetiological ingredient in chronic alcoholism. The primary alcoholic has experienced profound narcissistic need and entitlement deprivation during infancy and childhood. Unfortunately, most alcoholics have experienced consistent and devastating narcissistic injuries through subsequent developmental eras. This theory of alcoholism is interpersonal and intrapersonal in nature. It is generally similar to the deprivation model, which suggests that alcoholics have experienced global early life deprivation.

Environmental-psychological theories of alcohol addiction and abuse (Heath, 1983) associate parental, familial, geographic, and situational variables with patterns of alcohol use and abuse. Thus, 70 percent of teenagers who have nondrinking parents do not imbibe. It has been found that when both parents are drinkers, about 80 percent of their teenage sons and/or daughters are drinkers (Forrest, 1983c). Growing up in a slum or ghetto may influence drinking patterns. Social environments do influence such factors as the social acceptability of drinking, drinking styles and behaviors per se, attitudes associated with drinking, and the roles of alcohol in the culture. The incidence of alcoholism is relatively low in societies that maintain a total abstinence attitude. However, the incidence of alcoholism is high in societies that maintain inconsistent and ambivalent attitudes toward the use of alcohol. Alcoholism rates are also high in societies that have very permissive attitudes toward the use of alcohol and drinking to intoxication (Zimberg, 1982).

The French have a very high rate of alcoholism. Alcoholism is low in the Moslem countries. Alcohol use, abuse, and addiction are high in the United States, Ireland, and the Soviet Union. Jews have a low rate of alcoholism; however, alcohol abuse and addiction are rising among American Jews. Blacks have a high incidence of alcoholism. Native Americans (Forrest, 1976) have been devastated by alcoholism. Obviously, a plethora of environmental-psychological variables are associated with various individual and cultural patterns of alcohol use, abuse, and addiction.

PSYCHOPATHOLOGICAL PROCESSES IN ALCOHOLISM

It is apparent that the specific aetiology of alcoholism is unknown. The various biologic, psychological, and environmental processes discussed thus far can be considered as predisposing factors in alcoholism. Unfortunately, the precise role and cybernetic "weight" of these factors in the aetiology of alcohol addiction also remains unclear.

Alcoholism develops in a progressive manner that is relatively unique for each alcoholic. The developmental process of alcoholism involves an individualized interaction effect of biological, psychological, and environmental variables. This interaction effect constitutes the psychopathology of alcoholism. The experience of intensive psychotherapy with alcoholic persons provides the therapist with an intimate awareness and understanding of the intrapersonal, interpersonal, familial, and environmental sources of psychopathology in alcoholism. Therapy relationships with alcoholics can sometimes help clarify the roles of physical and medical factors in the development and maintenance of alcoholism.

The narcissistic need and entitlement deprivation model of primary alcoholism (Forrest, 1983b) attempts to integrate the influences of biological, intrapersonal, interpersonal, and environmental processes in the aetiology and psychopathology of alcoholism. This model is presented in Table I.

As indicated in Table I, the fundamental aetiological factors in primary alcoholism are interpersonal and intrapersonal. Secondary aetiological factors in alcoholism are genetic-biophysiological and involve brain chemistry, blood sugar, metabolism, endocrine, and other physiologic processes. Thus, pervasive early-life narcissistic injury in combination with familial, interpersonal, self-concept, self-dialogue, and genetic-biophysiological processes create and contribute to the psychopathology of alcoholism. According to this model, the developmental role and consequences of various biophysiological variables in the psychopathology of alcoholism cannot be delineated. However, the impact and developmental consequences of pervasive early-life narcissistic need and entitlement deprivation upon the development of the alcoholic character structure, personality, and adjustment style are clearly shown in this model of alcoholism.

Early-life narcissistic injury occurs primarily within the rubric of mother-object-significant others relationships. The experience of consistent and pervasive narcissistic need and entitlement deprivation facilitates the development of the alcoholic character structure and adjustment style. Narcissistic needs refer to the basic physical needs of the infant and child. Infantile and childhood narcissistic needs include feeding, elimination, holding and touching, communicative interaction, temperature control, and generalized "mothering." Narcissistic needs always include significant psychological components. However, the most basic physical survival needs of infants and children are referred to as narcissistic needs.

TABLE I.
The Psychopathology of Alcoholism

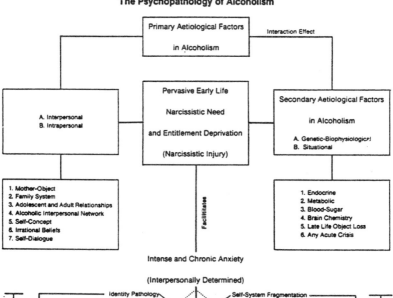

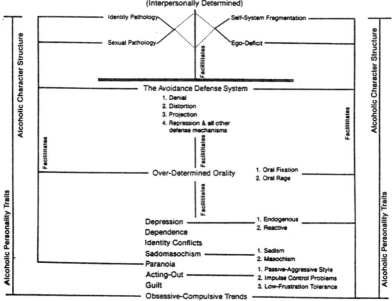

These needs are narcissistic because they are self-sustaining and self-oriented. Psychological illness, physical illness, developmental deficit, and even death can occur as a result of narcissistic need deprivation.

Narcissistic entitlements refer to the emotional and psychological components of the mother-infant-child relationship that convey to the developing person a basic sense of adequacy, self-worth, dignity, respect, and generalized well-being. The healthy and adequate fulfillment of narcissistic entitlements fosters a sense of being loved, valued, and needed. This process facilitates the capacity for healthy early-life self-respect and self-love that eventually enables the person to love others. The capacities for empathy, adaptive object-attachments, and rational social concern evolve from healthy early-life narcissistic need and entitlement gratification. Obviously, narcissistic needs and narcissistic entitlements involve various physical, psychological, and interpersonal components. The concept of narcissistic injury is used interchangeably with the concept of narcissistic need and entitlement deprivation throughout this text.

It is important to point out that human beings are almost totally dependent during the stages of infancy and childhood. Infants and children cannot provide for their own life-sustaining narcissistic gratifications. Significant others must provide adequate narcissistic supplies for the infant and child. Paradoxically, the narcissistic needs and entitlements of the evolving person are very much other-person-oriented!

Infants and children do not choose their parents. The nurturing and parenting skills of the alcoholics' parents or surrogate parents have been inadequate. This unfortunate reality is largely a measure of random chance. However, this reality plays a crucial role in the development of the psychopathology of alcoholism. The interpersonal and intrapersonal experiences of the alcoholic during infancy, childhood, adolescence, and adulthood have been consistently disturbed. Most alcoholics (Ackerman, 1978; Wegscheider, 1981; Wilsnack, 1982; Black, 1983; Forrest, 1983b, 1984) have experienced early-life abuse and neglect. Parental death, sibling death, separation, divorce, and other more psychological forms of object loss are common denominators in alcoholism and addiction (Paolino and McGrady, 1977; Knauert, 1980; Martin, 1982; Khantzian, 1983). Alcoholics have experienced consistent lifelong parental and familial criticism and psychological abuse. Some have experienced a great deal of early-life physical abuse and violence.

Pervasive infantile and early childhood narcissistic injury is a primary precursor to the development of characterologically determined acute and chronic anxiety and panic. The alcoholic has experienced consistent anxiety and near terror within the context of the mother-infant relationship. This process fosters self-system fragmentation and ego-deficit. Fears and intense anxiety associated with issues of annihilation, abandonment, rejection, and intimacy are also basic to the character structure of the alcoholic.

Alcoholics have not experienced a healthy symbiotic fusion and closeness with the mother-object. Intimacy and consensual validation are distorted in highly anxious mother-infant relationships. Thus, the narcissistic injuries that alcoholics sustain within the early-life mother-infant relationship result in (1) chronic interpersonally-determined anxiety, (2) self-system fragmentation or ego-deficit, (3) intimacy conflicts, (4) identity disturbance and ego-boundary pathology, and (5) sexual problems. Alcoholics are anxious within the context of their relationships with people. The anxiety of the alcoholic is interpersonally determined, target specific, and directly proportional to the degree of intimacy experienced in any human relationship or encounter. Alcoholics also manifest various sexual problems (Forrest, 1983a). Sexual pathology is prototypically associated with self-system fragmentation and identity disturbance. Alcoholics tend to feel inadequately masculine or feminine (Menninger, 1938; Fenichel, 1945; Wilsnack, 1973, 1982; Forrest, 1983a).

In order to control or bind catastrophic levels of infantile and childhood anxiety, the alcoholic develops an avoidance defense system (Forrest, 1983c). The avoidance defense system is constructed vis-à-vis the overdetermined utilization of denial, distortion, and projection defense mechanisms. The avoidance defense system serves the purpose of binding anxiety by keeping threatening affects, feedback, and reality external to the self. The avoidance defense system is also a defense against intimacy. Thus, the alcoholic avoids or externalizes a significant degree of early-life narcissistic injury through the use of denial, distortion, and projection defenses. Alcoholics also repress and suppress the many painful realities of their childhoods. Indeed, the alcoholic utilizes all of the defense mechanisms in the service of his or her addiction. The specific defense mechanisms that constitute the avoidance defense system are quite primitive. These defense mechanisms are basic to the alcoholic character structure. They are overdetermined and become pathologically functional between the ages of eighteen months and four years.

The avoidance defense system also enables the alcoholic to remain out of touch with self-perceptions, feelings and affects, and self-dialogue. The avoidance defense system is a defense against the external world as well as the internal self. Denial defenses represent the most primitive method for totally rejecting and blocking out reality. Distortion defenses involve changing or bending reality operations. Reality is then less threatening and less painful. Projection allows the alcoholic to blame others and the external world for threatening feelings and uncomfortable realities. Avoidance tactics are basic to the psychopathology of alcoholism.

Disturbed orality is basic to the pathology of alcoholism. Psychoanalysts and Freudian personality theorists (Knight, 1937; Fenichel, 1945; Freud, 1953) view alcoholism as an oral fixation. In actuality, the analysts and Freudians (Bratter, 1984) have not been active in the psychoanalysis and treatment of alcoholics and addicts. There is also a dearth of systematic and in-depth psychoanalytic literature dealing with the psychopathology of alcoholism.

The prototaxic oral feeding experiences of the alcoholic have extinguished anxiety and provided tension reduction and pleasure. The basic security operations of alcoholics are orally fixated and orally overdetermined. Oral gratification has been the alcoholic's primary and perhaps only consistent form of infantile gratification. Infantile feeding, breast contact, and the various sources of mothering that accompany the feeding process constitute the relative experiential antithesis of narcissistic need and entitlement deprivation. These processes and realities facilitate the development of the alcoholic's characterological oral fixation. Alcoholic beverages become the symbolic equivalent of milk for alcoholics. Infants ingest milk, experience tension and anxiety reduction, and then consistently sleep or become stuperous. Alcoholics ingest alcohol, experience anxiety reduction and a plethora of other affective and cognitive changes, drink to the point of intoxication, and then consistently pass out, sleep, or become stuperous.

The pervasive orality of the alcoholic is destructive, fused with anger and rage, and cannibalistic. Infants express primitive feelings of anger and rage vis-à-vis the oral dynamism. Screaming, crying, "nipple attack," and biting or chewing are basic components of the infantile and childhood oral behavioral repertoire. Alcoholics have experienced a great deal of oral gratification early in life, and they have also developed a characterological style that involves the oral management of anger and rage. Alcoholics orally cathect their angry feelings against the self and others. Thousands of alcoholics literally drink themselves to death. These are examples par excellence of oral suicide. Alcoholics also verbally and orally attack, criticize, castrate, and destroy significant others. The oral pathology of the alcoholic is ultimately self-destructive and masochistic.

Alcoholism is a disorder that involves dependency pathology. Alcoholics are pathologically dependent. Dependency conflicts are fused with the oral dynamism. Pervasive infantile narcissistic need and entitlement deprivation experiences impede the development of a healthy symbiotic, dependent mother-infant relationship. Intense and chronic mother-infant-child anxiety also impedes the process of establishing and resolving primitive early-life dependency needs. An infantile and early childhood symbiosis or ego-fusion with the mother object is a basic prerequisite for developing the capacity for healthy self–other differentiation and eventual independence. Alcoholics have a primitive need to be mothered. They look for significant others who will nurture them and meet their inordinate dependency needs. Many alcoholics are passive-dependent. Some attempt to reject their intense dependency needs by manifesting a counter-dependent adjustment style. Alcoholism per se is dependency. Alcoholics are overly-dependent and thus prone to developing smoking addictions, eating problems, caffeine dependence, and other patterns of substance abuse and addiction (Marcovitz, 1983).

An overdetermined oral character structure is associated with pathological dependence and depression. Early-life narcissistic injury results in depression. The depressive conflicts of alcoholism (Della-Giustina and Forrest, 1979; Forrest, 1983c) are essentially endogenous. However, many alcoholics manifest neurotic or reactive depressions. A few alcoholics become psychotically depressed after entering treatment and establishing sobriety. These psychotic depressions tend to be short-term. The early-life interpersonal and intrapersonal world of the alcoholic has been depressive. Many alcoholics drink in order to cope with depression. Women alcoholics (Blume, 1984; Wilsnack, 1984) tend to manifest more depression than male alcoholics. Alcohol is a central nervous system depressant. Eventually, alcoholics make themselves depressed through the addiction process.

The ego pathology and identity conflicts of the alcoholic precipitate the development of an overdetermined sadomasochistic character structure. During infancy and childhood, the alcoholic has been sadistically hurt by significant others. These sadistic early-life transactions with significant others involve emotional and physical pain. There may or may not be a primary sexual component in the early-life sadistic experiences of the alcoholic. The infant is enraged as a result of being narcissistically injured by significant others, and attempts to sadistically retaliate. Unfortunately, infants and children also incorporate and internalize the experience of narcissistic injury. Thus, the ego-structure of the alcoholic includes a very powerful and destructive masochistic component. The alcoholic behaves according to the unconscious and preconscious dictate, "I deserve to be punished." As with young children, alcoholics cannot rationally and logically comprehend that they do not "deserve" to be hurt and sadistically punished.

The masochism of alcoholism involves inflicting pain upon the self. Alcoholism is a form of masochism. Alcoholics inflict pain upon themselves via fights, physical injuries, automobile accidents, divorces, arrests, job losses, suicide, emotional problems, and family problems. Alcohol-induced liver disease, neurologic impairments, gastrointestinal problems, and other bodily system disorders are excellent examples of masochism and self-destruction. The sadism of alcoholism involves inflicting pain upon significant others and objects tangential to the self. Alcoholics verbally and physically destroy their spouses, families, and loved ones (Forrest, 1980). They kill thousands of people on our highways each year. The sadistic retaliations of the alcoholic consistently result in masochistic self-reprisals. Sadism and masochism are bipolar as well as ego-syntonic components of the self-system. Therefore, the character style of the alcoholic is sadomasochistic (Schad-Somers, 1982; Forrest, 1983c).

An inadequately consolidated nuclear sense of self (Forrest, 1983c) contributes to the development of paranoid trends and a paranoid character structure. Basic identity conflicts and unresolved questions about the self facilitate paranoia and a paranoid world view. Alcoholics are often overtly suspicious, guarded, defensive, and nontrusting. Very early in life, alcoholics have learned that they cannot trust other human beings. Narcissistic need and entitlement deprivation experiences teach the alcoholic that significant others are potential sources of harm, danger, and catastrophic threats.

Alcoholics manifest chronic feelings of inadequacy, inferiority and self-doubt. Alcoholics feel inadequate in a sexual and gender sense (Wilsnack, 1973; Forrest, 1983c). The identity and sexually determined paranoid trends of the alcoholic can be related to bisexual and homosexual conflicts (Menninger, 1938; Fenichel, 1945). However, very few alcoholics are explicitly homosexual in object choice. Alcoholics feel inadequate as human beings, not simply as sexual beings. The alcoholic also creates paranoid feelings and thoughts via the addiction process. Alcohol facilitated deviant behaviors and roles, blackouts and memory problems, and cognitive confusion can actively contribute to paranoid thinking and the outcropping of paranoid ideation.

Acting-out pathology is central to alcoholism. Historically, clinicians (Fenichel, 1945; Knauert, 1979; Pattison, 1983; Forrest, 1983c) have tended to diagnose alcoholics as character-behavior disorders, sociopathic or psychopathic personalities, and passive-aggressive personalities. The complex issue of differential diagnosis will be discussed in the following chapter. The alloplastic, acting-out behaviors of the alcoholic serve the purpose of binding or controlling intense anxiety associated with early-life narcissistic injury. Many alcoholics report that they were hyperactive as children and adolescents. Low frustration tolerance, restlessness, poor stick-to-itiveness, and constantly "being on the go" are behavioral characteristics that describe most alcoholic persons.

Alcoholics cope with chronic and acute anxiety by acting out. Alcoholism per se can be viewed as an acting-out or impulse disorder. Sexual and aggressive acting out are basic components of the alcoholic adjustment style. The alcoholic acts out sexually in order to compensate for underlying feelings of sexual inadequacy. Acting out represents a neurotic solution to basic identity conflicts and self-system fragmentation. Alcoholics are able to feel more adequately male or female through their sexual relationships.

The acting-out behaviors of the alcoholic are invariably destructive. Alcoholics consistently hurt themselves and significant others by acting out. Acting out is also a defense against acting in. The alcoholic attempts to avoid the emotional pain and hurt that is associated with acting in as compared with the process of acting out. Alcoholics are afraid of their feelings and internal struggles. Yet, they destroy themselves physically and psychologically by avoiding the reality of their internal being. Acting out is a defense against intrapersonal and interpersonal intimacy. These factors contribute to the alcoholic's impaired capacity for forming healthy, loving attachments with significant others. The spouse and family of the alcoholic are devastated by these realities. They cannot understand the grandiose, impulsive, self-centered, iconoclastic, and cavalier behaviors and attitudes of the alcoholic. The alcoholic's manipulative, exploitive, and "conning" behaviors are ultimately self-destructive as well as destructive within the marital and familial relationships.

Obsessive-compulsive psychopathology is a fundamental component of the alcoholic character structure and behavioral style. The alcoholic is an obsessive-compulsive sui generis. The purpose of the obsessive-compulsive dynamism is also to bind and control anxiety associated with early-life narcissistic injury (Marcovitz, 1983). An obsessive-compulsive character structure precedes the onset of alcohol addiction. This style of adjustment is characterized by orderliness, frugality, perfectionism, rigidity, and stubbornness (Salzman, 1968; Rachman and Hodgson, 1980; Forrest, 1983c). Obsessive-compulsives also avoid feelings and affects. They are prone to philosophizing, rationalization, procrastination, ambivalence, grandiosity, depression, and struggle with intrusive homosexual thoughts.

Alcoholics drink compulsively. They are not able to consistently drink one or two alcoholic beverages. The alcoholic drinks in order to become intoxicated, and this process usually involves a pattern of compulsive alcohol ingestion. It is very difficult for many clinicians to understand that alcoholics are simply unable to control their drinking. Most alcoholics intermittently attempt to control or stop their drinking. Many are "on guard" against the compulsive urge to drink following the establishment of sobriety. Alcoholics also tend to be compulsive workers and perfectionists. Indeed, alcohol addiction is only one facet of the alcoholic's globally compulsive adjustment style.

Alcoholics are obsessive. They manifest many irrational fears, and some are phobic. Ritualistic and magical thinking are basic ingredients of the alcoholic cognitive style. Alcoholics are obsessed with alcohol and drinking. Alcoholics often obsessively attend to liquor advertisements and media advertisements that pertain to drinking.

The obsessive and compulsive components of the alcoholic character structure (1) reinforce each other, (2) are ego-syntonic, and (3) serve the addiction process. Alcohol addiction is an obsessive-compulsive disorder (Forrest, 1983c).

Affective pathology is also associated with alcoholism. Guilt is a core-affective ingredient in alcohol addiction. Indeed, most alcoholics experience chronic guilt conflicts (Forrest, 1983c). The alcoholic's guilt conflicts are associated with depression, early-life narcissistic injury, and alcohol-facilitated irresponsible behavior. Alcoholics struggle with chronic irrational guilt feelings. Irrational guilt feelings stem from early-life experiences that condition the alcoholic to believe that he or she is unloveable, inadequate, worthless, and a failure. Adult alcoholics continue to experience these destructive self-perceptions and affects. Feelings of low self-esteem synergize neurotic guilt conflicts and depressive symptoms.

The rational guilt conflicts of alcoholics are determined in the here and now. Alcoholics make themselves feel guilty vis-à-vis their alcohol-facilitated irresponsible and irrational behaviors. It is appropriate for the alcoholic to experience guilt following a drunken debauch or after assaulting his or her spouse or children. Alcoholics make themselves guilty on hundreds of occasions. The process of continually making oneself feel guilty as a result of drinking is inappropriate and neurotic. However, the capacity to internalize guilt can be a favorable prognostic indicator of treatment outcome. Guilt can play an important role in the recovery from alcoholism. Guilt, remorse, and intrapersonal conflicts *push* many alcoholics into sobriety and recovery. Unresolved guilt also contributes to the physical and psychological destruction of many alcoholic persons.

The alcoholic adjustment style and character structure are globally pathological and paradoxically adaptive (Forrest, 1983c). The adjustment dynamisms discussed thus far in this chapter also determine or shape the processes of (1) spouse selection, (2) marital adjustment, and (3) family adjustment. Alcoholics and children of alcoholics (Black, 1983) tend to recreate their experiences within the original alcoholic family system regarding the creation of subsequent alcoholic family systems. This repetition compulsion is basic to the psychopathology of alcoholism.

The *behavioral* style and behavioral pathology of alcoholism include anxiety, low frustration tolerance, depression, anger, acting-out and impulse control problems, low self-worth, negative self-concept, dependence-independence struggles, identity and sexual problems, defensiveness and rigidity, pervasive orality, generalized self-defeating style, chronic interpersonal problems, guilt, inability to tolerate intimacy and form healthy object attachments, grandiosity and an over-idealized self-image, irrational fears, and obsessive-compulsive trends. These behaviors are manifest and overt before the onset and during the course of alcoholism for most, if not all, alcoholics. Although the behavioral style of every alcoholic is relatively unique, these behaviors are central to the areas of conflict that most alcoholics experience. Recovery from alcohol addiction is behavioral. Long-term sobriety and effective alcoholism treatment (Emrick, 1980) precipitate various adaptive behavioral changes. However, the alcoholic behavioral repertoire (Liebson and Bigelow, 1983) and character structure are always relatively recalcitrant to change.

THE ALCOHOLIC INTERPERSONAL NETWORK

The alcoholic character structure is shaped and determined during infancy and childhood. The various subsequent developmental life stages may also influence character structure and personality development. Adolescent and adult relationships affect behaviors, emotions, cognitions, and global adjustment. Indeed, there is an ever-present and increasingly interpersonal thrust throughout the lives of most human beings.

Parental and peer group modeling affect the drinking behaviors of adolescents. Peer-relevant factors immediately and directly (Forrest, 1983b) shape such characteristics of specific drinking episodes as quantity consumed, speed and duration of drinking, and beverage type. Adolescent drinking companions (Blane, 1982) are chosen on the basis of "affinity in drinking styles and attitudes." Teenage alcoholics and alcohol abusers socialize and drink together. The teenage drinker experiences considerable "peer pressure" that reinforces alcohol and drug use and abuse. Adolescent alcoholics are invariably engaged in an interpersonal network that actively and consistently reinforces drinking. The adolescent alcoholic interpersonal network involves drinking peers, drinking adults, people that purchase alcoholic beverages for the young drinker, and virtually all other people who "enable" and reinforce the addiction process. Thus, parents and other family members, teachers, drinking cohorts and "friends," bartenders and liquor store owners, and even the police may be active participants in the adolescent alcoholic interpersonal network.

The adult alcoholic interpersonal network also plays a crucial role in determining and shaping the alcoholic's drinking behaviors. Adult alcoholics tend to socialize with other alcohol abusers and alcoholics. The alcoholic interpersonal network includes all people who reinforce and maintain the addiction process. Thus, work colleagues who drink with the alcoholic each evening, the compliant spouse and children, parents, and bartenders are usually key people in the alcoholic interpersonal network. The skid row or Bowery drinking milieu has an alcoholic interpersonal network. Skid row alcoholics "share" a bottle of wine, "con" the liquor store owner for alcohol, and actually take each other to the hospital in crisis situations. So-called *closet drinkers* and addicted housewives often depend upon the taxicab driver and the liquor store owner to maintain their addictions. In sum, people always play important roles in the initiation and maintenance of the addiction process. It can be hypothesized that the alcoholic cannot function alcoholically in the absence of his or her involvement with an alcoholic interpersonal network. The alcoholic interpersonal network shapes the alcoholic's beliefs, attitudes, feelings, behaviors, values, cognitions, and life-style.

It is important for the psychotherapist to realize that the alcoholic interpersonal network reinforces and supports a plethora of deviant behaviors. In addition to drinking and alcoholic behaviors, the alcoholic interpersonal network can reinforce global socially deviant roles and behaviors. Thus, sexual and violent acting-out behaviors might be associated with the alcoholic's enmeshment in an AIN (alcoholic interpersonal network). Poor career choices, inappropriate occupational behaviors, divorce, child neglect or abuse, drunk driving, indecent exposure, and a multiplicity of other socially deviant roles and behaviors can be actively reinforced and synergized by the AIN.

Recovery from alcoholism is usually predicated upon the termination of involvement with an alcoholic interpersonal network. The psychotherapist needs to actively reinforce the recovering alcoholic's movement toward people and social situations that do not support and maintain drinking and social deviance. The recovery process is both interpersonal and intrapersonal. Recovering persons need to develop new friendships and object attachments. They also need to terminate many of their old malignant relationships. It is impossible for the alcoholic to actualize healthy sobriety, growth, and change while remaining statically attached to the AIN.

SUMMARY

The psychopathology of alcoholism is complex and multifaceted. Alcoholism is a disorder of individual differences. Alcoholism is a progressive disorder. Behavioral scientists (Zimberg, 1982) continue to investigate the various aspects of alcohol abuse and alcohol addiction. It is known that there are several different forms of alcoholism, as well as different alcoholism treatments (Pattison, 1983). The specific aetiology of alcoholism is not known. Several aetiological theories of alcoholism were outlined in this chapter. Alcoholism is a familial disorder that appears to be multivariantly determined (Forrest, 1983c).

The psychopathology of primary alcoholism was elucidated in this chapter. The differential diagnosis of primary alcoholism (Knauert, 1979, 1982) is based upon such criteria as (1) an extended history of tissue dependence, (2) initial drinking experiences resulting in intoxication and "relief", (3) an intense relationship or "love affair" with ethanol, (4) medical complications specific to alcoholism, (5) absence of an underlying primary psychiatric disorder, (6) history of primary life trauma(s) specifically associated with drinking and intoxication, and (7) early-life deprivation, abuse, or object loss. The differential diagnosis of alcoholism distinguishes between primary, secondary, and reactive types of alcoholism. Secondary alcoholism occurs as a response to serious underlying psychiatric disorder (schizophrenia, character disorder, or affective disturbance). Reactive alcoholism occurs in response to a specific life crisis (object loss, divorce, job loss). The differential diagnosis of alcoholism has been explored by several alcoholism researchers and clinicians (Forrest, 1978; Knauert, 1979; Pattison, 1980; Zimberg, 1982; Gottheil, Druley, Skoloda, and Waxman, 1983).

Pervasive early-life narcissistic need and entitlement deprivation or narcissistic injury results in the psychopathology of primary alcoholism and is closely associated with the pathology of the other alcoholisms. Characterologically determined intense anxiety, identity pathology, oral fixation, avoidance defenses, depression, dependence, acting out, sadomasochism, guilt, and an obsessive-compulsive style constitute the basic psychopathology of alcoholism. The vicissitudes of alcoholism pathology are intrapersonal and interpersonal. Alcoholics are conflicted within. Alcoholism is also a *people* problem and interpersonal disturbance is central to this disorder.

The addiction process per se creates and reinforces the psychopathology of alcoholism. Thus, alcoholics make themselves progressively more depressed, anxious, compulsive, impulsive, manipulative, and sexually conflicted as a result of drinking. During the early and middle stages of the addiction process (Forrest, 1978), drinking and intoxication reduce or neurotically extinguish many of the alcoholic's sources of conflict. This process is reversed later in the developmental course of alcoholism. Drinking reinforces and synergizes the alcoholic's various conflicts during the later stages of the addiction process.

Drinking alcoholics are involved in interpersonal networks and relationships that actively reinforce and maintain their aberrant alcoholic behaviors. The alcoholic interpersonal network (AIN) reinforces a plethora of inappropriate and deviant social behaviors. The spouse, children, and friends of alcoholics often engage in a diversity of enabling and permitting roles that maintain the addiction process. Alcoholism recovery is, in many respects, contingent upon the alcoholic's ability to disengage from the alcoholic interpersonal network and form new and healthy nondrinking object attachments. Psychotherapists need to play an active role (Bratter, 1984) in helping their alcoholic patients establish new friendships and adaptive group memberships.

Chapter II

DIFFERENTIAL DIAGNOSIS AND THE DIAGNOSTIC PROCESS IN INTENSIVE ALCOHOLISM PSYCHOTHERAPY

INTRODUCTION

The role of diagnosis is controversial in the treatment of psychiatric and psychological disorders. Many behavioral scientists (Rogers, 1952; Szasz, 1961; Glasser, 1965; Szasz, 1974, 1976) believe that psychiatric diagnoses result in patients being stigmatized, alienated, and even persecuted. Indeed, it has been repeatedly suggested (Szasz, 1976) that psychiatric diagnoses often become labels that are destructive and medically iatrogenic. Historically, mental patients have received a plethora of medical and psychological treatments that were destructive. In the not too distant past, mental patients were tortured, flogged, institutionalized for life, castrated, and burned at the stake. These persons were in various ways identified, stigmatized, persecuted, and labeled lunatics or insane.

Modern psychiatry and clinical psychology are based upon the medical model of treatment. Many other behavioral science disciplines also utilize medically-oriented treatment models and interventions. Diagnosis is the cornerstone of modern medicine. Elaborate and very sophisticated medical technologies have been developed to diagnose and assess cardiac problems, brain pathology, gastrointestinal problems, and the various other human subsystems. These diagnostic technologies have greatly enhanced the global efficacy of modern medicine and contributed to the health and well-being of millions of people.

The general psychiatric viewpoint of aberrant behaviors, affects, cognitions, and adjustments is disease oriented. Thus, most, if not all, forms of psychopathology are viewed as diseases or caused by underlying medical-biophysiological factors. Psychiatric and psychological diagnoses are based upon medical-biological theories and assumptions. The process of establishing a psychiatric diagnosis is similar to that of establishing other medical diagnoses. However, the patterns of behaviors, affects, cognitions, and living that are associated with different psychiatric labels or diagnostic categories may or may not reflect the presence of an underlying disease process.

Psychiatrists, psychologists, social workers, and other behavioral scientists have developed various tests, rating scales, physical procedures, and methods for assessing and diagnosing emotional problems. There are many physical-medical treatments for emotional problems and mental illness. These treatments are usually prescribed upon the basis of a psychiatric or psychological diagnosis. The psychotropic medications are physical treatments for anxiety, depression, and schizophrenia. Lithium is often used in the treatment of manic-depressive illness. Electroconvulsive (ECT) treatment is sometimes employed with patients who are diagnosed as severely or psychotically depressed. Thousands of hospitalized chronic schizophrenics have received ECT and other somatic treatments. Several years ago, lobotomies were routinely performed on aggressive and violent mental patients. Behavioral scientists often place emotionally disturbed people in hospitals and other controlled environments in order to establish an accurate diagnosis and provide adequate physical and psychological treatments. Hospitalization can also be initiated in order to assure the physical safety of the patient and society.

It is apparent that behavioral scientists manifest a diversity of beliefs about the roles and relevance of diagnosis in the treatment of psychological problems. The Rogerian, existential, and humanistic therapists (Forrest, 1978) have actively moved away from the use of diagnosis in their treatment efforts. Many of the newer schools of counseling and psychotherapy do not emphasize the importance of diagnosis as such in therapy (Glasser, 1965; Harris, 1969; Ellis, 1979). Medically trained psychotherapists generally continue to utilize the medical model of diagnosis and treatment. Most therapists are ambivalent about the role of diagnosis in psychotherapy. However, all therapists and mental health workers are confronted with the realities of routinely making diagnoses and being versed in diagnostic nomenclature in order to receive reimbursement for their professional services by the health insurance industry!

This chapter clarifies (1) the role of diagnosis in alcoholism treatment, (2) dimensions of the diagnostic process, and (3) differential diagnosis of the alcoholisms. These issues tend to be inadequately understood by many psychotherapists and alcoholism clinicians.

THE ROLE OF DIAGNOSIS IN ALCOHOLISM TREATMENT

Physicians, psychotherapists, and mental health workers tend to underdiagnose alcoholism. Health providers that are themselves recovering alcoholics tend to overdiagnose alcoholism (Lawson, Pertosa, and Peterson, 1982). Nearly one-third of admissions to general hospital psychiatric units are alcoholics and drug abusers; 15 to 50 percent of general hospital medical service patients are treated for alcoholism or alcohol-related medical complications; 25 to 30 percent of patients treated in hospital emergency rooms are alcoholic, and alcoholism is the number one discharge diagnosis for Medicare and Medicaid patients in New York County general hospitals (Zimberg, 1982). A significant percentage of general psychotherapy outpatients manifest serious chemical dependency problems.

As discussed in Chapter One, alcoholism is a disorder that involves the overdetermined utilization of denial, distortion, projection, repression, and avoidance defenses. Therefore, an initial step in the psychotherapy of alcoholism is that of accurately assessing and diagnosing the patient's drinking behavior. The clinician needs to utilize the clinical interviewing process, medical history, familial and social history, psychological testing, legal and work history, and possibly medical diagnostic testing in order to accurately diagnose and assess the patient's drinking behavior. It can also be helpful to include the patient's spouse or other family members in the initial diagnostic evaluation. These individuals can often provide important feedback relative to the patient's drinking behavior and global adjustment style. The clinician also needs to realize that the patient's spouse and other family members sometimes distort, deny, and overreact to the drinking. A few of these individuals are themselves alcoholics or drug abusers.

The psychotherapist finds in some cases that he or she is unable to accurately diagnose the patient after one or two clinical interviews. In these situations, I have often found it efficacious to schedule the patient to come in for three or four subsequent diagnostic-treatment sessions. These subsequent diagnostic-therapeutic sessions are scheduled at two to three week intervals. This diagnostic strategy allows the therapist to evaluate the patient's behavior, affect, and cognitive style over relatively extended periods of time. Furthermore, some of these individuals eventually appear to be "hung over" and in other ways demonstrate that they manifest a serious drinking problem. This procedure also allows the therapist and patient to develop a relationship that can foster patient honesty, trust, and openness relative to the drinking issue. This procedure is also helpful in identifying individuals who are not alcoholics or alcohol abusers.

Once the clinician has formulated a diagnostic impression of the patient, this formulation is openly and honestly shared with the patient (Forrest, 1978). Thus, the clinician might share with a patient that based upon his or her clinical experience, research data, medical and legal data, and spouse input that he or she believes that the patient has (1) no drinking problem, (2) primary alcoholism, or (3) another appropriate clinical category of alcoholism or alcohol abuse. It is also appropriate for the clinician to openly tell the patient that he or she has not been able to formulate a precise diagnosis or assessment of the patient's drinking behavior. This procedure is usually followed by implementing the diagnostic strategy outlined earlier for difficult cases.

The diagnostic technique of openly discussing the diagnostic formulation with the patient facilitates several sources of psychotherapeutic gain. First of all, this procedure is not steeped in distortion or denial. This technique involves honesty, genuineness, and reality. It lets the patient know exactly how the therapist perceives his or her drinking. Furthermore, this technique helps minimize therapist involvement in "patsy" roles (Steiner, 1971).

Importantly, this strategy assesses the alcohol abuser or alcoholic's readiness for therapy and treatment. Alcoholics that are not motivated or committed to therapy sometimes respond to this technique by failing to make subsequent treatment appointments or by seeking out another therapist. Many alcoholics and alcohol abusers are somewhat upset about hearing their diagnoses but respond very favorably to this strategy by committing themselves to the treatment process. These individuals often verbalize a sense of relief associated with knowing that someone else knows or understands their problem. Diagnosis literally means "knowing through."

This technique incorporates the magic of words (May, 1973) and is tantamount to the therapist saying "Your problem is known and has causes — we can do something to effect constructive and positive change." This strategy also helps some alcoholics and alcohol abusers begin to accept and deal with the various stigmas that are associated with these labels and behaviors. Finally, the technique of openly discussing the diagnostic formulation with the patient implicitly defines (1) the need or lack of need for treatment, (2) treatment goals, and (3) areas of psychotherapy or treatment outcome assessment. This technique is also confrontation oriented (Forrest, 1982). It represents the therapist's first systematic attempt to resolve the alcoholic's avoidance defense system. Diagnostic sharing can be an integral component in therapeutic relationship building.

DIMENSIONS OF THE DIAGNOSTIC PROCESS

Diagnosis is process oriented. The diagnostic process begins when the patient enters the therapist's office and begins to communicate and interact with the secretary or other office personnel. Some patients arrive for their initial therapy session intoxicated. Many alcoholics and drug abusers are overtly angry, depressive, manipulative, and confused in their initial interactions with office personnel and the therapist. Alcoholic patients frequently advise the secretary that they do not have a drinking problem but that they have decided to come in for an alcohol evaluation at the request of their spouse or family. Increasing numbers of people are being court ordered to complete professional alcohol assessment and alcohol education classes. Most of these people have been arrested for drunk driving (DUI, DWI) or other alcohol-related legal offenses. These individuals tend to be angry and hostile about being "ordered" to complete an alcohol evaluation.

A few alcoholics and alcohol abusers enter treatment as a result of a sincere desire to either stop drinking or control their drinking. Some of these individuals may have previously completed several residential alcoholism treatment programs. A few have been in outpatient psychotherapy with one or more therapists for varying periods of time. Many of these people have never been involved in any form of prior professional or self-help alcoholism treatment.

In all of these clinical situations, an accurate clinical assessment and diagnosis of the patient's drinking behavior is essential to successful treatment. Sometimes people are inappropriately referred to the psychotherapist for alcoholism treatment. These individuals may have psychological problems but may not be alcoholics or alcohol abusers. Obviously, it is clinically inappropriate and unethical to treat such individuals for alcoholism or chemical dependency. People are frequently referred to psychologists and psychiatrists for such mental health problems as depression, marital difficulty, anxiety, sexual dysfunction, and poor impulse control. Many of these individuals are alcohol dependent or consistently abuse alcohol and/or other drugs (Zimberg, 1982; Forrest, 1983a).

Clinicians sometimes misdiagnose alcoholics and, as a result, fail in their treatment efforts. It is very difficult, if not impossible, to successfully treat a seriously depressed person vis-à-vis intensive psychotherapy and antidepressant psychotropic medication if that person consumes a pint or quart of vodka each evening! It is, therefore, also clinically inappropriate and unethical to treat people for depression or another primary psychiatric/psychological disorder when they are actually alcoholics or addicts. Clinicians need to be very astute and sensitive in their diagnostic work.

As touched upon earlier, the clinician actively explores the patient's drinking history and drinking behaviors, medical history, social and family history, legal history, and vocational status during the initial one or two hours of assessment. Psychological testing and medical screening can be vital components of the initial diagnostic workup. Consultation with the patient's spouse, employer, parents, children, and/or other family members can be diagnostically beneficial. The clinician explores each of these components of the diagnostic process in a careful and in-depth fashion.

The initial diagnosis and diagnostic impression of the patient's drinking behavior is not always concrete or final. It is important for the clinician to realize that (1) the patient's initial diagnosis will not always be final, (2) that diagnosis is process oriented rather than static in nature, and (3) in a few cases, the patient's diagnosis may change rather radically. The therapist also needs to point out to the patient early in the treatment process that the patient's initial diagnosis is not "cast in cement." The psychotherapeutic process always reveals and uncovers diagnostic elements that were not readily apparent during the initial hours of patient assessment. Indeed, the in-depth psychopathology of each primary alcoholic is always relatively unique and can perhaps only be elucidated and comprehended in relation to the medium of intensive psychotherapy.

Male primary alcoholics often indicate to the psychotherapist that they have rarely struggled with depression and affective problems. The therapist may accurately diagnose these individuals as "primary alcoholics" but find after several hours of patient sobriety and work in psychotherapy that they are also reactively, neurotically, or endogenously depressed (Della-Giustina and Forrest, 1979). These patients also tend to be confused, frightened, and surprised by their depressive symptomatology. A few alcoholics become psychotically depressed following the establishment of sobriety and engagement in treatment. It can be easy for the newly recovering alcoholic to use depression and guilt in the service of his or her addiction. Indeed, depression and affective disturbance are frequently associated with relapse.

In many respects, the diagnostic process continues throughout the course of psychotherapeutic treatment. Most alcoholics experience a slip or massive regression while in therapy (Forrest, 1978, Forrest, 1979b). The patient's attempts to control drinking and massive regressions in therapy often prove diagnostic and therapeutic. Alcoholics need to neurotically prove to themselves and their therapists that they are alcohol dependent. The alcoholic patient's attempts to drink while in therapy also provide the therapist with diagnostic data pertaining to (1) depression and affective pathology, (2) rage and impulse control, (3) identity and sexuality, (4) marital and family adjustment, and (5) cognitive style. The psychotherapist continues to evaluate and diagnose the patient's global adjustment style throughout the treatment process, and even during subsequent follow-up contacts.

DIFFERENTIAL DIAGNOSIS OF THE ALCOHOLISMS

There are several different types or forms of alcoholism (Pattison, 1980; Pattison, 1984). Therefore, it is important for clinicians and psychotherapists to be able to accurately diagnose these different alcoholisms. On one level, the differential diagnosis of alcoholism entails differentiating between a serious drinking problem and a plethora of other psychiatric/psychological syndromes. Once the clinician has established that a patient manifests a serious drinking problem, he or she is then confronted with differentially diagnosing the type of drinking problem or alcoholism. An accurate differential diagnosis is essential to (1) the development of an adequate individualized treatment plan, (2) utilizing treatment interventions that are associated with aetiology, (3) research and data collection, and (4) reimbursements for treatment and professional services.

Jellinek (1960) was a pioneer in the scientific classification and diagnosis of alcoholism. According to Jellinek (1960), alpha alcoholism is a dependence on the effects of alcohol to relieve emotional and/or physical pain. Alpha alcoholics have not lost the ability to control their drinking, they do not experience acute alcohol withdrawal symptoms, there is not a progression of the disease process, and these drinkers experience primarily interpersonal problems as a result of drinking.

Beta alcoholism does not involve physical or psychological dependence on alcohol. These drinkers do experience significant medical problems as a result of progressive daily drinking in combination with poor nutritional habits. This form of alcoholism often occurs in countries that accent and reinforce daily wine drinking as a social custom.

Jellinek (1960) described Gamma alcoholism as an addiction to alcohol with loss of control over drinking. Gamma alcoholism is very prevalent in the United States and is associated with the disease/medical model of alcoholism. Severe physical, psychological, and social deterioration is also basic to Gamma alcoholism.

Delta alcoholism has the same basic characteristics as Gamma alcoholism. However, Delta alcoholics may be able to stop drinking for short periods of time. Jellinek (1960) also described Epsilon alcoholism as episodic or periodic "binge" drinking. It is important to point out that Jellinek's diagnostic categories of alcoholism scientifically reinforced the "disease concept" of this disorder and greatly influenced professional and lay beliefs, treatments, and models of alcohol abuse. This general model posits that alcoholism is (1) a disease, (2) chronic and progressive, and (3) results in death in the absence of effective treatment.

Knight (1937) suggested that primary alcoholism is a basic disorder that occurs (1) in the absence of a coexisting psychiatric disorder, or (2) the psychiatric disorder develops after the onset of alcoholism. Secondary alcoholism develops after the onset of a major psychiatric disorder. Recently, several clinicians (Knauert, 1979; Tarter, 1983) have indicated that there are three basic diagnostic categories of alcoholism: (1) primary alcoholism, (2) secondary alcoholism, and (3) reactive alcoholism.

Primary alcoholics (Knauert, 1979, 1983) "do not have an underlying psychiatric disorder and have not experienced a specific life event that triggered their excessive alcohol consumption." These individuals manifest an intense relationship with alcohol, and this relationship seems to be present when they discover the effects of drinking. They deny their dependence upon alcohol and primitively relate to alcohol as a close friend or love object. Inconsistent parenting and narcissistic injury (Forrest, 1983c) are basic components in primary alcoholism. Parental drinking problems are often associated with primary alcoholism. Hyperactivity, depression and impulse control problems, craving for alcohol, drinking while alone and under stress, and a long history of heavy drinking are essential characteristics of the primary alcoholic (Forrest, 1983c;

Tarter, 1983). Many primary alcoholics return to a relatively normal intrapersonal and interpersonal adjustment style following the cessation of drinking.

Secondary alcoholism (Knauert, 1979, 1983) occurs in individuals that use alcohol as a medication to cope with a severe, underlying psychiatric disorder. Some manic-depressives, schizophrenics, borderlines and character disorders, and neurotics abuse and/or become addicted to alcohol. Such individuals use alcohol as a medication. However, many of these individuals do not develop a physical dependency (Forrest, 1983c). Secondary alcoholics often experience an acute exacerbation of their psychological problems following detoxification. Male secondary alcoholics with underlying thought disturbance tend to become acutely paranoid, agitated, and disorganized following detoxification. The onset of serious psychological/psychiatric disturbance preempts the onset of alcohol abuse and/or alcohol addiction in secondary alcoholism. An accurate diagnosis of secondary alcoholism (Zimberg, 1982) can be made after the patient has been totally abstinent for three–four weeks. Gross psychiatric symptomatology in the absence of drinking is essential to this diagnosis. Appropriate treatment of the basic psychiatric disorder usually results in the amelioration of secondary alcoholism.

Reactive alcoholism (Knauert, 1979; Zimberg, 1982) occurs in response to a traumatic life event. The reactive alcoholic does not have a history of alcoholism or alcohol abuse prior to the experience of a trauma such as object loss, job loss, serious accident, or disease. These individuals often initiate a history of alcohol abuse and/or alcohol dependence shortly after the death of a spouse, child, parent, or other loved one. Reactive alcoholism occurs frequently among the elderly. The reactive alcoholic attempts to repress and cope with threatening feelings associated with object loss via intoxication. These individuals may progress in their drinking to the stage of tissue dependence. Sobriety and a therapeutic resolution of the patient's affects associated with object loss are keys to the successful treatment of reactive alcoholics. Indeed, many of these patients have an excellent treatment prognosis.

The Diagnostic and Statistical Manuals II (1968) and III (1980) of the American Psychiatric Association include several diagnostic categories that are specifically related to alcohol use, abuse, and addiction.

The DSM–II diagnostic code for alcoholism (303) is "for patients whose alcohol intake is great enough to damage their physical health, or their personal or social functioning, or when it has become a prerequisite to normal functioning. If the alcoholism is due to another mental disorder, both diagnoses should be made."

The DSM–II (1968) identifies the following types of alcoholism: Episodic excessive drinking (303.0) is defined as "if alcoholism is present and the individual becomes intoxicated as frequently as four times a year, the condition should be classified here. Intoxication is defined as a state in which the individual's coordination or speech is definitely impaired or his behavior is clearly altered;" Habitual excessive drinking (303.1) diagnosis is "given to persons who are alcoholic and who either become intoxicated more than 12 times a year or are recognizably under the influence of alcohol more than once a week, even though not intoxicated." Alcohol addiction (303.2) is diagnosed "when there is direct or strong presumptive evidence that the patient is dependent on alcohol. If available, the best direct evidence of such dependence is the appearance of withdrawal symptoms. The inability of the patient to go one day without drinking is presumptive evidence. When heavy drinking continues for three months or more, it is reasonable to presume addiction to alcohol has been established." Other (and unspecified) alcoholism (303.9) is not defined.

The DSM–II also has several diagnostic codes and criteria for drug dependence (304): drug dependence, barbiturates (304.2), drug dependence, cannabis sativa-hashish, marijuana (304.5), drug dependence, cocaine (304.4), etc. Alcoholic psychoses (291), delirium tremens (DT's, 291.0), Korsakov's psychosis (291.1), alcohol paranoid state (291.3), acute alcohol intoxication (291.9), alcoholic deterioration (291.5), and pathological intoxication (291.6) are additional alcohol determined diagnostic categories that are delineated in the DSM–II.

The DSM–III (1980) defines alcohol abuse (305.0X) as "need for daily use of alcohol for adequate functioning, inability to cut down or stop drinking, repeated efforts to control or reduce excess drinking by 'going on the wagon' or restricting drinking to certain times of the day, or switching from spirits to beer or wine; binges; occasional consumption of a fifth of spirits (or its equivalent in wine or beer); amnestic periods for events occurring while intoxicated (blackouts); continuation of drinking despite a serious disorder that the individual knows is exacerbated by alcohol use; drinking of nonbeverage alcohol."

Work absenteeism, violent behaviors, job loss, legal problems, and family and interpersonal conflicts are associated with this diagnostic category. This overall pattern of consumption needs to be manifest for at least one month in order to make this diagnosis. The DSM–III diagnostic criteria are established regarding pattern of alcohol use, functional impairments, and duration.

The DSM–III (1980) also delineates criteria for the diagnosis of alcohol dependence (303.9X). This diagnostic category is similar to that of alcohol abuse in the realms of alcohol use and functional impairments. However, these problems are (1) more severe, and (2) there must be evidence of physiological/tissue addiction to alcohol via tolerance and/or withdrawal symptoms. The clinical concepts of *tolerance* and *withdrawal* are defined in the DSM–III. In essence, the DSM–III views alcohol abuse (305.0X) as a pathological but nonaddictive pattern of alcohol use, and alcohol dependence (303.9X) as physiological addiction to alcohol.

The various DSM–III alcoholism diagnoses are listed in the category of Substance Use Disorders. The digit coding system indicates the course of the specific drinking disorder. The DSM–III also includes several diagnoses of alcoholism in the category of Substance-Induced Organic Mental Disorders: Alcohol Intoxication (303.00), Alcohol Withdrawal Delirium (291.00), Alcohol Amnestic Disorder (291.10), Dementia Associated with Alcoholism (291.2X), Alcohol Hallucinosis (291.30), Alcohol Idiosyncratic Intoxication (291.40), and Alcohol Withdrawal (291.80). Each of these diagnostic categories are clearly delineated in the DSM–III. For example, Alcohol Intoxication (303.00) is defined as "maladaptive behavior due to recent ingestion of alcohol. This may include aggressiveness, impaired judgment and other manifestations of impaired social or occupational functioning. Characteristic psychological signs include loquacity, impaired attention, irrationality, euphoria, depression and emotional liability."

Many clinicians (Zimberg, 1982) believe that the DSM–III classification of alcoholism and alcohol-related disorders is much better than other models. The DSM–III model is multiaxial, with axis 1 and axis 2 representing specific psychiatric syndromes and disorders, 3 representing nonmental disorders, 4 representing recent psychosocial stressors, and 5 representing the patient's highest level of recent adaptive functioning.

There are several psychological tests (Forrest, 1978; Zimberg, 1982) that can be very useful in the differential diagnosis of the alcoholisms and substance abuse. Many clinicians find that the consistent use of one or two of these test instruments for alcoholism assessment over a period of several years greatly enhances their diagnostic accuracy and acumen.

The Minnesota Multiphasic Personality Inventory, or MMPI (Dahlstrom and Welsh, 1960), is quite helpful in the assessment of alcoholism. The MMPI is a self-administered, true–false, 400 item (short form) personality test. A few specific MMPI profiles (Forrest, 1978) are consistently associated with alcohol abuse, alcoholism, and substance abuse. The 2–7–4 profile is most consistently indicative of alcoholism and/or an addictive personality makeup. This particular profile configuration indicates the presence of a personality structure and life-style characterized by moderate-severe depression, obsessive-compulsive trends, poor impulse control, anxiety, irrational fears and phobias, irresponsibility, immaturity, and acting out. The 4, 3–4, or 4–3 and 4–9 MMPI profile configurations are also frequently associated with alcoholism, alcohol abuse, and chemical dependency. All of these profiles can additionally be associated with prescription drug abuse and/or addiction, polydrug use, and various other patterns of addictive behavior. Impulse disorder, inadequate personality features, passive-aggressive behaviors, irresponsibility, and immaturity are the central behavioral and life-style characteristics that occur with 4, 3–4, 4–3, and 4–9 configurations.

It is important that the MMPI validity scales (L, F, and K) be within normal limits in order to accurately infer that these profiles are suggestive of problems with alcohol and/or other chemicals. The 2–7–4 profile is most consistently associated with alcohol dependence. The extremely elevated 4–9 profile ($t < 90$ for both 4 and 9) is more often associated with sociopathic personality, severe impulse disorder, or antisocial personality. Most sociopaths or psychopaths (Forrest, 1983c) are users and often abusers of alcohol and/or other mood-altering drugs. However, very few psychopaths establish a long-term alcohol tissue addiction.

The MacAndrew Alcoholism Scale (MacAndrew, 1965) is an instrument that was designed for the explicit purpose of assessing alcoholism and drinking behavior. This instrument utilizes forty-nine items from the MMPI to assess alcoholism, and it has demonstrated good validity and reliability. Obviously, the MacAndrew Alcoholism Scale is much quicker and easier to administer, score, and interpret than the Minnesota Multiphasic Personality Inventory.

Horn, Wanberg, and Foster (1974) developed the Alcohol-Use Inventory (AUI) for the purpose of evaluating and assessing drinking behavior. The AUI is a 147 item, self-administered, quartile-scored instrument. This diagnostic tool includes such scales as social benefit drinking, obsessive-compulsive drinking, loss of control when drinking, psychoperceptual withdrawal, nonalcoholic drug usage, daily quantity of alcohol, and drinking provoked marital conflict. The AUI also includes general alcoholism and alcoholic deterioration scales.

The Michigan Alcoholism Screening Test (MAST) and the Self-Administered Alcoholism Screening Test (SAST) (Selzer, 1971; Morse and Swenson, 1975) are brief tests that evaluate alcohol use and alcohol-related problems. The SAST has been employed to evaluate alcoholism in relation to the nonaddicted spouse. This instrument can be clinically accurate and helpful in situations involving alcoholics that are not cooperative in the diagnostic and treatment processes. The MAST is used rather widely in alcoholism treatment programs, and it also has good reliability and validity.

Various medical or physiological tests (Zimberg, 1982) have been devised to diagnose alcoholism. One test of abnormal liver function (serum gamma-glutamyl transferase or GGT) appears to be quite useful in diagnosing alcoholism (Schuckit, 1981). The amino acid metabolism test, the mean corpuscular volume of red blood cells test, and computer analysis of the SMA–12, SMA–6, and CBC tests can be helpful in diagnosing alcoholism (Shaw, Lue and Lieber, 1978; Eckardt and Feldman, 1978; Ryback, Eckardt, and Paulter, 1980). The biochemical diagnosis of alcoholism is most adequately conducted via the evaluation of several physiological processes.

A final consideration in the differential diagnosis of the alcoholisms involves the coexistence of various psychiatric syndromes with alcoholism. Alcohol addiction and/or alcohol abuse can occur in combination with neurosis, affective disturbance, character-behavior or personality disorder, schizophrenia, brain syndrome, borderline, and narcissistic personalities. Secondary alcoholism occurs in some schizophrenics, borderlines, and chronic depressives. These individuals use alcohol as self-medication. It can be difficult to establish an accurate differential diagnosis in these cases. Clinicians will find it diagnostically efficacious to hospitalize these individuals or place them in an alcohol-free environment. Once the patient has been alcohol and drug free for several days to a few weeks, the therapist will be able to accurately assess the role(s) of drinking in the patient's overall adjustment style. Alcoholic hallucinosis may resemble an acute schizophrenic episode. However, the psychotic symptoms associated with alcohol withdrawal usually go into remission in a few days. To the contrary, schizophrenics who abuse alcohol continue to be "crazy" after they have terminated all drinking for days, weeks, or years. A few chronic alcoholic patients evidence a chronic paranoid/schizophrenic adjustment following the establishment of long-term sobriety (Forrest, 1983c).

Psychotherapists need to be able to provide appropriate treatments for patients that manifest alcoholism and a coexisting psychiatric disorder. Thus, some schizophrenics need to be detoxified and then treated for schizophrenia and alcoholism vis-à-vis long-term intensive psychotherapy, psychotropic medication (phenothiazines), self-help, vocational rehabilitation, etc. Borderline patients tend to abuse alcohol and/or other drugs (Kernberg, 1975; 1976; Forrest, 1983c). These individuals (Forrest, 1983c) are behaviorally, affectively, and cognitively similar to the primary alcoholic. They are impulsive, chronically depressive, interpersonally and sexually conflicted, angry and enraged, anxious, identity conflicted, and lonely. These patients need alcoholism/addiction treatment in combination with long-term therapy, antidepressants and/or phenothiazines, residential care, and self-help (Alcoholics Anonymous, Narcotics Anonymous, etc.).

Alcoholism results in acute and chronic brain dysfunction (Cala and Mastaglia, 1981; Sena, 1984). Chronic alcoholism can result in cerebral atrophy and such neurological impairments as Korsakoff's syndrome, Wernicke's syndrome, Marchiafava's disease, or polyneuropathy (Forrest, 1978). Alcoholic patients that manifest such neurological signs as confusion, memory impairment, ataxia, speech difficulties, and confabulation after several weeks of total abstinence need to be referred for neurological examination, CT scan, and an EEG. It can be relatively easy for the clinician to confuse organic brain impairment with acute or chronic alcohol intoxication.

Depression and anxiety are basic ingredients (Forrest, 1983c) in the primary alcoholic character structure. Acting out is also a basic characteristic of the alcoholic. However, less than ten percent of alcoholics manifest a sociopathic or psychopathic personality disorder. Most alcoholics experience chronic problems involving guilt, remorse, depression, anxiety, shame, and low self-esteem. Some alcoholics are in need of antidepressant medication, a short-term minor tranquilizer, or long-term treatment with a major tranquilizer. It is imperative that the psychotherapist observe and treat the alcoholic while he or she is sober in order to utilize psychotropic medications appropriately. Every alcoholic is prone to polydrug abuse and dependency. Therefore, physicians must be very cautious when they prescribe any mood-altering chemical to an alcoholic.

The minor tranquilizers (Librium, Valium, etc.) can be very useful in the treatment of alcohol withdrawal (DT's). However, many alcoholics want to continue taking these medications after they have successfully withdrawn from alcohol. Alcoholics are prone to switching addictions, and many actually become addicted to Valium® or Librium®. Alcoholics also drink alcohol in combination with prescribed medications. For these reasons, it is always important for the therapist to (1) accurately diagnose drinking disorders, (2) assess concomitant psychological/psychiatric problems and disorders, and (3) provide appropriate treatments based upon differential diagnosis.

The following case study demonstrates the global problem of differential diagnosis in alcoholism treatment.

CASE 1. Tyler O. was a fifty-four-year-old assembly line worker. He was referred for an "evaluation" by his company EAP (Employee Assistance Program) coordinator due to conflicts with other employees, taking "pills," job absenteeism and "strange behavior." The supervisor also indicated to the therapist during the initial phone call referral contact that Tyler frequently appeared to be "hung over" in the mornings.

The patient was angry, depressive, quite anxious, and reported feeling generally "stressed" during the first consultation session. He indicated that he had been divorced twice and that his present marital relationship was diffusely conflicted. Mr. O. had three children within the context of his first two marriages and one child with his present wife. He had been employed by the same large corporation for over twenty years. The patient stated several times that he did not like his job and that the "company" was responsible for many of his problems. He repeatedly referred to his immediate job supervisor as a "cocksucker." The patient paced about the office, swore a great deal, and appeared to be diffusely angry.

When questioned by the therapist about his use of alcohol, drugs, and medications, the patient stated that he had "taken every prescription drug under the sun." He did not feel that he had a "drinking problem," although he indicated "I periodically drink too much." He also indicated to the therapist that he sometimes drank in combination with prescribed psychotropic medication. The patient had taken various prescribed psychotropic medications daily for a period of fifteen years. He had taken Thorazine®, Elavil®, Librium®, Valium®, Limbitrol®, Dilantin®, phenobarbital, and other psychotropics for varying periods of time during these fifteen years. Mr. O. indicated that many of these medications "seemed to help control my problems" for a few weeks, but that none of them "really worked." The patient said that he had been in several psychiatric hospitals over the past twenty-five years and that he had been "treated" by various physicians, psychologists, psychiatrists, social workers, and clergy members.

At the close of the initial consultation hour, the patient verbalized to the therapist that he was struggling to control sexual feelings for his sixteen-year-old stepdaughter. He indicated that he had never been sexually active with his stepdaughter, but that he found her sexually attractive and stimulating. He pointed out that he was partially impotent and a premature ejaculator with his wife, and that their sexual relationship was poor. The patient also stated that he had decided to stop taking his prescribed medications "on my own." He completed the Minnesota Multiphasic Personality Inventory (MMPI) at the close of the hour, and told the therapist that he would call for another appointment next week. At this point, the therapist encouraged the patient to (1) make a commitment to intensive psychotherapy and (2) consult with his physician about stopping medication.

The patient would not consent to having the therapist contact his physician.

The patient called for an appointment and was seen in therapy the following week. His overall MMPI profile (2–7–4) was suggestive of an addictive personality makeup with impulse control problems, depression, severe interpersonal difficulties and paranoid trends. The patient's behavioral and cognitive styles reflected anger, impulse disorder, and passive-aggressiveness. He was not grossly disorganized or psychotic. The patient discussed his conflicted childhood and adolescence. His mother had abandoned the family when he was nine years old and, in essence, he had been parented by an angry, cold, and punitive father. The patient's oldest son was an "alcoholic and drug addict" who had been incarcerated several times. The patient revealed that he had "discovered" how his company was overbilling customers for "millions of dollars" and stated that "they" (the company) would have him killed if they "found out" that he possessed this knowledge. Furthermore, he emphasized that he wanted to be "drug free." He had discussed entering a residential alcoholism and drug rehabilitation program with the company EAP coordination in order to help him stop taking psychotropic medication. In spite of the therapist's suggestion to discuss this issue with his physician, the patient emphasized that he did not want his doctor involved in this "decision." He ended this session by telling the therapist that he would call if he decided to come in for another session.

Five days after this session, the therapist was contacted by the patient's EAP coordinator. The patient was in a residential treatment center at that time. He had asked to be placed in a residential addiction treatment center in order to become totally abstinent from prescription medication and alcohol. The company agreed to this treatment alternative, and the patient entered a twenty-one-day treatment facility.

Nearly three weeks after the patient completed residential treatment, he called the therapist and scheduled a conjoint therapy session. At the beginning of this session, the patient stated "I feel better than I have in twenty years" and that he wanted to "get started working on my marriage and family problems." He appeared to be less agitated, less depressive, and more in control. During this session, the patient's wife revealed that the patient had been incestuously involved with his stepdaughter some six years earlier. The patient admitted this but became very upset and angry with his wife for disclosing this issue to the therapist. Mrs. O. also indicated that Mr. O. had beaten her on several occasions. She stated that he consistently abused her and the children "in a psychological way." Furthermore, Mrs. O. stated that "they" were morbidly afraid of Mr. O. The patient pointed out that Mrs. O. had been sexually involved with her father throughout adolescence.

The O.'s were seen in four subsequent conjoint therapy sessions. During the third conjoint session, Mrs. O. announced that she had consulted with a lawyer and that she had decided to get a divorce. The patient became enraged upon being told of his wife's decision to get a divorce. He verbalized that under the circumstances of a divorce, "they" (meaning the family system) "might all be better off dead." Mrs. O. did, in fact, initiate a divorce, and the patient was removed from the house via a legal restraining order. Mrs. O. indicated in conjoint therapy that she had been concerned about Mr. O.'s "constant pill popping" for years, and that she knew that he should not drink alcohol and take medication. During this phase of treatment, Mrs. O. called the therapist late one evening following a heated argument and "shoving match" with the patient. Mr. O. got on the phone and told the therapist that Mrs. O. was accusing him of molesting their nine-year-old daughter. The incest issue involving the youngest daughter was the focus of the final conjoint therapy session. This matter was immediately referred to the local Department of Social Services for investigation. Both daughters were also referred for individual psychotherapy. The patient vehemently denied any sexual involvement with this daughter. However, DSS recommended that Mr. O. be removed from the home, and a highly structured and supervised visitation program was initiated for the patient.

The couple had a long history of sexual problems. Mr. O. was partially impotent and a premature ejaculator. He did not trust his wife and "suspected" that she had been involved in several extramarital affairs. It was his belief that extramarital affairs were "evil," and that all sex should be restricted to the immediate family system. The patient told the therapist that he had found "a lot of used rubbers in our septic tank, and they sure as hell aren't mine." He described his wife as sexually quite responsive, i.e. "hotter than a damned firecracker." Mrs. O. denied having ever been involved in any extramarital affairs. She felt that Mr. O. would kill her if she became involved with other men.

Both Mr. and Mrs. O. decided to continue in individual psychotherapy after the divorce process had been initiated. Mr. O. was seen in seven subsequent individual therapy sessions over a period of some four months. Mrs. O. remained active in therapy and was seen in fifteen sessions over a six-month time interval.

Mr. O. continued to be enraged, depressive, manipulative, and psychosomatically conflicted. His work relationship with colleagues and supervisors deteriorated. The patient was sporadic in attending treatment sessions in spite of his therapist's continued messages that he needed to be seen every week or twice each week. The patient indicated to the therapist in one of his final sessions that he had read about "vital depression" in a *Psychology Today* article, and that this had been his "problem" for twenty-five years. He made an appointment with a psychiatrist who prescribed the antidepressant medication discussed in the magazine article. During his final contact some three weeks later, the patient indicated that this

medication was not "working" and that he had started taking another
medication. He indicated that he had also initiated therapy with another
psychologist and was undergoing "primal therapy."

Mrs. O. spent several hours in treatment dealing with her disturbed
relationship with her father, Mr. O., and men in general. She improved
significantly in treatment and received a job promotion. She continued to
be convinced that Mr. O. had sexually molested their youngest daughter
and felt guilty about not having intervened earlier. She continued to be
extremely fearful of Mr. O. She also indicated that she had infrequently
encountered her former husband in different nightclubs, and that he was
"up to his old tricks in drinking and taking pills." Several months later,
Mrs. O. remarried and moved to another state.

This case study encompasses several interesting diagnostic
problems. The patient was not an alcoholic. He was an episodic
alcohol abuser. He had also been psychologically dependent upon
psychotropic medication. However, this patient was clearly in
need of appropriate psychotropic medication and long-term, intensive psychotherapy. In effect, Mr. O. had been a chronic mental
patient, although he was able to work and only required periodic
hospitalization. The patient was a very angry, explosive, and poorly
controlled person. He was also depressive, very manipulative,
anxious, and manifested a number of psychosomatic complaints
(fatigue, low back pain, headaches, respiratory difficulties, etc.).
The patient had serious sexual conflicts and was incestuously
involved with his oldest stepdaughter. Indeed, he was a spouse and
child abuser. His marital, familial, and vocational adjustments
were pathologic and tenuous. Additionally, the patient's oldest
son was described as an "alcoholic and drug addict."

Clinically, this patient manifested a borderline personality with
clear-cut addictive features. Kernberg (1975, 1976, 1980) has astutely
elucidated the borderline and narcissistic personality syndromes.
A chronic adjustment style involving severe impulse-control
problems, severely conflicted interpersonal relationships, rage,
chronic depression and anxiety, fragmented identity, addictive
trends, self-destructiveness, and intermittent psychiatric hospitalization characterizes borderline personality organization (Kernberg,
1975; Masterson, 1981). The patient's MMPI profile (2–7–4–6) is
diagnostically suggestive of (1) anxiety reaction with alcoholism
in a passive-aggressive personality, (2) depressive reaction with

alcoholism, (3) passive-aggressive personality with alcoholism, or perhaps (4) schizophrenia, or (5) schizoid personality (Gilberstadt and Duker, 1965). The MMPI also indicated that Mr. O. was impulsive, irresponsible, obsessive-compulsive, and paranoid.

The diagnosis of the alcoholisms can be relatively easy or quite difficult for the clinician. There are many caveats and paradoxes associated with the diagnostic process. Yet, accurate assessment of the patient's drinking behavior and basic adjustment style are essential to the process of implementing effective treatment interventions.

SUMMARY

The behavioral science professions are ambivalent about the roles and relevance of "diagnosis" in the treatment of psychiatric/ psychological problems. Many psychiatric diagnoses are simply *ic* labels that generally infer mental illness and "sickness" (Szasz, 1976; Forrest, 1978). Many "schools" of counseling and psychotherapy rejected the use of diagnostic categories or labels during the 1960s and early 1970s.

Accurate diagnosis is essential to the efficacious treatment of people with alcoholism and drinking problems. The clinician needs to thoroughly explore the patient's style of drinking and drinking history, medical history, family and social history, legal history, and work history in order to accurately diagnose the alcoholisms. Medical tests, psychological tests, and clinical interviews with the patient's spouse, family members, or employer may contribute to the diagnostic process. The clinician openly shares his diagnostic formulation with the patient. This particular therapy/ diagnostic strategy facilitates treatment gain vis-à-vis (1) resolving denial and the avoidance defense system, (2) minimizing therapist scotomization, (3) conveying a sense of therapist competence, honesty, and a sense of hope, and (4) defining the need for treatment and a basis for treatment related process-outcome assessment.

Diagnosis of the alcoholism is always a process. A patient's diagnosis may change during the course of therapy. Diagnosis or literally "knowing through" occurs in-depth as the therapy relationship intensifies.

There are several different types or forms of alcoholism. The Jellinek (1960) alcoholism types were delineated. The characteristics of primary, secondary, and reactive alcoholics were also elucidated. *The Diagnostic and Statistical Manuals* II (1968) and III (1980) of the American Psychiatric Association include several diagnostic categories of alcoholism and alcohol abuse. These diagnostic classifications were discussed.

Several psychological and medical/physiological tests are used to diagnose alcoholism and evaluate drinking behaviors. The Minnesota Multiphasic Personality Inventory (MMPI), MacAndrew Alcoholism Scale, Alcohol Use Inventory (AUI), and Michigan Alcoholism Screening Test (MAST) are psychological tests that are very useful in the assessment and diagnosis of alcohol use. Liver function tests, the amino acid metabolism test, and other medical tests can be helpful in diagnosing alcoholism.

The alcoholisms can coexist with several psychiatric disorders. Various patterns of alcoholism occur in combination with neurosis, affective disturbance, personality disorder, borderline and narcissistic conditions, schizophrenia, and brain syndrome. Psychotropic medication and relatively different treatment interventions are often appropriate in the therapeutic management of these patients. It is estimated (Zimberg, 1982) that fifty percent of alcohol-addicted women seen in therapy manifest a concomitant depressive disorder, while five percent of alcoholic males manifest a depressive disorder.

The case study included in this chapter demonstrates the various difficulties that sometimes occur in assessing alcoholism and drinking behavior. This patient had a long history of episodic alcohol abuse and prescription drug dependence. However, he manifested a borderline personality adjustment style and was not an alcoholic.

Chapter III

EARLY STAGES OF INTENSIVE ALCOHOLISM PSYCHOTHERAPY

INTRODUCTION

The early stages of intensive alcoholism psychotherapy encompass the initial two to four months of weekly therapy. Most primary alcoholics need to be actively committed to the therapy process for a period of eight months to two years in order to achieve long-term sobriety and concomitant personality change and growth. Weekly one hour psychotherapy sessions are essential to successful treatment during the early stages of treatment. Some patients need to be seen twice a week during this phase of treatment. Relapses or massive regressions (Forrest, 1978) do occur in the psychotherapy of alcoholism. Additional weekly treatment sessions can be a situational deterrent to relapse. Most patients need to be seen two or three times per week immediately following a massive regression. Intensive alcoholism psychotherapy is often initiated while the patient is in residential treatment. It is efficacious to see these patients on a twice-a-week basis prior to beginning outpatient psychotherapy.

The initial one to four hours of therapist-patient contact are devoted to assessment and diagnosis. These early therapist-patient interactions are also therapeutic. The psychotherapist is consistently able to evaluate the patient's readiness and motivation for treatment during these sessions. The patient's initial interactions with secretaries and other clinic staff members can also be viewed as diagnostic and therapeutic.

Aside from these early encounters with the patient, the basic psychotherapeutic process during the first 15 to 25 sessions entails (1) establishing a working and productive therapeutic alliance, (2) developing a program of recovery, and (3) essentially completing the genetic reconstruction phase of treatment. Many patients are able to develop the rudiments of a program of recovery within the initial two or three hours of treatment. The process of establishing a working and productive therapeutic alliance is more difficult and involves several hours. Indeed, maintaining a productive therapeutic relationship is an ever-present goal in effective psychotherapy with alcoholics. A working and productive therapeutic alliance is *established* during the initial 15 to 20 hours of psychotherapy. Genetic reconstruction work is initiated during the phase of patient assessment and the earliest therapy sessions. The basic therapeutic focus between sessions 4, 6, and 15 encompasses genetic reconstruction work.

This chapter elucidates the (1) structural components of intensive alcoholism psychotherapy, (2) dimensions of the working and productive therapeutic alliance, (3) roles and functions of genetic reconstruction work in alcoholism psychotherapy, (4) initial strategies of confrontation, and (5) initiating an addiction focus in the treatment process. These therapeutic issues are explored within the context of the early stages of intensive alcoholism psychotherapy. A case study and actual therapy vignettes are also included in this chapter.

STRUCTURAL COMPONENTS OF
INTENSIVE ALCOHOLISM PSYCHOTHERAPY

The psychotherapist openly discusses his or her diagnostic impression of the patient's drinking behavior *with the patient*. This therapeutic procedure is usually employed after the second or third contact hour with the patient. The therapist also briefly explains to the patient the clinical meaning of *primary alcoholism* and points out that there are different types of alcoholism. It is important for the therapist to explore the patient's motivation for entering psychotherapy during the initial one to three sessions. A few patients are self-motivated to enter treatment. Some have been court ordered into treatment. Many alcoholics seek out professional help when they are faced with a marital, familial, or vocational crisis.

The therapist-patient dyad must be committed to the psychotherapeutic process. In essence, both the therapist and the patient need to be committed to the work that psychotherapy entails. If the psychotherapist feels that an alcoholic patient is not sufficiently motivated and "ready" for therapy, he or she needs to openly share these perceptions and beliefs with the patient. It may be appropriate to refer such individuals to another therapist or treatment facility. Some alcoholics may tell the therapist that they do want to begin therapy, but with another therapist. Therapists need to help their alcoholic patients actively and openly explore their global readiness to enter psychotherapy very early in the treatment process. In sum, a good therapist-patient "fit" is an essential prerequisite to effective intensive alcoholism psychotherapy.

The psychotherapist needs to explain to the patient that effective treatment will require several months of therapeutic work and commitment. It is unrealistic and clinically inappropriate to suggest to primary alcoholics that recovery and personality change will occur after a few therapy sessions. The therapist also needs to assess the primary alcoholic's willingness to make a commitment to the goal of total abstinence during the initial treatment sessions. Total abstinence is always the most basic treatment goal in the intensive psychotherapy of primary alcoholism. It is essential that the therapist and the patient be committed to achieving the goal of patient abstinence. Therapists need to be firm and consistent in maintaining this treatment goal. Many primary alcoholics state that they have decided to enter therapy in order to learn how to "control" their drinking. Some believe that they are "problem drinkers" or "drunks" but deny that they are "alcoholics" as compared with physiologic-psychologic alcohol addiction. It is clinically inappropriate to attempt to do intensive psychotherapy with primary alcoholics who are not willing to commit themselves to the treatment goal of total abstinence. Obviously, this basic issue must be therapeutically resolved in the initial treatment sessions. Therapist and/or patient inconsistency in accepting this basic treatment goal is tantamount to therapeutic impasse and ultimately treatment failure. Primary alcoholics that refuse to work toward the goal of total abstinence are not appropriate candidates for intensive alcoholism psychotherapy.

Once the therapist and patient are committed to the psychotherapeutic process, it is important to concretely develop the specific structural components of treatment. The structural components of intensive alcoholism psychotherapy are developed by the therapist and patient. These components of therapy are always based upon the relatively unique treatment needs of the patient. The structural components of intensive alcoholism psychotherapy constitute the basis for holistic health care and treatment. Primary alcoholism is a disorder or disease of the whole person. Thus, the alcoholic is intrapersonally, interpersonally, physically and spiritually disturbed, and conflicted. Effective alcoholism treatment helps the patient modify pathological affects, behaviors, cognitions, relationships, health maintenance patterns, and global life style behaviors.

The basic structural components of intensive alcoholism psychotherapy include (1) Antabuse® maintenance for 90 to 120 days, (2) weekly or twice weekly attendance of Alcoholics Anonymous, (3) weekly attendance of Al-Anon by spouse and/or other family members, (4) an active program of physical exercise (four to five, twenty-minute exercise sessions per week), (5) appropriate nutrition and basic health habits (three well-balanced meals per day, adequate sleep, avoidance of other addictive substances such as sugar, nicotine, caffeine, etc., possible weight control program), and (6) possible establishment of a spiritual or religious affiliation. These structural components of alcoholism treatment are adjuncts to intensive psychotherapy. They can be viewed as ingredients in effective alcoholism therapy. Intensive psychotherapy in addition to these structural components of treatment constitutes a program of recovery (Forrest, 1980; Forrest, 1983b) for the alcoholic.

The primary alcoholic needs to actively commit himself or herself to these structural components of intensive alcoholism psychotherapy during the initial four or five treatment sessions. The therapist and patient need to work together to develop the patient's individualized program of recovery. Some alcoholics cannot take Antabuse. Cardiovascular problems, gross neurologic complications, and liver dysfunction are but a few of the medical conditions that make it either unwise or impossible for alcoholics to be involved in an Antabuse maintenance program (Forrest, 1984). Many alcoholics refuse to take Antabuse or are morbidly afraid of this medication. Some alcoholics will attend AA only once a week, while others decide to attend several AA meetings each week. The patient may decide to walk, jog, swim, play tennis, lift weights, or ride a bicycle several times each week. Sometimes patients want to join a support group, attend church, or join a program such as *Weight Watchers*.

It is essential for the therapist and patient to develop the specific and comprehensive structural components of the treatment process. Furthermore, the patient needs to practice or actualize these treatment adjuncts on a very consistent basis. Very little therapeutic gain will be derived from exercising once a week or once a month. Antabuse should be taken two or three times each week. Sporadic AA attendance will not significantly benefit most alcoholics. Seeing the therapist every three or four weeks is ineffective treatment. Skipping meals several days a week, staying up all night, or dieting two or three days each week can contribute to treatment failures. Consistency in actualizing these structural components of intensive alcoholism psychotherapy is the key to successful treatment and recovery.

These structural components of intensive alcoholism psychotherapy provide the patient support and reinforce abstinence. Prosocial learning, adaptive time structuring, and a generalized sense of well-being are also facilitated by these structural components. Antabuse is a physical and psychological deterrent to drinking. Antabuse enables the therapist and patient to establish a relationship framework that eventually fosters sobriety and healthy personality and behavioral change. Alcoholics learn experientially within the context of Alcoholics Anonymous that other alcoholics have recovered!

The following case study is utilized throughout the remainder of this text to demonstrate (1) the developmental course of primary alcoholism, and (2) the developmental process of intensive alcoholism psychotherapy. All of the therapy vignettes presented in the following chapters are taken from actual therapy sessions involving Jack G. and the author.

CASE PRESENTATION: The patient, Jack G., was referred for alcoholism treatment by the coordinator of a U.S. Army Employee Assistance Program (EAP). Jack was a fifty-three-year-old retired Army First Sergeant. He had been employed by the Civil Service as a cook for thirteen years following his military retirement. The patient's wife was German. The G.'s had no children. However, the patient had been married several years earlier and had one son with his first wife. His present wife was also a Civil Service employee.

Mr. and Mrs. G. came to the initial therapy/diagnostic session. They were interviewed separately and conjointly on this occasion. The patient also completed the Minnesota Multiphasic Personality Inventory (MMPI) and the Alcohol Use Inventory (AUI). Mr. G. indicated in the first clinical interview that he had a "drinking problem." He had received residential alcoholism treatment at a military alcohol and drug center some two years earlier. The G.'s had also been involved in sporadic outpatient counseling for over one year. The patient had received two DUI's (Driving Under the Influence of Alcohol) during the past three-and-one-half years. He had been arrested, jailed, and court-ordered to attend alcohol education classes for the last DUI. He stated "I drink *almost* every day—usually about a pint of vodka and a few beers each day." He consumed "three or four" beers each morning before going to work. The patient had to report for work each morning at 5:30 AM.

Mrs. G. referred to her husband as a "damned drunk." She indicated that the patient had been continuously intoxicated throughout the duration of their eighteen-year marriage. She associated their marital arguments, communication problems, and general living problems with Jack's drinking. She also stated "Jack's no good in bed." Apparently, he had been impotent for a few years. Mrs. G. also verbalized that she felt Jack was "hopeless." She wanted Jack to enter therapy, but she was not willing to be involved in treatment. It was her stated belief that "Jack has the goddamned problem, not me."

The patient scheduled a second therapy session, indicating that he "had to come for treatment, or lose my job." He was quite resentful about his wife's refusal to enter therapy. The patient was anxious and physically "shaky" at this session. He stated that he had been attempting to "taper off on my own" since the first session. He had been taking medication for hypertension for over two years. He also reported having chronic low back pain, stomach problems, and a "bad liver." Jack stated that his "nerves" had been bad for several years and that he took prescription Librium when he "couldn't take it any more."

During the second therapy/diagnostic session, the therapist (1) indicated to the patient that he felt that the patient manifested primary alcoholism, (2) that long-term intensive psychotherapy and other appropriate alcoholism treatments could help the patient recover, (3) discussed the patient's MMPI and AUI results, and (4) referred the patient for a complete medical examination. The patient's MMPI profile (2–7–4–3) indicated serious depressive, obsessive-compulsive, anxiety, psychosomatic, and impulse control conflicts. This particular MMPI profile is consistently associated with chronic alcoholism, an addictive personality structure and polydrug use, abuse, and addiction. His AUI profile included high quartile scores on the mental benefit drinking, obsessive-compulsive drinking, postdrinking worry, guilt, fear, drinking to change mood, prior use of external help to stop, loss of control when drinking, DT's and hangovers, daily quantity of alcohol, drinking provokes marital conflict, and general alcoholism scales.

This patient was subsequently seen in seventy-six individual psychotherapy sessions over a period of eighteen months. His wife refused to enter individual or conjoint therapy. She also refused to attend Al-Anon. The patient attended a few Alcoholics Anonymous meetings early in treatment but generally resisted any consistent and meaningful involvement in AA. After nearly fourteen months of successful outpatient therapy, the patient experienced a massive regression. He then continued in outpatient psychotherapy and eventually successfully terminated treatment. When last contacted for follow-up evaluation, the patient had been totally abstinent for three years. He was not attending AA and had not reentered therapy. Jack reported that he and his wife "were still having our ups and downs" and that their "sex life is about the same."

Mr. G. was ambivalent about initiating psychotherapy. However, at the point of treatment engagement, he was quite fearful of losing his job as a result of drinking. He also feared the possible legal consequences of further drinking. The patient manifested a very dependent-symbiotic relationship with his wife. He terminated his Civil Service employment some seven months after beginning psychotherapy. The marital relationship continued to be severely pathologic in spite of the patient's abstinence and constructive behavioral change.

During the third psychotherapy session, Jack and the author worked to construct the specific structural components of the treatment process. The following therapy vignette was taken from this session.

Doctor F: So, what are you willing to do in order to get better—to recover? What can you do in addition to therapy?

Jack G: You mentioned that last week, Doctor—I've thought about it. I did get the physical and I've only had 2 or 3 beers this week—no vodka, and I feel a lot better. I've tried AA and it didn't help—Oh, my doctor doesn't want me to take antabuse either. My goddamned blood pressure is too high!

Doctor F: So you've thought about a program of recovery?

Jack G: Yeah—only nothing worked in the past—maybe I really didn't want to quit. I know I'm killing myself, but shit—it seems like I never learn—Ha, Ha, Ha.

Doctor F: I suspect that you weren't consistent with what you tried to do in order to stop drinking in the past... Do you eat breakfast and three meals a day? How about an exercise program—do you work out four to five times a week—like walking or swimming—maybe riding a bike?

Jack G: Ha, Ha—I've been drinkin' about a six pack of Bud for breakfast for the last three or four years—I don't eat right and the only exercise I get is work! Used to go fishin' and huntin'...

Doctor F: You're basically sober now—I want you to make a commitment to start eating breakfast and regular meals.

Jack G: Well, er—I can give it a try. That exercise idea sounds like a lot of work—I'm sure as hell not going to get up at 4:00 AM and try to run ten miles! Piss on that—walking might be good, though...

Doctor F: So you're ready to make the commitment to eating right—breakfast and a proper diet. How about walking fifteen or twenty minutes, three or four times a week for a start? I don't want you to overdo it—it would be good for you to discuss this with your physician. How about AA or maybe attending church or getting involved with a support group?

Jack G: AA's just a bunch of drunks... Besides, my wife won't even go to Al-Anon. She goes to church two or three times each week... guess I should go, but I'm tired on Sundays.

Doctor F: Would you be willing to give AA another try—perhaps once a week for 12 to 15 weeks?

Jack G: Yeah, maybe. I need to think about it.

Doctor F: It takes more than weekly therapy to recover. It takes a lot of *consistent work!*

This therapy vignette demonstrates how the psychotherapist helps the patient develop a treatment format or structure that promotes recovery and holistic health care. It is important for the therapist and patient to develop the structural components of treatment very early in the psychotherapeutic process. A few alcoholics resist developing a program of recovery. Successful therapy occurs when patients are committed to a program of recovery. The development and implementation of the structural components of intensive alcoholism psychotherapy constitutes the initiation of the actual therapeutic process. It is often necessary for the therapist and patient to spend two to five hours developing the concrete structural components of treatment.

Intensive alcoholism therapy is consistently ineffective with patients that fail to develop a structural recovery program. For this reason, it is appropriate to terminate treatment with primary alcoholics who are unwilling to develop a structural program of recovery within the context of the initial five to fifteen psychotherapy sessions. These individuals need to be referred to another therapist, treatment agency, or engaged in other appropriate treatment modalities. They are not good candidates for intensive alcoholism psychotherapy.

THE THERAPEUTIC ALLIANCE
IN INTENSIVE ALCOHOLISM PSYCHOTHERAPY

The therapeutic relationship begins to develop during the initial therapist-patient interactions. Relationship building is an essential ingredient of the diagnostic phase of treatment. The working and productive therapeutic alliance encompasses the therapist's basic belief and awareness that the primary alcoholic can benefit from psychotherapeutic treatment. The psychotherapist expects his or her alcoholic patients to (1) terminate their alcoholism, (2) modify or extinguish the behavioral repertoire that maintains and supports their alcoholism, and (3) actualize life-style growth and change.

The therapeutic alliance is based upon the psychotherapist's fundamental comfortableness with alcoholics. This therapist characteristic also involves the simple capacity to like alcoholics. Many psychotherapists are uncomfortable with alcoholics and some refuse to treat these individuals (Bratter, 1980). Therapists who abuse mood-altering chemicals are generally unsuccessful in their therapeutic interactions with alcoholics. The working and productive therapeutic alliance is also constructed vis-à-vis the therapist's sensitive and in-depth understanding of the psychopathology of alcoholism.

Facilitative psychotherapy relationships evolve as a process. They do not simply occur as a function of several hours of therapist-patient contact. The therapist and patient need to be equally committed to creating a therapy relationship that is a potent and meaningful vehicle of change. Mutual trust, respect, and concern are essential ingredients of the therapeutic alliance. Primary alcoholics (Forrest, 1983c) experience intense anxiety and threat within the context of intimate human encounters. However, therapist support and sensitivity enable the alcoholic to struggle with and eventually resolve interpersonal anxiety. The basic humanness and relatedness of the therapeutic alliance is curative. Alcoholics prototaxically fear narcissistic injury, destruction, and annihilation as a function of intimacy. However, these patients experience a sense of comfortableness with self, the therapist, and significant others that adaptively generalizes after the working and productive therapeutic alliance has been established.

Key therapist ingredients in the development and maintenance of a working and productive therapeutic alliance include non-possessive warmth, empathy, concreteness, and genuineness (Truax and Carkhuff, 1967; Forrest, 1978). These therapeutic characteristics pertain to the therapist's ability to (1) accept the alcoholic patient unconditionally, (2) be affectively and cognitively attuned to the patient's feelings, experiences, and behaviors, (3) communicate to the patient an understanding of this awareness, and (4) be open to his or her own experience within the therapeutic encounter. Furthermore, the therapist is able to honestly and genuinely express his or her feelings, beliefs, and experiences with the patient. The psychotherapist is a "real person" within the therapeutic encounter. Effective therapists are able to consistently provide high levels of nonpossessive warmth, empathy, genuineness, and concreteness *throughout* the course of their psychotherapy relationships with primary alcoholics.

The therapeutic alliance is also nurtured and strengthened in relation to the therapist's consistent communication of respect and dignity for the alcoholic. The psychotherapist needs to interact with alcoholic patients in a manner that conveys a deep sense of dignity, respect, and worth for the patient. Therapist activity is essential to the process of effective alcoholism psychotherapy. It is sometimes necessary for the therapist to hospitalize alcoholics. This form of limit setting may initially anger the patient. However, the therapist needs to value the worth of the alcoholic to the extent that he or she is willing to actively intervene in the patient's life. Such interventions can be life-sustaining in the treatment of primary alcoholics. Therapy involves actively teaching the alcoholic self-respect, dignity, and self-worth.

These *core conditions* of the therapeutic alliance facilitate recovery. However, the essential therapist ingredients in effective intensive alcoholism psychotherapy constitute the necessary but not always sufficient conditions for creating adaptive personality and behavioral change. The working and productive therapeutic alliance involves strategic therapist interpretations, confrontations, and self-disclosure. Many alcoholics also need to be involved in assertiveness training, prosocial training, homework assignments, relaxation training, self-help alternatives, and career or vocational guidance programs. The successful intensive psychotherapy of alcoholism demands that the therapist possess a multimodel therapeutic armamentarium.

The following therapy vignette illustrates the rudimentary process of establishing a working and productive therapeutic alliance. This vignette was taken from the sixth therapy session with Jack G.

> *Jack G:* At least I don't feel so damned nervous about coming in here ... Actually, I'm startin' to kinda look forward to our sessions.

> *Doctor F:* You must feel good about being sober ... perhaps the positive changes you've begun to experience make it easier to be in therapy?

> *Jack G:* Yeah ... but I trust you, Doc ... I'm comfortable

talking with you because you seem to understand me... are you sure you're not a drunk? Ha, Ha.

Doctor F: We're starting to get to know each other better.

Jack G: It's always been hard for me to get close to people. Like I told you, I've always been a loner—hell, my wife doesn't even know me—sometimes I wonder if I know myself?

Doctor F: Therapy can be a bit scary ... especially if you've always been a loner or uncomfortable with people. Do you know why you've been a loner or afraid of relationships?

Jack G: Hell, my whole family was like that... my dad was a drunk and couldn't deal with anything and both my parents left us when we were just kids... Yeah, a lot of people have shit on me... but you get over it and by God, I don't let anybody hurt me any more!!

Doctor F: So you learned very early in life that people can let you down ... your parents hurt you.

Jack G: That's for sure! My first wife treated me like shit too... I've even been in rehabilitation programs where my counselors didn't seem to give a damn about me... Guess that's the story of my life... Ha, Ha.

It is apparent from this therapy vignette that the patient had experienced a good deal of narcissistic injury throughout his life. It was difficult for Jack to trust people and risk real interpersonal attachments. The therapeutic alliance is an intense human relationship. A working and productive therapeutic alliance fosters the development of the patient's ability to tolerate interpersonal intimacy and relatedness. Indeed, the therapeutic alliance provides the primary alcoholic with a corrective emotional experience that facilitates sobriety and global adaptive personality change.

The therapeutic alliance is strengthened via the process of ongoing therapeutic work. Intensive alcoholism psychotherapy cannot take place in the absence of a working and productive therapeutic alliance. A rupture in the therapeutic alliance is tantamount to treatment termination and treatment failure.

GENETIC RECONSTRUCTION WORK
IN INTENSIVE ALCOHOLISM PSYCHOTHERAPY

Genetic reconstruction work in intensive alcoholism psycho-therapy refers to the psychotherapeutic structuring of the treat-ment relationship in a fashion that focuses primarily upon the patient's early life experiences, behaviors, affects, and cognitions. The genetic reconstruction phase of treatment basically encompasses sessions four or five through fifteen. During this stage of the psychotherapy process, the therapist and patient explore the patient's experiential past in-depth. The patient's experiential past constitutes the explicit treatment focus at this time. Although the genetic reconstruction phase of therapy is not limited to these early treatment sessions, later therapeutic work of this type is far less intensive and less affective for the patient.

Alcoholism is a neurotic solution to painful and traumatic early life narcissistic injuries. Alcoholics neurotically avoid and deny their experiential histories through drinking and intoxication. Yet, drinking alcoholics are chronically fixated in the past and future. One basic therapeutic task of the psychotherapist is that of helping the primary alcoholic patient explore his or her past in the absence of intoxication. Genetic reconstruction work is also a very important component of the working and productive thera-peutic alliance.

Most alcoholic patients are ambivalent about sharing and disclosing their early-life experiences with the psychotherapist. The clinician needs to understand the patient's anxiety and am-bivalence associated with working through his or her early life experiences. Yet, the therapist needs to consistently and supportively help the patient begin to talk about the many painful realities of his or her past. This therapeutic technique eventually enables the patient to rationally comprehend and understand his or her past. This treatment strategy also helps resolve the patient's over-determined repression and avoidance defense mechanisms that are associated with early-life narcissistic injury. As the genetic reconstruction phase of intensive alcoholism psychotherapy be-gins to unfold, the patient begins to discover that he or she no longer experiences the compulsion to neurotically escape the past through drinking. The urge to drink diminishes or is extinguished. Chronic feelings of anxiety, depression, rage, and guilt that are associated with the patient's experiential past are also resolved. Genetic reconstruction work enables the alcoholic patient to grow and resolve the global conflicts and bondage of the past.

Alcoholics are ambivalent about exploring their early-life experiences with the therapist for a plethora of reasons. Self-exploration and genetic reconstruction work can be painful, emotional, and somewhat traumatic. Unconsciously and preconsciously, the patient is fearful and very anxious about discussing the various experiential realities of his or her past. Most alcoholics have put a great deal of long-term neurotic energy into the processes of repressing, denying, and avoiding their pasts. Patients are often simply embarrassed to honestly share their early-life experiences with another human being. It is also important for the psychotherapist to realize that alcoholics have paradoxically and adaptively survived their catastrophic early-life experiences largely as a function of repression and the avoidance defense system (Forrest, 1983c). In the absence of developing the alcoholic characterological makeup, it is reasonable to assume that many of these individuals would have become schizophrenics.

Genetic reconstruction work is initiated following the patient's commitment to total sobriety and the psychotherapeutic process. I have found that this therapeutic strategy is most efficaciously initiated by focusing first upon the patient's high school and late adolescent years. The psychotherapist then proceeds to shift the therapeutic focus to the patient's junior high school or early adolescent years and then to grade school and childhood. This therapeutic procedure becomes progressively more regressive in a developmental sense. Beginning the genetic reconstruction phase of intensive alcoholism psychotherapy by focusing upon experiences associated with late adolescence results in (1) less intensive affective conflict for the patient, (2) a lowered incidence of premature treatment termination or "fleeing" from treatment, and (3) a strengthening of the therapeutic alliance that eventually provides a therapeutic relationship and structure that can endure the work of childhood reconstruction.

The therapist needs to spend several therapy hours helping the patient explore and partially resolve experiences and material associated with the various developmental life stages. Thus, it is important for the therapist to allow the patient to partially work through late adolescent material before progressing to early adolescent or later childhood experiences. A complete resolution or working through of the various sources of conflict and pathology associated with different developmental life stages occurs during the middle and later stages of intensive alcoholism psychotherapy.

Alcoholics and other addicts (Bratter, 1984; Forrest, 1984) are noted for their resistance to psychotherapy. These patients also tend to terminate treatment prematurely and flee from affectively oriented therapies (Forrest, 1982). Therefore, the genetic reconstruction phase of therapy generally proceeds from superficial, nonthreatening content to highly affective and ego-dystonic therapeutic content. Therapist sensitivity and appropriate timing are essential ingredients in effective genetic reconstruction work. Alcoholics fear their feelings and the emotions that are associated with their early-life experiences. Premature and untimely genetic reconstruction work precipitates acute anxiety in many of these patients and results in iatrogenic treatment termination.

Genetic reconstruction work eventually reveals the Procrustean bedrock of the patient's pathology and character structure. The patient's basic feelings of inadequacy, self-defeating behaviors, and self-system fragmentation are the result of pervasive early-life narcissistic need and entitlement deprivation. The patient's extensive history of narcissistic injury soon becomes the focus of the genetic reconstruction phase of therapy. The patient's defensive style and avoidance defense system are also modified vis-à-vis the utilization of this treatment technique. Here-and-now behaviors, cognitions, and affects become more understandable and amenable to change as a result of genetic reconstruction work. Genetic reconstruction work enables the alcoholic to (1) accept the reality of being an alcoholic, (2) rationally comprehend the various realities associated with being and becoming an alcoholic, and (3) begin to modify the pattern of defensive armoring and characterological rigidity that is basic to the alcoholic adjustment style. Alcoholism recovery is very much contingent upon the ability of the therapist-patient dyad to significantly modify the patient's avoidance defense system and characterological rigidity.

A therapeutic resolution of the primary alcoholic's narcissistic pathology (Forrest, 1983c) is facilitated by genetic reconstruction work that focuses upon the patient's early-life experiences with significant others. The patient needs to openly and honestly explore his or her early-life mother-father-sibling and family system object relations with the psychotherapist. Alcoholics vacillate with regard to feelings of self-worth. Hypernarcissism, grandiosity, and megalomania are defenses against profound feelings of worthlessness, inadequacy, and low self-esteem. Genetic reconstruction of the patient's early-life object relations results in the development of a more consistent and realistic sense of self. Power fantasy ideation and the alcoholic narcissistic character style can be modified through genetic reconstruction work.

A therapy vignette taken from the thirteenth treatment session with Jack G. clearly demonstrates the importance and efficacy of genetic reconstruction work in intensive alcoholism psychotherapy.

Doctor F: You've told me several times that people have really hurt you and let you down all your life . . .

Jack G: Yeah . . . I guess it pretty much started with my folks. Like I told you a few weeks ago, my parents left us kids alone . . . I don't like to talk about it . . . it upsets the hell out of me . . .

Doctor F: It upsets you to talk about your parents?

Jack G: Yeah . . . it always has . . . but then, I haven't told anyone about it except Ilsa (the patient's wife).

Doctor F: It? You mean how your parents hurt you?

Jack G: Uh, right . . . when I was ten years old, I woke up one morning—it was in July and school was out . . . There wasn't anyone at home except us kids . . . Shawn was about six and Laura was about a year old (at this point, the patient's eyes became tearful and he began to experience difficulty talking) . . . God dammit, I've got to tell you this.

Doctor F: We can talk about this whenever you're ready . . . it's a painful subject to talk about.

Jack G: No, I'm ready to get it out . . . I thought that Mom and Dad had just gone to work, that they would be back later . . . So I got the girls up and fed them. We all slept in the same bed and there was a new pair of jeans and a five-dollar bill on the foot of the bed. Anyhow, my folks never came back (the patient began to sob and became very upset). God damn, how could they do that?? I took care of the girls for about a week and finally went to the neighbors when we ran out of food . . .

Doctor F: So your parents actually left you . . . they abandoned all of you.

Jack G: You bet your sweet ass . . . and I've hated both of 'em for it for over forty years! I went to work on the neighbor's farm and some other neighbors took Shawn in . . . the welfare department put Laura in an institution or orphanage . . . I've never seen her again (the patient was crying, shaking, and quite agitated).

Doctor F: I can understand why you've kept this to yourself . . . it makes me feel sad listening to you . . . we're going to need to talk about this more.

Jack G: At least the neighbors treated me ok . . . they fed me and worked my ass off . . . when I was seventeen, I joined the Army and . . . well, I guess the Army became my family.

The patient had been severely traumatized by the experience of parental abandonment. Indeed, narcissistic injury had been an ever-present reality component of much of the patient's life. The patient avoided and repressed his devastating childhood experience of parental abandonment. A working and productive therapeutic alliance eventually enabled the patient and therapist to openly explore the patient's emotionally devastating past.

Genetic reconstruction work helps the primary alcoholic (1) rationally understand and resolve early-life narcissistic injuries, and (2) modify characterological rigidity. Genetic reconstruction work is an essential ingredient in effective intensive alcoholism psychotherapy. Continued intoxication and a generally maladaptive adjustment style are persistent realities in the absence of extensive genetic reconstruction work in alcoholism treatment.

INITIAL STRATEGIES OF CONFRONTATION IN INTENSIVE ALCOHOLISM PSYCHOTHERAPY

Confrontation is a fundamental ingredient in successful intensive alcoholism psychotherapy. Psychotherapy interventions with primary alcoholics tend to be ineffective in the absence of the therapist's utilization of timely and strategic confrontations. Historically, psychotherapists have been reluctant to use confrontation techniques in their treatment relationships. Confronting "brittle" and inadequate persons within the confines of the counseling relationship was believed to result in decompensation and iatrogenic treatment (Adler and Myerson, 1973; Forrest, 1982). However, recent psychotherapy approaches (encounter groups, gestalt therapy, reality therapy, rational emotive therapy, behavioral modification, primal therapy, etc.) are increasingly confrontational in theory and practice. Confrontation is a basic component in all effective systems of counseling and psychotherapy.

It is difficult to precisely define confrontation as a unique strategy of psychotherapy. What constitutes a strategy of confrontation for one therapist may or may not be interpreted as such by another therapist. The patient may or may not perceive the therapist's *intended* confrontation as a confrontation! However, confrontation techniques in psychotherapy can be defined as therapeutic interventions that (1) imply force, activity, and focus the patient's attention upon self, (2) heighten self-awareness, (3) provide the patient with direct interpersonal feedback relative to the therapist's global or specific perceptions of the patient, (4) teach the patient to attend to self and the therapist, and (5) provide the patient with reality-oriented feedback via the psychotherapist.

Facilitative confrontation interventions are employed by the psychotherapist through the medium of the working and productive therapeutic alliance. Rational and effective confrontation interventions in intensive alcoholism psychotherapy always incorporate high levels of therapist nonpossessive warmth, empathy, genuineness, and concreteness and support (Truax and Carkhuff,

1967; Forrest, 1979a). It is important for the therapist to consistently confront the alcoholic patient regarding his or her profound sense of love, concern, and compassion for the patient. Psychonoxious confrontations occur in psychotherapy when the therapist is (1) not genuinely concerned about the overall well-being of the patient, (2) insensitive to the patient's overall adjustment style, or (3) interacting with the patient in a pathological therapeutic manner as a result of countertransference dynamics.

Confrontation techniques contribute to the development of a working and productive therapeutic alliance and foster the process of genetic reconstruction work. The psychotherapist's efficacious confrontations also help modify the alcoholic's avoidance defense system and foster healthy, non-patsy-oriented therapist behaviors. Confrontation interventions reinforce patient commitment to sobriety and induce adaptive internal conflict. Primary alcoholics often experience pain and concomitant growth as a result of the therapeutic, timely, and ongoing confrontations of the psychotherapist.

It is important for the therapist to be aware of the historic roles of confrontation in most alcoholics' lives. Alcoholics have been angrily and abusively confronted by parents and significant others throughout childhood, adolescence, and adulthood. Alcoholics also tend to confront other human beings in a diversity of parataxic ways. Thus, the alcoholic can be expected to respond emotionally and irrationally to the therapist's initial confrontation interventions. In juxtaposition to these patient realities associated with confrontation treatment strategies, it is equally important to point out that many therapists experience a great deal of difficulty utilizing this particular therapy technique. Psychotherapists tend to be warm, nurturant, supportive, and passive. Therapists have been trained to utilize a myriad of non-confrontation-oriented treatment interventions. Several "schools" of psychotherapy train therapists to be inactive, reflective, and passive. In sum, there are a plethora of intrinsic therapist and patient factors which contribute to problems and conflicts in the utilization of confrontation techniques in intensive alcoholism psychotherapy.

The alcoholic is "confronted" in a variety of ways during the initial contact with the therapist or treatment center. Completing a social history form, interactions with the receptionist, and filling out insurance forms, or paying for professional services can all be viewed as confrontations. The psychotherapist initially confronts the alcoholic in a therapeutic sense vis-à-vis the process of openly discussing the patient's diagnosis. In effect, the therapist's verbal message "in my opinion you have alcoholism" is a very direct therapeutic confrontation.

Therapists need to be very sensitive and skillful in their use of confrontation interventions early and throughout the process of intensive alcoholism psychotherapy. Premature, affective, high-impact confrontations (Forrest, 1982) frequently result in treatment termination. Alcoholics tend to flee from the psychotherapy relationship when they are confronted in a very personal and premature manner. The therapist's confrontations need to be "controlled" early in the treatment relationship. Controlled confrontations provide the patient with reality-oriented feedback that conveys a point of emphasis, usually a matter of feeling or opinion upon the part of the therapist that is somewhat dissonant with the self-perceptions or beliefs of the patient. This form of confrontation does not threaten the patient or the psychotherapy relationship. On the contrary, controlled confrontations communicate to the patient a sense of the therapist's honesty, authenticity, therapeutic acumen, and a willingness to work and help the patient resolve his or her addiction.

The next therapy vignette was taken from the fourth psychotherapy session with Jack G. This vignette shows the clinical importance of appropriately timed and "controlled" therapist confrontations during the early stages of intensive alcoholism psychotherapy.

Jack G: I've probably been an alcoholic for ten or fifteen years . . . at least my wife says so . . . Ha, Ha.

Doctor F: You referred to yourself as a "problem drinker" in our first session.

Jack G: Yeah . . . well, what's the difference . . . problem drinker or alcoholic?

Doctor F: In some ways, there aren't any differences, but in other ways, there are important differences. It is apparent to me that you have alcoholism...you're an alcoholic. Your health problems, the arrests and job problems, your test results...even your wife's opinion...plus your drinking history all mean to me that you have alcoholism. You are physically and psychologically *addicted* to alcohol.

Jack G: I guess I don't like that word "alcoholic"...but I sure as hell can't control my drinking. I've tried that a thousand times and it never worked...I always end up drunk sooner or later.

Doctor F: It's hard to accept that you're an alcoholic...you don't like that word.

Jack G: That's for damn sure! You know, thinking back about it, I've never really *believed* that I was an alcoholic. Even when I went to treatment before, I believed that I had a drinking problem...and you know, I always thought I could learn how to control my drinking...that was the answer!

Doctor F: By viewing yourself as a problem drinker, you never really had to make the commitment to completely stop drinking and do the work to recover.

Jack G: That sure makes sense.

In spite of alcohol determined arrests, liver dysfunction, marital problems, and vocational difficulties, the patient continued to deny that he was an alcoholic. This therapy vignette demonstrates how the therapist needs to confront alcoholics about the reality of their addiction early in the treatment process. Therapists need to confront alcoholics in an empathic, supportive, and generally nonthreatening manner early in therapy.

Confrontation techniques are an important part of the psychotherapist's armamentarium. These therapist interventions contribute to the development of a working and productive therapeutic alliance, and they also facilitate the genetic reconstruction phase of treatment. Indeed, confrontation strategies are essential to all phases of intensive alcoholism psychotherapy.

INITIATING AN ADDICTION FOCUS
IN INTENSIVE ALCOHOLISM PSYCHOTHERAPY

An ever-present addiction focus must be maintained throughout the process of intensive alcoholism psychotherapy. It is appropriate for the therapist to set this precedent during the earliest treatment sessions. The psychotherapist carefully and accurately assesses the alcoholic's pattern of consumption during the diagnostic interviews. Subsequently, the therapist spends a few minutes of each psychotherapy session focusing explicitly upon the patient's drinking behavior per se.

During the initial 15 to 20 therapy sessions, it is helpful for the clinician to spend 10 to 15 minutes of each therapy hour focusing upon the patient's drinking history, style of drinking, and urge or compulsion to drink. Many primary alcoholics struggle with the urge to drink on a daily basis for several weeks. Some of these individuals become obsessed with drinking after three or four months of treatment, but experience relatively no difficulty abstaining early in therapy. It is important for the therapist to understand the patient's drinking history. A few patients manifest an extended history of remaining totally abstinent for a few weeks or even several months followed by weeks or months of chronic intoxication. Specific therapeutic interventions can be implemented to modify the patient's historic drinking pattern, and progress in therapy can be measured as a function of maintaining an ever-present addiction focus.

It is clinically appropriate and therapeutic for the therapist to actively question the patient about his or her feelings and thoughts about drinking between sessions. The therapist may need to reinforce the patient's intensification of AA participation, exercising, or other therapeutic adjuncts in the face of a continued and emotionally upsetting craving for alcohol. The patient may also need to be seen two or three times a week in therapy on a short-term basis in order to extinguish the intermittent compulsion to drink. Progress in psychotherapy is not measured according to the sole criterion of abstinence. However, very little psychotherapeutic progress can be actualized during the initial stages of treatment in the absence of patient abstinence.

The following therapy vignette was taken from the sixth session with Jack G. Although Jack had been completely sober for several weeks at this time, he continued to think about drinking and periodically struggled with the "urge" to drink.

Doctor F: How long has it been now since you've had anything to drink?

Jack G: About two months . . . you know I don't think about that much . . . actually, I'm trying not to think about drinking- . . . it's easier that way.

Doctor F: You try not to think about drinking . . . does that mean that you're afraid to think about it . . . by thinking about drinking, you might actually make it easier to drink?

Jack G: I don't know . . . I sure as hell don't want to start drinking again! A lot of people in AA seem to be busy telling everybody how long they've been sober . . . that's a bunch of shit to me.

Doctor F: It's hard to stay sober.

Jack G: Yeah . . . I've thought about how good a cold beer would taste . . . especially when I'm out working in the yard on a hot day! Ha, Ha . . . hell, one beer is too much and a thousand beers aren't enough if you know what I mean . . . Ha, Ha!

Doctor F: So you remind yourself of the consequences of drinking if you really feel the urge . . . what else can you do when you feel the urge to drink?

Jack G: Uh . . . get my ass to a meeting . . . if I need to, I'll call you . . . is that O.K.?

Doctor F: I'd rather have you call me than get drunk . . . going to an extra AA meeting or working out are also good alternatives.

It is difficult for the primary alcoholic to achieve sobriety and remain committed to psychotherapy and an abstinent life-style. The psychotherapist needs to help the patient explore his or her feelings about drinking and abstinence, craving for alcohol and drinking behaviors per se. The patient needs to realize that only he or she can struggle with these issues and do the work essential to recovering and maintaining abstinence. However, the patient is not alone in this struggle. Therapists need to be advocates that are committed to helping their alcoholic patients develop more rational and adaptive patterns of living.

SUMMARY

The early stages of intensive alcoholism psychotherapy encompass the first two to four months of weekly treatment. Some alcoholics need to be seen twice a week at this time. The initial 15 to 25 hours of psychotherapy involve (1) establishing a working and productive therapeutic alliance, (2) developing a structured program of recovery, (3) essentially completing the genetic reconstruction phase of treatment, (4) implementing confrontation techniques, and (5) initiating an addiction focus.

The therapist-patient dyad needs to develop a structured program of recovery for the patient early in the treatment process. The basic structural components of intensive alcoholism psychotherapy include (1) Antabuse maintenance for 90 to 120 days, (2) active participation in Alcoholics Anonymous, (3) active participation in Al-Anon for family members, (4) an exercise program, (5) nutritional stabilization, and (6) possible establishment of a spiritual or religious affiliation. These structural components of alcoholism treatment are holistic health adjuncts to intensive psychotherapy. The patient needs to be actively committed to the psychotherapy relationship and these treatment adjuncts for several months in order to fully recover from primary alcoholism.

The therapeutic alliance begins to develop during the initial therapist-patient interactions. Successful psychotherapeutic treatment of the alcoholic is contingent upon the therapist's sense of basic comfortableness with alcoholics. A working and productive therapeutic alliance is constructed vis-à-vis the therapist's sensitive and in-depth understanding of the psychopathology of alcoholism. Therapist qualities of nonpossessive warmth, empathy, genuineness, and concreteness contribute to the establishment of a working and productive therapeutic alliance. The therapeutic alliance is also strengthened by the therapist's communication of respect and dignity for the patient. Successful psychotherapeutic work with alcoholics requires that the therapist be able to skillfully implement multimodel treatment interventions.

Genetic reconstruction work in intensive alcoholism psychotherapy refers to the therapist's structuring of the helping relationship in a fashion that focuses primarily upon the patient's early-life experiences. This phase of therapy is essentially completed during the first fifteen sessions. The genetic reconstruction phase of treatment is very affective and difficult for the patient. A developmental framework for implementing genetic reconstruction work was outlined. This treatment strategy helps the patient (1) understand and resolve early-life narcissistic injuries, (2) modify the avoidance defense system, and (3) accept the reality of being an alcoholic.

The uses of confrontation techniques in intensive alcoholism psychotherapy were discussed. Confrontation techniques focus the patient's attention on self, heighten self-awareness, provide reality-oriented feedback, and teach new behaviors. Confrontation strategies contribute to the development of a productive therapeutic alliance and foster the genetic reconstruction work. Constructive and psychonoxious confrontation strategies were discussed. Premature, affective, and high-impact therapist confrontations often result in the patient's movement away from the therapy relationship. Controlled confrontations need to be utilized during the early stages of intensive alcoholism psychotherapy.

Psychotherapists need to maintain an addiction focus throughout the course of intensive alcoholism psychotherapy. The therapist should spend 10 to 15 minutes of each therapy hour exploring the patient's feelings about drinking, sobriety, and the urge to drink. Specific treatment interventions can be implemented to modify the patient's historic drinking pattern, and progress in therapy can be measured by maintaining an ever-present addiction focus.

The primary alcoholic needs to be committed to the treatment goal of total abstinence throughout the course of intensive alcoholism psychotherapy. Some patients are abstinent when they initiate treatment. Others need to be detoxified or hospitalized prior to initiating psychotherapy. In general, these individuals should be referred for medical detoxification if they are unable to "taper off" or detoxify themselves on an outpatient basis during the initial four to six sessions with the psychotherapist. Primary alcoholics that have a history of serious medical problems and/or are beginning to experience acute alcohol withdrawal at the time of treatment engagement should always be referred immediately for medical evaluation and treatment before intensive alcoholism psychotherapy is initiated.

A case study was presented early in the chapter. Several actual therapy vignettes were taken from the psychotherapeutic treatment of this case. These vignettes were utilized to demonstrate the various early stages of intensive alcoholism psychotherapy that were discussed throughout this chapter.

Chapter IV

MIDDLE STAGES OF
INTENSIVE ALCOHOLISM PSYCHOTHERAPY

INTRODUCTION

The middle stages of intensive alcoholism psychotherapy involve the fifth through tenth month of treatment. Most primary alcoholics need to be seen in weekly therapy during this stage of treatment. A few patients are ready to begin every other week or once-a-month therapy at the end of ten to twelve months of intensive alcoholism psychotherapy. Drinking relapses or massive regressions tend to occur most frequently between the fourth and sixth month of intensive therapy with primary alcoholics that are highly motivated for treatment. Therefore, the psychotherapist will need to see some patients more than once a week during this particular time.

Alcoholics that remain actively committed to the psychotherapy process for several months are generally very motivated to remain abstinent and engaged in treatment. The vast majority of these patients have an excellent treatment prognosis. In the clinical experience of the author, it is realistic to expect at least seventy percent of these individuals to remain totally abstinent for three to five years following psychotherapy termination. Many of these patients will remain sober and continue to recovery for several years and perhaps life. These patients actualize a diversity of healthy behaviors and life-style changes. It is a deeply rewarding experience for the psychotherapist to observe and actively participate in the recovery process of such patients.

The early stages of intensive alcoholism psychotherapy provide much of the therapeutic grist for the middle stages of the treatment process. More specifically, the genetic reconstruction phase of therapy exacerbates most of the alcoholic's prototaxic sources of anxiety and conflict. These various sources of patient pathology and dissonance must be adequately worked through in order to result in basic personality growth, behavioral change, and long-term abstinence.

Massive regressions during the middle stages of intensive alcoholism psychotherapy are stressful for the patient, therapist, and the patient's family. It is beneficial for the spouse and family members of the primary alcoholic to be involved in personal therapy (Wegscheider, 1981; Black, 1981; Lawson, Peterson, and Lawson, 1983). The therapeutic management of relapse and therapy of nonaddicted family members of the patient can constitute additional treatment issues that need to be managed during the middle stages of intensive alcoholism therapy. The patient's will to live and recover is truely tested through the middle stages of therapy. Resistance, transference, and countertransference issues are especially germane to this phase of treatment.

A major therapeutic task that needs to be accomplished during the middle stages of intensive alcoholism psychotherapy involves shifting the treatment style to a more cognitive behavioral orientation. The early stages of intensive alcoholism therapy are basically supportive, relationship or Rogerian, and analytically-oriented. The middle stages of treatment require that the psychotherapist utilize rational-emotive, reality, and cognitive behavioral therapy modalities in combination with depth-psychology and analytically-oriented strategies of intervention.

This chapter explores (1) insight, interpretation, and self-awareness in intensive alcoholism psychotherapy, (2) resistance, transference, and countertransference, (3) initiating a here-and-now therapy orientation, (4) cognitive-behavioral interventions, (5) sex counseling and sex therapy, (6) confrontation techniques, (7) maintaining an addiction focus, and (8) relapse. These treatment issues are considered from the perspective of the middle stages of intensive alcoholism psychotherapy. This chapter also includes several therapy vignettes that demonstrate the content, process, and outcome of the middle stages of alcoholism treatment.

INSIGHT, INTERPRETATION, AND SELF-AWARENESS
IN INTENSIVE ALCOHOLISM PSYCHOTHERAPY

Facilitating patient insight and self-awareness are basic goals of intensive alcoholism psychotherapy. These goals are primarily accomplished during the middle and later stages of the therapy process. The genetic reconstruction phase of treatment provides most of the basic cognitive, behavioral, and affective content that the patient needs to understand, integrate, and resolve. Indeed, the patient must develop an enhanced degree of insight and self-awareness associated with a plethora of matters that are elucidated and brought to a conscious level of awareness via the genetic reconstruction process. Insight and self-awareness refer to the accurate perception and experience of the total self. Heightened insight and self-awareness result in the patient's ability to better understand unconscious and preconscious processes, global cause and effect relationships, and symbolic meanings.

Paradoxically, many primary alcoholics are unconsciously and preconsciously aware of their basic neurotic conflicts. These individuals attempt to deny, avoid, and repress self-oriented insight and awareness through intoxication. They have been chronically unable to modify and resolve their various neurotic struggles. Many alcoholics *consciously* choose to avoid painful self-awareness by drinking. Alcoholics are afraid of self, others, and the phenomenal world. Alcoholics also morbidly fear self-awareness. Alcoholism is a disorder that involves the neurotic management of self-oriented insight and awareness.

The process of therapeutically enhancing the patient's insight and self-awareness is often accompanied by fear and intense anxiety. However, personality growth and behavioral change occur as a result of insight and reality-oriented self-awareness. The psychotherapist structures the therapy relationship in a manner that facilitates the patient's development of a greater capacity for rational, reality-oriented personal insight and self-awareness. The process of intensive alcoholism psychotherapy facilitates a relationship context which enables the patient to openly explore self-perceptions, feelings, behaviors, and relationships. The therapist also directly contributes to the patient's capacity for insight and self-awareness through the use of interpretation. The psychotherapeutic process elevates the patient's unconscious and preconscious self-oriented perceptions and processes to the conscious level of experience.

Interpretation is one of the most fundamental treatment techniques that psychotherapists can use to potentiate patient insight and self-awareness (Kernberg, 1975, 1980). Appropriately-timed therapist interpretations help to modify the alcoholic's overdetermined use of regression and the avoidance defense system. The therapist must consistently explore and make interpretations that are associated with the patient's alcoholism per se. Alcoholics scotomize their relationships with alcohol and other mood-altering chemicals. The *drug-person* relationship is consistent grist for the middle stages of intensive alcoholism psychotherapy. Alcoholics have very little insight into the nature of their profound and destructive alcohol dependence. Indeed, the psychotherapist's ongoing reality-oriented interpretations relative to the patient's addiction are prerequisite to the (1) patient's ego-syntonic acceptance of being an alcoholic, and (2) modification of the patient's various parataxic perceptions and beliefs that maintain the addiction process.

The interpretative process is primarily centered around the resolution of pathologic behaviors, cognitions, and affects that stem from (1) early-life narcissistic injury and subsequent chronic interpersonal and intrapersonal conflicts, (2) chronic affective disturbance involving anxiety, depression, and anger; (3) characterological rigidity and the avoidance defense system, (4) identity and sexual disturbance, and (5) a sadomasochistic character style. The therapist needs to help the alcoholic patient rationally integrate the realities of the past that are associated with chronic narcissistic injuries. This process enables the patient to understand and thus change present-oriented behaviors, feelings, and thoughts that are rooted in his or her pathologic experiential past. The therapist explains to the patient that these experiences were, in fact, depressing, threatening, and painful. The patient has been chronically enraged at his or her parents and significant others. Avoidance-oriented defenses and the alcoholic character style evolve as an adaptive and functional response to pervasive early-life narcissistic injury. The psychotherapeutic process is devoted to the patient's rational elucidation of these issues. Therapists need to actively interpret and explain to the patient how identity and sexual conflicts and the punishment of self and others are processes that occur in the present as a result of early-life narcissistic need and entitlement deprivation.

Most primary alcoholics experience both anxiety and a sense of catharsis as a function of therapy-induced insight and self-awareness. These patients tend to initially respond to the therapist's interpretations and their enhanced self-insight by blaming parents, circumstances, and tangential objects for their alcoholism and life struggles. It is imperative that the therapist continue to utilize the interpretative process to enable the patient to (1) stop blaming others for his or her alcoholism and life problems, (2) internalize and struggle with these issues in a self-oriented fashion in the here-and-now, and (3) eventually grow beyond the pathology of the past. Thus, interpretation is a therapeutic tool that fosters sobriety and responsible living (Glasser, 1965). Acting-out conflicts are also resolved and extinguished vis-à-vis the therapist's use of interpretations that facilitate an internalization of conflicts.

Another major focus of the middle stages of intensive alcoholism psychotherapy involves affects and feelings (Forrest, 1984). Alcoholics flee from psychotherapy when the therapist prematurely effects an intense therapeutic focus upon the patient's feelings and emotions. The patient's feelings and affective conflicts have historically operated in the service of the addiction. Primary alcoholics are unable to productively and rationally explore their internal struggles and feelings during the early stages of intensive alcoholism psychotherapy. These patients allow their feelings to neurotically control their behaviors and cognitions. Indeed, most alcoholics live and behave in accord with the equation $\frac{E}{I}$. The E in this equation refers to Emotions and the I refers to Intellect (Martin, 1980).

The therapist needs to maintain a consistent focus upon the patient's feelings and affect during the middle stages of intensive alcoholism therapy. Affective conflicts usually contribute to the patient's drinking compulsion as well as global living problems. It is usually most efficacious for the therapist and patient to explore the patient's present feelings and then interpretatively associate these affects with historic or long-term affective conflicts. The therapist begins this process by simply helping the patient begin to talk and communicate openly about his or her feelings. Alcoholics tend to be grossly out of touch with their feelings. They repress their feelings, they fear their emotions, and they are unable to express feelings and affect. Most alcoholics are unable to accurately label such personal affects as depression, rage, anxiety, fear, and guilt.

Effective intensive alcoholism psychotherapy results in a significant resolution of the patient's affective pathology. Thus, it is realistic to expect the patient to become less anxious, less depressive, and less angry and enraged as a function of treatment. Alcoholics utilize ethanol to partially extinguish and control threatening affects. The psychotherapy relationship per se is a more rational and functional vehicle for changing and managing emotions and affective conflicts.

In-depth self-exploration, interpretative work, insight, and self-awareness are essential therapeutic ingredients of the middle stages of successful intensive alcoholism psychotherapy. Obviously, these therapeutic ingredients are key factors in all stages of effective alcoholism therapy. It is also important to emphasize that insight, interpretation, and self-awareness are not the only elements that contribute to the middle stages of successful intensive alcoholism therapy. Yet, the primary alcoholic's capacities for personality growth, behavioral change, and alcoholism recovery are limited in the absence of a psychotherapy experience that fosters the development of reality-oriented and rational insight and self-awareness.

The following therapy vignette was taken from the twenty-sixth session with Jack G. At this point in the treatment process, he had been totally abstinent for over six months and was generally improved. The patient was beginning to develop a more insightful and rational understanding of his persistent problems in the realm of male-female relationships.

Jack G: We talked about that last week ... really, we've talked about my relationships with women a lot.

Doctor F: Yes. When we finished last week, you were talking about how you've been hurt or disappointed by so many women.

Jack G: Oh, yeah ... my real mother probably hurt me the most ... at least I can talk about her and all that now without getting so damned upset. You know, my first wife ran out on me too ... she ran off with one of my Army buddies. Hell, that was years ago. We got married when I was twenty years old.

Doctor F: You had mentioned before that your first marriage ended in divorce, but you didn't go into the specifics of how it ended.

Jack G: Yeah, she was no goddamned good. She screwed around on me. We were only married about two years. She got a divorce when I was overseas, so I wasn't even there when it ended.

Doctor F: So she was unfaithful. She left with one of your friends?

Jack G: That's right. Hell, I met her in a bar. As a matter of fact, we were both drunk when we got married! Ha, Ha! Guess I should have known better ... but I was hittin' it pretty good in those days.

Doctor F: So alcohol played a role in that marriage and divorce.

Jack G: Sure it did. You know, she was a real heavy drinker and so was my mother ... maybe my mother was an alcoholic? Dad was an alkie for sure.

Doctor F: Both of those women hurt you ... They left you and both of them drank a lot.

Jack G: My first wife hurt me more than I let on ... I remember crying about her a lot, but I sure never told anybody ... gettin' those divorce papers was hell. You know, I said to myself then that I'd never trust another goddamned woman ... by God, I didn't even get close to women for years after that ... I mean I didn't talk to 'em, didn't dance with 'em and didn't even try to screw 'em! Ha, Ha!

Doctor F: So you weren't about to get hurt again... You didn't want anything to do with women. You must have gotten lonely... you eventually got married again.

Jack G: Yeah... I guess I married Ilsa about eight years after my divorce... I was about 30 then and knew what the hell was goin' on... she was out to get me for over a year... and she's stuck by me for over 20 years!

Doctor F: It must have been difficult for you to get close to her... to trust her, or maybe even trust your buddies when you were dating her?

The patient had experienced a plethora of relationship conflicts with women. This therapy vignette shows that Jack was beginning to understand how his early-life experience of being abandoned by his mother was associated with his subsequent relationships with women. He was also cognizant that alcohol had played an important role in many of his relationships with women. At this point in the therapy process, Jack continued to repress and scotomize many realities associated with being rejected by his father, his inability to trust other males, and the behavioral and dynamic similarities between his mother, first wife, and present wife.

Primary alcoholics develop a reality-oriented sense of self-awareness and insight during the middle stages of intensive alcoholism psychotherapy. This reality-oriented insight and self-awareness is associated with (1) early-life narcissistic injury, (2) affective disturbance, (3) avoidance defenses, (4) sexual and identity problems, (5) sadomasochism and acting out, and (6) self and alcoholism. The psychotherapist consistently utilizes interpretation and other therapeutic techniques in order to help the patient develop insight and self-awareness. Increasing the patient's global levels of reality-oriented insight and self-awareness constitutes a deterrent to further drinking and facilitates healthy personality growth and behavioral change.

RESISTANCE, TRANSFERENCE, AND COUNTERTRANSFERENCE IN INTENSIVE ALCOHOLISM PSYCHOTHERAPY

Resistance in intensive alcoholism psychotherapy refers to the patient's various movements away from recovery and the therapy relationship. The alcoholic is ambivalent about initiating and maintaining sobriety, being committed to the psychotherapy relationship, and changing other ineffective patterns of behavior. Unconsciously, preconsciously, and consciously, the alcoholic simply resists alcoholism recovery.

Alcoholics that are basically not motivated (Forrest, 1978b) to maintain sobriety and remain in therapy usually terminate treatment during the early stages of intensive alcoholism psychotherapy. When the patient is highly motivated to recover, he or she usually experiences a great deal of positive reinforcement to remain abstinent and committed to the psychotherapy process during the initial weeks and months of treatment. Many patients are keenly aware of feeling physically better, receiving praise, and thinking more clearly and rationally at this time. Family, marital, and sexual relationships often seem to improve dramatically following a few weeks of sobriety and treatment engagement (Lawson, Peterson, and Lawson, 1983). A few primary alcoholics experience extreme resistance to recovery and treatment vis à vis severe depressions, agitation and personality disorganization during the early stages of therapy. Unfortunately, many of these individuals terminate treatment prematurely.

At any rate, it is during the middle stages of intensive alcoholism therapy that many patients begin to consciously understand and struggle with various sources of resistance. A drinking relapse is the best example of resistance. Canceling therapy sessions, missing or forgetting sessions, consistently being late for appointments, missing AA meetings, maintaining an inconsistent exercise program, or "forgetting" to take Antabuse are also classic forms of resistance. Failure to pay for treatment and late payments are additional indications of the patient's resistance. Indeed, any behavior that impedes the patient's recovery, commitment to therapy, or jeopardizes the therapeutic alliance can be viewed as resistance.

The psychotherapist needs to sensitively point out, discuss, and confront the patient's various resistances to treatment and recovery *as they occur* in therapy. It is imperative that therapists not deny and avoid these very important dimensions of the psychotherapy process. Therapist scotomization of the patient's resistances can precipitate a diversity of psychonoxious phenomena. These therapist transactions can reinforce drinking, irresponsibility and acting-out, and further resistance. When the patient misses an appointment or begins to exercise on a sporadic basis, the therapist should inquire about the possible meaning of these behavioral changes. The therapist also needs to actively reinforce the need for consistency in maintaining a responsible behavioral style. Most importantly, the therapist needs to explore and interpret patient resistance from the framework of the therapeutic relationship. It is appropriate for the therapist to ferret out how the patient is feeling about the therapist, self, the therapeutic process, and other issues that are associated with the therapeutic alliance per se whenever resistance becomes a manifest reality in intensive alcoholism psychotherapy.

It can be relatively easy for most alcoholics to remain sober and involved in psychotherapy for several weeks. Practical, as well as internal, psychodynamic factors make it more difficult for these patients to remain sober and persist in psychotherapy for several months. These therapeutic realities must be faced and resolved during the middle stages of intensive alcoholism psychotherapy if the therapeutic process is to continue and be successful.

Transference conflicts become overtly and acutely manifest during the middle stages of intensive alcoholism psychotherapy. Transference is a Freudian (Freud, 1953) concept that refers to the patient's distorted or neurotic responses to the psychotherapist and the psychotherapy relationship. In essence, transference encompasses the patient's parataxic early-life experiences and emotions that stem from parental and family interactions. The patient begins to relate to the therapist as a father-figure, mother, or just significant other. Obviously, the patient's authority conflicts, affective conflicts, cognitive distortions, and generalized neurotic struggles are exacerbated as a result of the transference phenomenon in psychotherapy.

The primary alcoholic's transference distortions are usually repressed and relatively well-controlled during the initial weeks of therapy. However, after a few months of involvement in intensive psychotherapy, most patients begin to evidence a rather acute transference reaction. The therapeutic resolution of the transference neurosis (Freud, 1953; Kernberg, 1975, 1980; Masterson, 1981) is believed to constitute the essence of effective treatment. Traditional psychoanalytically-oriented theory (Fenichel, 1945) emphasizes that a therapeutic "cure" can only be effected through the successful therapeutic resolution of the transference neurosis.

The middle stages of intensive alcoholism psychotherapy involve the therapeutic resolution of transference problems that are associated with the patient's (1) authority conflicts, (2) control problems, and (3) narcissistic disturbance. Many of these patients begin to resent the therapist as an authority figure. They also feel controlled by the therapist and the therapy relationship. They are also angry about feeling out of control. Yet, in reality, they are only beginning to develop the capacity for self-control of thoughts, emotions, and relationships. At this time, the patient's bipolar narcissism begins to emerge in the form of an exaggerated sense of egocentricity and self, and world mastery. The patient's healthy identification with the psychotherapist evolves into a narcissistic struggle.

The psychotherapy relationship spontaneously contributes to the development of a transference neurosis. The intimacy, dependency, regression, symbiosis, and authority-power dynamics that characterize intensive psychotherapy relationships facilitate the emergence of a transference neurosis. Primary alcoholics are especially prone to experiencing transference problems in intensive psychotherapy. Their experiences involving narcissistic injury, parental abuse and authority problems, impulse control problems, effective conflicts and intimacy-relationship disturbance all contribute to the outcropping of resistance and transference conflicts in therapy.

There are several therapist roles and intervention strategies that help alcoholics resolve their transference conflicts during the middle stages of intensive alcoholism psychotherapy. First of all, therapists need to allow the transference relationship to develop.

Transference dynamics reveal many of the patient's most basic conflicts and personality problems. Therapists should not avoid or suppress the patient's transference pathology. Rather, the psychotherapist needs to experience the patient's transference pathology with the patient while maintaining a therapeutic stance of technical neutrality. Secondly, it is imperative that the therapist consistently point out and interpret the patient's transference conflicts. Thirdly, the psychotherapist needs to consistently help the patient distinguish between the transference realities of the past and those that are occurring within the context of the present psychotherapy relationship. The therapist also needs to differentiate self from the patient's transference images.

Very few alcoholics develop a transference psychosis during the process of intensive psychotherapy. However, many patients become moderately anxious and depressive as they begin to work through and resolve the transference neurosis. The therapist must consistently help the patient differentiate between (1) the past and present, (2) therapist and self, (3) self and significant others, and (4) affects that are present-oriented as opposed to experienced in the past. A good deal of therapist support and work are essential to the process of helping the alcoholic modify chronic transference-determined conflicts. This task is accomplished within the confines of the psychotherapeutically induced transference neurosis.

Countertransference is also a Freudian concept (Fenichel, 1945; Reik, 1948). The countertransference reaction refers to the therapist's inappropriate and neurotic reactions to the patient and the psychotherapy relationship. The psychotherapeutic process sometimes exacerbates the psychotherapist's unresolved infantile and familial conflicts. Thus, the therapist begins to interact neurotically with the patient as he or she did with early-life significant others. Countertransference reactions result in psychonoxious psychotherapy (Forrest, 1982).

Many psychotherapists and behavioral scientists refuse to treat alcoholics (Bratter, 1980, 1984). The decision not to work with alcoholics and chemically dependent patients can be very healthy and rational for some therapists. Such clinicians tend to consciously realize that their previous experiences and interactions with alcoholic family members, patients, and significant others have created unresolved personal conflicts that could result in countertransference problems in their treatment relationships with alcoholics. To the contrary, some therapists attempt to treat alcoholics and remain unaware of their personal countertransference conflicts which systematically contribute to treatment failures. Clearly, many psychotherapists are not well-trained and/or experientially equipped for the work of intensive alcoholism psychotherapy.

Inappropriate therapist rescuing transactions during the early stages of intensive alcoholism psychotherapy set the stage for serious countertransference problems later in the treatment process. There are many pitfalls and dilemmas related to therapist-rescuing interventions. Many alcoholics need to be hospitalized or detoxified prior to entering outpatient psychotherapy. Some end up being legally committed to a hospital or inpatient alcoholism treatment facility. These rescuing transactions can be very appropriate and, indeed, lifesaving. However, therapist-rescuing interventions that involve helping patients avoid jail or other legal actions, free treatment, loaning patients money, and direct attempts to deter a divorce are clinically inappropriate. Therapist interventions that do not consistently help the patient assume responsibility for his or her behaviors can be viewed as unhealthy rescuing.

Alcoholics can be very adept at "arranging" for the therapist to give them such special favors as fee reductions, medical or psychological work releases, promotions, etc.. Therapists who allow themselves to be placated by their alcoholic patients assume the role of a "patsy" (Steiner, 1971). After the psychotherapist has assumed an unhealthy rescuer role early in the treatment process, he or she may become frustrated, enraged, and depressed about the patient's lack of progress and/or relapses during the middle stages of therapy. At this point in treatment, the therapist may actually change roles and become a persecutor (Forrest, 1982). Alcoholics have frequently assumed the role of a familial and social victim when they begin therapy. If the therapist changes roles later in therapy and becomes a patient persecutor, the victim role is further reinforced. Therapist persecutor roles are extremely iatrogenic and can result in suicidal acting out (Forrest, 1979b, 1982) upon the part of some primary alcoholics.

It is important for the therapist to be able to differentiate between healthy and unhealthy rescuing. Countertransference distortion that is associated with the therapist's anger, anxiety and depression over drinking relapses and poor treatment progress can be reduced by the utilization of therapeutic interventions that convey to the patient that he or she is responsible for self, drinking decisions, and other life issues. The therapist cannot assume responsibility for the patient. Furthermore, the therapist must be able to perceive the patient as a person who is capable of assuming responsibility for self. The patient is ultimately not a victim or scapegoat.

Therapists are not capable of magically and omnipotently restoring their alcoholic patient's mental health. Therapists cannot even control the drinking behavior of their alcoholic patients! These countertransference matters are closely tied to the psychotherapist's self-esteem and narcissism. Countertransference problems in the intensive psychotherapy of alcoholism often stem from the narcissistic struggles that occur between the therapist and patient. These patients challenge and confront the therapist's narcissism, self-worth, and professional sense of competence. The iconoclastic attitudes and behaviors of the alcoholic threaten some counselors. Alcoholic patients sometimes refuse to follow the therapist's suggestions and direct guidance. They may stop taking Antabuse, miss therapy sessions, and go on a drinking binge. They also disagree with their therapists, get angry, act out, and sometimes fail to recover. The therapist's countertransference reactions to all of these potential realities are frequently a function of various narcissistic dynamics.

The next psychotherapy vignette was taken from the thirty-first session with Jack G. The patient felt as though further treatment would be of limited benefit, and he consciously felt that the therapist and therapeutic relationship were anxiety-producing.

Doctor F: You have made excellent progress in therapy . . . I see a lot of positive changes and feel good about the work you've done.

Jack G: Yeah, eh . . . I really am kinda proud of myself. I feel better, look better . . . hell, I honestly feel like I'm ten years younger! It's amazing ... what a little sobriety and some therapy can do for a man ... Ha, Ha.

Doctor F: Yes ... We're getting where we need to go.

Jack G: You know, I mentioned last week about starting to meet every two or three weeks? I still think I'm ready for that ... What do you think? I mean, wh ... I've been sober and I'm not having the urge to drink any more ... plus, therapy is expensive and I've got a lot of yard work to do this summer.

Doctor F: Uh huh ... You feel like you're ready to cut down on therapy. We talked a bit about these issues last week. I was concerned when you mentioned that you hadn't been to a meeting in over two weeks.

Jack G: Well, to tell the truth, I haven't been getting a lot out of the meetings lately ... Seems like it always is the same speeches, the same stories, and the same old horse shit.

Doctor F: It's getting stale? I mean therapy and AA are getting "old"?

Jack G: Yeah ... don't get me wrong. I know that I still need to be in therapy and get to a few meetings, but hell, there's more to life than that! Besides, my wife has been pissin' and moanin' about all the time I spend at meetings and coming to see you. You know, sometimes I feel like all of you are runnin' my life. It's kinda like I'm still a kid ... And she's still drinkin' her damned beer two or three nights a week ... she's a good kraut! Ha. Ha.

Doctor F: Jack, I honestly don't believe that you're ready to begin every other week treatment ... and I'm also concerned about your not getting to AA meetings on a regular basis. The marital situation isn't resolved yet either. Your wife told you last week that you were easier to live with when you were drunk ... you were angry about that and she continues to get loaded once or twice a week ... it seems like you may be setting yourself up?

At this point in the treatment process, Jack had actualized many gains. The patient had been sober for several months and was beginning to come to grips with marital dissonance. He was also much less depressed, less angry, more controlled, and no longer acutely agitated. The patient's overall insight was improved, and he had made substantial gains in the area of resolving narcissistic-sadomasochistic pathology. Nevertheless, he very much needed to continue in weekly psychotherapy. His resistance to therapy and continued AA involvement is clearly evident in this vignette. Transference conflicts are also apparent in the vignette. The therapist's countertransference was well controlled in this session.

Resistance, transference, and countertransference dynamics are basic therapeutic issues that emerge and need to be resolved during the middle stages of intensive alcoholism psychotherapy. The therapist must help the patient explore, understand, and work through these treatment components. It is important for the patient to develop conscious awareness and insight into his or her resistance to therapy. Recovery is based upon this reality. The patient must also overcome transference conflicts. Effective intensive alcoholism psychotherapy is based upon the therapist's timely, skillful, and consistent interpretations of the patient's resistance and transference distortions. The psychotherapist must also be able to maintain (1) a therapeutic style, and (2) treatment relationships that are relatively uncontaminated by countertransference pathology.

INITIATING A HERE-AND-NOW THERAPY ORIENTATION IN INTENSIVE ALCOHOLISM PSYCHOTHERAPY

The initial diagnostic and assessment interviews with the patient involve a significant here-and-now focus. The patient's behaviors, mannerisms, verbal and communicative interactions, and overall temporal orientation are centered in the here-and-now during these sessions.

The early stages of intensive alcoholism psychotherapy also include a rather limited but consistent here-and-now focus. However, a great deal of therapeutic time and effort is devoted to exploring and uncovering the patient's past during the early stages of therapy.

As discussed in Chapter Three, the therapeutic alliance develops in the here-and-now but also evolves as a function of the process of genetic reconstruction work and confrontation interventions. The genetic reconstruction stage of therapy is almost explicitly past-oriented. The therapist's addiction focus is both here-and-now and past-oriented.

As the psychotherapeutic process begins to move into the middle and later stages of treatment, the therapist needs to shift the content and focus of therapist-patient interactions to the here-and-now. The therapeutic movement and focus into the here-and-now is a gradual and consistent process. Eventually, the basic grist of treatment becomes centered in the here-and-now. The therapist-patient dyad centers on present behaviors, relationships, cognitions, and affects. Dynamics of the psychotherapeutic relationship are centered in the present. Present-oriented realities constitute the struggles of life and the challenges of recovery. Indeed, the patient needs to learn how to live in the present and overcome problems in the here-and-now. Psychotherapy cannot change or bring back the past. The patient's pathological past is overcome and resolved through relationships and intrapersonal realities that occur in the present.

The therapist's consistent integration and synthesis of prior therapeutic material and the patient's past-oriented behaviors, feelings, relationships, thoughts, and experiences form an integral component of the shift into a here-and-now therapeutic focus. Primary alcoholics behaviorally act out their conflicted and neurotic pasts in the here-and-now. The psychotherapist must help the patient (1) consciously understand and accept the conflicts and pathology of his or her past, (2) integrate the various relationships and roles of past-oriented problems and inappropriate behaviors with present problems and conflicts, and (3) behave, think, and feel appropriately and adaptively in the present.

Psychotherapy enables the alcoholic to stop repressing and denying his or her global past. The patient is no longer terrified and catastrophically anxious about the past. Thus, therapy helps the patient live and experience life in a far less threatening here-and-now. The patient is freed from the neurotic bondage of the past. These dimensions of therapy make it simply easier for the alcoholic to stop drinking and begin to live a life that is more rationally centered in the present. Alcoholics must reexperience, resolve, and simply come to grips with their pasts, while *sober*, in order to begin to live more adaptively in the here-and-now.

The therapist needs to consistently point out to the patient that past hurts and painful experiences occurred in the past, and that the patient had no control over most of these transactions. At the same time, the therapist must stress to the patient that he or she has a great deal of control over present behaviors, feelings, relationships, and thoughts. Therapists also need to consistently help their alcoholic patients exercise healthy control over their lives by actualizing more rational choices and decisions in the here-and-now.

Obviously, the therapeutic here-and-now focus consistently includes present thoughts, feelings, and impulses that are associated with drinking and alcohol. The psychotherapist or counselor needs to actively explore the patient's current drinking adjustment. It is important to point out gains that occur as a function of sobriety. In some situations, the therapist may be able to circumvent a relapse by interpreting and exploring the patient's preconscious "set ups" to reinitiate drinking. It is also important to avoid lengthy segments of therapy that are focused around previous drinking episodes and alcohol-facilitated debauches. Effective therapy sessions are not "drunk-a-logs" that center around lengthy and continuous explorations of past drinking episodes.

The next therapy vignette demonstrates the therapist's role in maintaining a here-and-now therapeutic focus. This vignette was taken from the thirty-fourth session with Jack G. At this point in the treatment process, the patient had begun to preconsciously struggle with the compulsion to drink.

Jack G: I did have a lot of good times drinking . . . hell, I drank for fifteen or twenty years without having any serious problems . . . we used to get drunk a lot on the weekends and holidays when I was still on active duty.

Doctor F: Alcoholism doesn't usually develop overnight . . . you probably did have a lot of positive drinking experiences, but that was a long time ago.

Jack G: Yeah, it was a few years back. I remember a two-week drunk that ole Sgt. W. and I went on when we were stationed at Fort B., Georgia ... hell, we both got busted when we came back to post ... I should have learned something from that, but then I got my stripe back in less than two months.

Doctor F: It sounds like your drinking *was* a problem then. Let's switch gears. You mentioned several times last week that you had been thinking about drinking ... uh, how good a beer or two would taste ...

Jack G: Well, er ... Yeah, I have been thinking more about drinking the last couple of weeks. Sure, I'd like to have a couple of cold ones, but I'd never stop at two ... we've had some old friends over to the house and my wife always makes sure they have plenty of beer ... uh, they make sure to drink it up.

Doctor F: And that's triggered your thoughts about drinking?

Jack G: Well, I just go to bed if it gets to bothering me too much ... and I know what would happen if I tried to drink a beer or two ... Shit, it'd be "Katy, bar the door" ... Ha, ha ... But it does piss me off sometimes ... I mean that I can't drink and my wife and friends can.

Doctor F: So what have you been doing this week when you think about drinking ... you go to bed when the drinking bothers you at home. What else? Are you able to tell your wife how you're feeling about the drinking? How about the meetings? Are you talking about your thoughts and feelings about drinking at the AA meetings?

The patient was experiencing a good deal of overt conflict over the issues of his wife and friends drinking and his own desire to be able to drink. He was unable to verbally resolve these issues with his wife. The therapist avoided a lengthy therapeutic focus upon the patient's prior drinking experiences (drunk-a-log) by shifting the content of the session to the here-and-now. Alcoholic patients often avoid the reality of their present feelings and thoughts about drinking by discussing previous drinking experiences. This dynamism can be an unconscious attempt to avoid, deny, and repress the present compulsion to return to drinking.

The middle stages of intensive alcoholism psychotherapy involve a progressively more intense and systematic therapeutic focus on here-and-now issues. The therapist centers the content of therapy around the patient's present feelings, cognitions, relationships, and behaviors during the middle stages of intensive alcoholism psychotherapy.

COGNITIVE-BEHAVIORAL INTERVENTIONS
IN INTENSIVE ALCOHOLISM PSYCHOTHERAPY

During the middle and later stages of intensive alcoholism psychotherapy, the therapist may need to utilize specific cognitive-behavioral treatment techniques in order to help some patients overcome or modify select patterns of ineffective behavior. These treatment strategies can be viewed as therapeutic adjuncts. Cognitive-behavioral treatment techniques supplement and contribute to the efficacy of intensive alcoholism psychotherapy. Cognitive-behavioral strategies of therapy do not constitute an adequate holistic treatment approach for primary alcoholism. Recently, behavioral psychologists and therapists (Sobell and Sobell, 1975; Polich, Stambul, and Armor, 1978) have advocated the use of various short-term behavioral treatments for chronic alcoholics. These treatments, as well as attempts to behaviorally condition alcoholics to control their drinking, appear to be generally unsuccessful (Emrick, 1980, 1983).

Cognitive-behavioral strategies of alcoholism treatment can be very appropriate and therapeutically efficacious when combined with extended, intensive alcoholism psychotherapy. These strategies of treatment are based upon the principles of social learning theory. Applied social learning theory (Wellman and Evans, 1978) makes three primary assumptions regarding deviant (alcoholic) behavior: (1) all voluntary behavior is learned, (2) since behavior is learned, it can be "unlearned" or extinguished, and (3) the problem area is the maladaptive behavior per se. Maladaptive or ineffective behavior is learned responses and nothing more.

Cognitive-behavioral treatments simply attempt to modify or extinguish maladaptive and inefficient patterns of thinking, behaving, and emoting.

There are several relatively specific strategies of cognitive-behavioral therapy. These treatment modalities should be utilized according to the unique needs and problems of each alcoholic patient. Unfortunately, every alcoholic that enters any residential alcoholism treatment programs receives several cognitive-behavioral treatments. It is important to realize that all alcoholics are not in need of a particular behavioral treatment. The primary models of cognitive-behavior therapy that are used in alcoholism treatment and rehabilitation include relaxation training and self-hypnosis, assertion training, prosocial modeling, multimodal interventions, Antabuse maintenance, and behavioral contracting. Thought stopping, flooding, imagery training, biofeedback, chemically-based aversion therapy, and verbal aversion or covert sensitization therapy are additional cognitive-behavioral techniques that have been utilized in alcoholism treatment programs.

Most of these behavior therapy techniques can be employed during the middle and later stages of intensive alcoholism psychotherapy. It is imperative that the therapist apply these treatment techniques appropriately and in accord with the individual needs of each patient. Successful alcoholism rehabilitation can be related to the process of matching appropriate patients with appropriate therapists and appropriate treatments (Pattison, 1983, 1984).

Most alcoholics (Forrest, 1983c) experience chronic anxiety and stress. Alcohol is a general depressant that acts on the peripheral and central nervous systems. Alcoholics drink in order to extinguish anxiety. Alcohol pharmacologically and psychologically reduces the alcoholic's feelings of tension, anxiety, stress (Yost and Mines, 1984), and fear. The alcoholic's drinking response becomes habitual or chronic and maladaptive. The process of intensive alcoholism psychotherapy also evokes a good deal of anxiety and stress for many alcoholics. Thus, the psychotherapist can use relaxation, meditation, and self-hypnosis techniques to help the patient relax and reduce threatening affects. Relaxation therapy techniques reduce physiological and psychological arousal states. These techniques also reinforce the patient's commitment to psychotherapy and facilitate the potentially threatening process of self-examination.

It is often efficacious to schedule several consecutive twenty to thirty-minute therapy segments for relaxation training or self-hypnosis during the middle stages of intensive alcoholism therapy. This can be done when the patient is feeling generally anxious or in the face of a situational therapeutic exacerbation of anxiety-producing content. The relaxation therapy segments are conducted during the last half of the therapeutic hour. The patient is instructed to lie on the couch or recliner and close his or her eyes. Several relaxation or self-hypnosis techniques can then be employed to facilitate anxiety and stress reduction. Visual imagery, concentration on different muscle groups, deep breathing, trance induction, and direct suggestion measures extinguish tension and anxiety. The patient is told to practice these techniques three or four times each week between therapy sessions. Most alcoholics can subsequently utilize these stress management techniques (Solomon, 1983) after treatment termination or in crisis situations.

Many alcoholics are behaviorally passive, dependent, and inadequate. These individuals can usually benefit from assertion training. However, alcoholics that are angry, violent, poorly controlled, and overly aggressive should not receive standard assertion training. The process of intensive alcoholism psychotherapy will enable the therapist to ferret out appropriate candidates for assertion training.

Assertion training is implemented in order to help the alcoholic patient express anger and other affects, give feedback, stand up for his or her rights, and confront others without feeling anxious or guilty. The goals of assertion training need to be tailored to the individual patient. Assertion therapy is generally appropriate for patients who experience maladaptive anxiety that inhibits the expression of appropriate feelings and the performance of adaptive behaviors. Assertive behavior refers to all socially acceptable expressions of personal rights and feelings (Wolpe, 1969). Primary alcoholics need to learn how to express and deal with feelings of anger and resentment more rationally and appropriately.

There are several methods whereby the psychotherapist can

implement assertion training techniques in the therapeutic process. Patients can be referred to another therapist or group for assertion training. The therapist can devote several specific time-limited segments of a few regular therapy sessions to assertion training. The author has found that the process components of the middle stages of intensive alcoholism psychotherapy make the psychotherapeutic relationship per se a natural vehicle for assertion work. The resistance, transference, and countertransference struggles and dynamics that occur during the middle stages of therapy can be interpretatively used to teach and condition the patient to assertively express feelings and thoughts. The therapeutic alliance provides an appropriate context for the patient to learn, try out, and practice assertive behaviors. The psychotherapist can also monitor and provide feedback relative to the patient's assertive behaviors. Role playing, cathartic expression, and rehearsal are other techniques that the therapist can use to help the alcoholic patient learn more appropriate assertive behaviors. Homework assignments can also be a helpful treatment adjunct.

It is important for the therapist and patient to clearly distinguish between assertive and aggressive behaviors. Some alcoholics find it difficult to make this differentiation regarding behaviors, thoughts, and feelings. The patient's inappropriate or neurotic management of assertive behaviors is grist for the psychotherapeutic process.

The therapeutic relationship is a consistent prosocial modeling and training experience for the patient. Alcoholics identify with their therapists. Indeed, they emulate, model, and incorporate many of the therapists' behaviors, values, and beliefs. For these reasons, it is important for the psychotherapist to model a plethora of appropriate prosocial behaviors, beliefs, values, and attitudes. Countertransference conflicts can be related to the unconscious and preconscious behaviors and beliefs that the therapist models.

Research (Bandura, 1969) indicates that most learning phenomena resulting from direct experiences can occur on a vicarious basis as a result of the observation of other individuals' behaviors and the consequences of that behavior. Alcoholics have spent thousands of hours learning and modeling socially inappropriate, unacceptable, and even bizarre behaviors within the contexts of family, self, and the alcoholic interpersonal network (Forrest, 1983c). Intense, affective modeling occurs in psychotherapy. Some alcoholic patients need more structured social skills training and habilitation rather than social rehabilitation. These individuals may need to be referred for group therapy and/or involvement in a highly structured social skills training program.

The middle stages of intensive alcoholism psychotherapy are especially conducive to prosocial modeling. A great deal of this learning and modeling occurs unconsciously and preconsciously. However, it is therapeutically germane for the therapist to consistently point out, interpret, and explore the patient's inappropriate social behaviors. The therapist needs to didactically teach some patients social skills and appropriate patterns of interpersonal behavior. Many of these individuals also need to be told and taught that (1) it is simply "OK" or socially appropriate to have feelings and emotions, and (2) there are several socially acceptable ways to express feelings. The interpersonal management of feelings is difficult for most recovering alcoholics. Therefore, the clinician must be able to facilitate prosocial learning and social skills training that is affectively oriented as well as cognitive-behaviorally oriented.

Multimodal therapy (Lazarus, 1981) incorporates the use of several cognitive-behavioral treatment techniques. Thus, the patient may receive relaxation training, assertion training, systematic desensitization, self-image modification, thought stopping, and prosocial training sometime during the course of treatment. Multimodal approaches attempt to modify maladaptive or ineffective patterns of behavior, thinking, emoting, and interacting. Different treatment techniques can be employed sequentially or simultaneously for the treatment of various problems.

Rational Emotive Therapy, or RET (Ellis, 1961, 1979), can be viewed as a multimodal treatment approach. RET theory stresses that it is not people or events in themselves that are emotionally upsetting, but rather the way in which the event is perceived by the client. A wealth of clinical and research data support the overall effectiveness of rational emotive therapy (Ellis, 1979, 1981). Albert Ellis has developed a variety of practical, ingenious, and humorous therapy techniques that help patients understand, overcome, and dispute their irrational beliefs and self-defeating behaviors.

Glasser's Reality Therapy (Glasser, 1965, 1976) is also a multimodal treatment approach. This theory or model of therapy emphasizes behavior, responsibility, alternatives, the here-and-now, and reality-oriented problem-solving skills. Reality therapy (Forrest, 1978, 1984) is a very useful and effective treatment for alcoholism and substance abuse.

The therapist may need to utilize multimodal treatments during the middle stages of intensive alcoholism therapy. It is particularly important for the psychotherapist to consistently stress the role of generalized patient responsibility throughout all stages of alcoholism therapy. The basic reality operations of every alcoholic are impaired. This is a paradoxical issue, as very few alcoholics are overtly psychotic (Forrest, 1983c). Nonetheless, the therapist needs to continually help the patient accurately perceive reality and distinguish reality from nonreality or distorted thinking. These patients also must learn to anticipate and accept the consequences of their behavior. In short, the counselor can use multimodal treatments to help the primary alcoholic change and modify a diversity of relatively specific patterns of ineffective behavior, thinking, and emoting. Multimodal approaches need to be "fitted" to the individual needs of each client.

Antabuse (disulfiram) maintenance (Forrest, 1984b) can be a therapeutically efficacious cognitive behavioral alcoholism treatment. Antabuse therapy is a widely misunderstood alcoholism treatment modality. This medication produces extreme and acute physical illness when combined with ethanol. The physical symptoms of an Antabuse reaction include extreme nausea, vomiting, fall in blood pressure, extreme headache, blurred vision, breathing difficulties, and ataxia. Antabuse reactions are potentially lethal. This reaction is believed to occur (Schuckit, 1981) as a result of the accumulation of acetaldehyde as the first breakdown product of ethanol. A complete medical examination should be a basic prerequisite for Antabuse treatment. Patients with cardiac and other serious medical problems are not appropriate candidates for Antabuse treatment (Cahill, 1972). Psychotic and brain-impaired patients should not take Antabuse.

Antabuse is retained in the body (Ayerst, 1981) for as long as fourteen days after the patient has discontinued treatment. The accumulation of Antabuse in the body is a strong physiologic and psychologic deterrent to drinking for most alcoholics. The patient must ingest Antabuse daily for five to seven consecutive days during the initial stage of treatment. Patients can then be maintained indefinitely on a dose of 250 mg or 500 mg two or three times per week.

This treatment modality is aversive and alcohol-antagonizing. The patient cognitively understands the consequences of drinking in combination with Antabuse. A multiplicity of behavioral reinforcers also deter the alcoholic from drinking while taking Antabuse. However, Antabuse does *not* cure alcoholism or take away the compulsion to drink. There are no magical cures for alcohol addiction! Antabuse is not addictive or a mood elevator. Antabuse can be viewed as a healthy or adaptive "crutch" that simply reminds the alcoholic that he or she cannot drink.

It is imperative that the psychotherapist fully explains to the alcoholic how Antabuse works. As discussed in Chapter Three, Antabuse is a particularly useful treatment modality during the early stages of intensive alcoholism psychotherapy. Some patients decide to remain on Antabuse for six to twelve months. A few continue to take Antabuse regularly for many years. Alcoholics that respond favorably to Antabuse treatment (Mendelson and Nello, 1979) (1) "have a positive stated desire to abstain from alcohol," (2) "tend to be obsessive-compulsive and not prone to severe depression," (3) "are socially stable and socially competent," (4) "are usually not highly introspective," (5) "have a propensity to form dependent relationships with trusted figures," and (6) "tend to drink sporadically rather than continually and compulsively."

Whenever a patient experiences a relapse or perhaps several relapses during the middle stages of intensive alcoholism psycho-therapy, it is appropriate to initiate or reinitiate Antabuse treatment. It is also clinically appropriate to maintain court-ordered patients on Antabuse for the duration of their psychotherapeutic treatment. Many of these individuals are multiple offenders who seem to be unable to maintain sobriety in the absence of monitored Antabuse treatment. Antabuse treatment usually needs to be monitored by the therapist, treatment center, or legal agency. The patient's feelings and general response to taking Antabuse are excellent grist for the psychotherapeutic process.

The behavioral contract (Wellman and Evans, 1978; Forrest, 1984a) is a comprehensive treatment plan that is jointly constructed by the therapist and patient and possibly significant others (spouse, children, attorney, or employer). The behavioral contract is actually signed by all parties involved in its construction. The therapist and patient work out the exact treatment format (frequency of treatment, types of treatment, treatment goals, duration, etc.).

This cognitive-behavioral treatment modality is typically initiated early in the rehabilitation process. However, it may become necessary to (1) develop a behavioral contract, or (2) renegotiate the content of a previously established contract during the middle stages of intensive alcoholism psychotherapy. Patient resistance and/or lack of treatment progress during the middle stages of therapy may necessitate the development of a contract or content restructuring of a previously developed behavioral contract. Missing sessions, failure to pay for therapy and professional services, relapse, and other acting-out problems can often be resolved or minimized via the behavioral contract.

The behavioral contract is a method for concretely assessing the specific behaviors of the alcoholic. The primary sources of therapeutic gain afforded by this treatment strategy include (1) teaching the patient to deal more effectively with the matter of responsibility, (2) helping the patient make and keep commitments, (3) setting limits, (4) conveying therapist concern, (5) structuring the treatment process, and (6) allowing both patient and therapist to evaluate the process and outcome of treatment. Primary alcoholics respond individually to the processes of initiating and maintaining a therapeutic behavioral contract. The patient's ongoing reactions and responses to the behavioral contract are also content grist for the therapeutic process.

Several other cognitive-behavioral treatment techniques can be used effectively during the middle stages of intensive alcoholism psychotherapy. Indeed, the psychotherapist's armamentarium should include systematic desensitization, biofeedback, covert sensitization, imagery training, and various other cognitive-behavioral treatment techniques. These behavioral strategies of change are very effective adjuncts to the process of intensive alcoholism psychotherapy.

The following therapy vignette was taken from the thirty-fifth interview with Jack G. This treatment segment demonstrates how the therapist can integrate assertion training, prosocial training, and other direct behavioral therapy interventions within the context of intensive alcoholism psychotherapy.

Doctor F: We were talking about your wife's drinking last week... and that's been an issue that seems to come up pretty regularly.

Jack G: Yep! It still pisses me off, too.

Doctor F: Her drinking makes you angry. We've worked on that issue before. What are you doing to change the situation?

Jack G: Well, nothing I guess... I mean I've more or less given up. I've tried to tell her that it bothers me... like we've discussed. It seems like that doesn't help either... hell, she doesn't want to hear it... She really gets mad whenever I bring the subject up.

Doctor F: So you have tried to talk to her about it... about how the drinking makes you feel... how it affects you.

Jack G: Damned right! But it doesn't help... she still does it and I still get upset.

Doctor F: When have you tried to talk to her? I mean, do you bring the subject up at the time of the situation?

Jack G: Uh... well, when she says the D's or someone else is coming over for a party, I've tried to tell her to limit the drinking... stuff like that.

Doctor F: Perhaps you need to be more direct or more assertive... I think it would be quite appropriate for you to refuse to attend these parties at your home... You need to discuss or *tell* your wife this *prior* to the next party.

Jack G: She wouldn't like that a bit!

Doctor F: Uh huh... You've tried to honestly let her know

that the drinking and booze parties bother you . . . What other alternatives are there? Uh, I mean . . . what else can you do?

Jack G: I'm not sure . . . I guess I've really given up . . . like I said. What else could I do? You know, I could go do something else the next time . . . like go to the show or fishin' if they have a party.

Doctor F: That's one alternative . . . you could definitely extricate yourself from those situations. Rather than arguing or getting upset . . . even setting yourself up to drink, go do something else. If I were in your situation, that alternative would work for me. What else?

Jack G: You know, I really need to confront my wife about her drinking. I mean, she's not an alcoholic . . . at least, not like me, but she does have a problem . . . you've brought that issue up before, but I haven't really faced it . . . Uh, maybe I need to be more honest or like you say, "assertive" about *her* drinking!

Doctor F: So there are really a lot of alternatives for you to handle the problem better . . . I think the important issue is for you to choose an alternative and work at being consistent in applying it.

The drinking behavior of Mrs. G. had been a source of resentment and anxiety for Jack throughout treatment. He had been able to verbalize his concerns and feelings about this issue to the therapist for several weeks. However, he eventually "gave up" and stopped trying to modify this source of personal conflict. The therapist actively reinforced Jack's need to deal more effectively with this problem. Assertion training, modeling, examination of behavioral alternatives, and confrontation strategies were employed by the therapist in order to help Jack modify an ineffective pattern of behavior that involved coping with his wife's drinking.

Cognitive-behavioral strategies of intervention need to be utilized during the middle stages of intensive alcoholism psychotherapy. These treatment modalities are based upon the various principles of applied social learning theory. Cognitive-behavioral treatments should be applied according to the individual needs of the patient. Thus, some patients are in need of assertion training, while others may need relaxation training, prosocial training, systematic desensitization, or Antabuse maintenance. In reality, all primary alcoholics are in need of multimodal treatments. Cognitive-behavioral strategies of treatment can usually be employed as therapeutic adjuncts during the middle stages of intensive alcoholism psychotherapy. These interventions are integrated within the process of intensive alcoholism therapy.

SEX COUNSELING AND SEX THERAPY INTERVENTIONS IN INTENSIVE ALCOHOLISM PSYCHOTHERAPY

Most alcoholics (Forrest, 1978, 1983a) manifest sexual problems and conflicts. The alcoholic's sexual pathology stems from characterologically-determined identity deficit. These individuals experience chronic self-system fragmentation, blurring of the ego-boundaries, and a structural weakness of the ego. Recovering alcoholics often verbalize that they do not know who they are, and that they have been chronically confused about various identity issues. The various sexual conflicts of the patient can be associated with basic identity disturbance. Alcoholism per se also causes identity problems and ego-defusion.

Alcoholics are especially prone to developing sexual dysfunction problems. Narcissistic injury, faulty learning and conditioning, and the direct physiological consequences of chronic and/or acute intoxication contribute to the alcoholic's sexual dysfunctions. Alcoholism causes (Malatesta, Pollack, Crotty, and Peacock, 1982; Forrest, 1983a) neurogenic impotence, retarded ejaculation, orgastic inhibition, and frigidity. Indeed, all of the human sexual dysfunctions can be related to alcohol abuse and/or addiction. Acute or chronic intoxication can also precipitate deviant sexual behavior. Incest, rape, homosexuality, bestiality, child molesting, exhibitionism, and various other forms of deviant sexual behavior frequently occur as a function of acute intoxication or chronic alcoholism. Many studies (Forrest, 1983a) indicate that 40 to 70 percent of incestuous fathers are either alcoholics or alcohol abusers.

Heavy drinking synergizes the sexual and identity conflicts of the primary alcoholic. Alcoholics tend to neurotically manage their various sexual and identity conflicts by (1) overdetermined sexual acting out, or (2) avoiding sexual intimacy. The polymorphous sexual acting out of many male alcoholics (Menninger, 1938) is a defense against intense anxiety and fear associated with sexual relations and the opposite sex. Low self-esteem, castration fears, feelings of inadequacy and inferiority, and depression are also key ingredients in many alcoholics' sexual problems. Perhaps the most common form of sexual dysfunction that therapists encounter in their work with alcoholics and alcoholic couples involves desire and arousal (Forrest, 1983a) disorders. A surprising number of these individuals simply do not have sexual relations of any kind.

It is clinically inappropriate for the psychotherapist to initiate primary sex counseling and/or sex therapy interventions with alcoholics during the initial four to six months of treatment. A few of these patients openly discuss their sexual problems with the therapist early in therapy, and express a desire to "work" on these issues. Many alcoholics are afraid to discuss their sexual conflicts during the early therapy sessions. At any rate, these patients are not psychologically or physically ready to begin sex therapy until they have (1) established several months of total abstinence, (2) established a working commitment to the therapeutic alliance, (3) actively maintained a holistic program of recovery for several months, and (4) significantly resolved the underlying symptom structure that has caused and maintained their various sexual dysfunctions and/or deviations.

Alcoholics are invariably in need of basic sex education. These patients are guilty, confused, and poorly educated in the realm of human sexual behavior. The therapist must explain to some patients that masturbation is not "evil" and will not result in physical weakness. Many of these patients have been told that oral sex and anal sex are perversions. In sum, the psychotherapist needs to be a sex educator who both teaches the patient the basics of human sexual behavior and also challenges and disputes the patient's irrational sexual beliefs and attitudes (Ellis, 1980). Basic sex education sometimes results in the amelioration of the alcoholic's sexual dysfunction or sexual problems. More typically with these patients, basic sex education is an essential precursor to the therapist's initiation of sexual counseling and sex therapy.

Sex therapy is an essential ingredient in the successful intensive alcoholism psychotherapy of many alcoholics. Sex therapy interventions are usually initiated during the middle stages of intensive alcoholism psychotherapy. These interventions can be an integrated component of the process of intensive relationship therapy. It can be important for the therapist to refer some of these patients to a physician for a specific physical examination (pelvic or clitoral, blood sugar or diabetes, neurologic, etc.) prior to the beginning of sexual counseling and sex therapy. This phase of intensive alcoholism psychotherapy is typically limited to ten to fifteen actual treatment sessions.

If the patient has a spouse or is involved in a stable and meaningful heterosexual relationship, it is very helpful to include this person in the sex therapy. The spouse of the alcoholic (Forrest, 1983a) is also in need of basic sex education, and many of these individuals are sexually conflicted and/or sexually dysfunctional. A few manifest sexual deviation problems. The therapist needs to assess these various clinical issues. Obviously, the therapist can provide the spouse or lover with sex education and sex counseling. Severely conflicted spouses need to be referred for intensive individual therapy prior to beginning sexual counseling and sex therapy. It is inadviseable to attempt sex therapy when the spouse or lover is generally and/or severely sexually conflicted. Extended conjoint therapy is often indicated prior to beginning sexual therapy with these couples (Forrest, 1983a). The therapist may choose to initiate time limited conjoint relationship therapy as a prerequisite to sex therapy with these couples. It is also clinically appropriate to refer many of these couples to another therapist for conjoint treatment prior to beginning sex therapy. Considerable therapeutic experience and acumen is needed to actualize these important treatment decisions and responsibilities.

The actual sex therapy interventions that the therapist needs to implement depends upon the specific sexual dysfunction and problems of the patient and/or couple. In general, primary alcoholics require sex therapy interventions that foster sexual awareness, sexual technique, physical and psychological intimacy, and sharing.

Touching, caressing, massage, communicating, and sharing exercises are essential to the resolution of most sexual dysfunctions. Behavioral sex therapy techniques can be applied to extinguish deviant sexual response. Many alcoholics terminate their patterns of deviant sexual behavior following the establishment of long-term sobriety. Intoxication is central to the deviant sexual response of many of these patients. The psychotherapeutic relationship is always a vehicle for helping the patient define self, sexual needs and preferences, deviation, and relationship-oriented sources of sexual and identity conflict.

This therapy vignette was taken from the forty-first session with Jack G. It was the first of nine weekly conjoint therapy sessions that were conducted with Mr. and Mrs. G. Conjoint treatment was initiated for the specific purpose of helping the patient overcome long-term secondary impotence.

> *Doctor F:* Well, I'm certainly glad that you were willing to come in to work on the erection problem ... This phase of Jack's therapy will involve a few weeks ... Uh, probably 10 or 12 sessions with both of you.

> *Mrs. G:* I've wanted to have a better sex life for the last two or three years ... We used to have good sex before Jack got to drinkin' so much. Lately, it's seemed like Jack and me avoid sex ... We don't even talk about it any more ... I think he's embarrassed because he can't get it up ... Guess there's no lead in his pencil ... Ha, ha.

> *Jack G:* Yeah ... it is kinda embarrassing ... my drinking sure as hell didn't help our sex life ... I mean, the more I drank, the less interested in sex I got ... and maybe we just got too mad at each other to have sex ... Doctor F. and I have talked about that.

> *Doctor F:* Both of you seem to agree that your sexual problems were related to Jack's drinking.

> *Jack G:* I've noticed that I'm starting to get hard-ons again ... Uh, the last two or three months ... It's startin' to come back since I stopped drinking.

> *Mrs. G:* You know, I think we both have started talking to

each other more . . . ha, ha. At least we've started to like each other a little bit.

Doctor F: Perhaps you're both more able or ready to be affectionate . . . now that the booze is out of the picture.

Jack G: Things have been better for a few months, but the big thing for me was her drinking . . . We have been able to talk about that and Ilsa has finally agreed to stop having booze at our parties.

Mrs. G: I've cut down on my drinking too . . . I've thought a lot about it . . . Jack and I sure did a lot of drinking and partying over the years . . . and we did have a lot of fun before it became a problem.

Doctor F: Heavy drinking or alcoholism can cause many different kinds of relationship difficulties . . . including sex!

Mrs. G: That's for sure! Uh . . . I'm so happy about the progress that Jack has been making . . . maybe we're too old to be trying to have a better sex life, but better late than never . . . ha, ha.

Doctor F: You're not too old to have sex or enjoy sex . . . that's a myth! It sounds like both of you are interested in having good sex again, but maybe you're both a little bit afraid to try . . . or to even talk openly about your sexual "wants" or needs?

Jack G: Yeah . . . I have been embarrassed about being impotent . . . I want to have sex, but it's an embarrassing subject. Besides, she used to cut me down about it . . . uh, no lead in the pencil and limp dick . . . that sorta stuff.

Doctor F: It's important for both of you to remember that all that stuff occurred in the past . . . we can't change that, but both of you can work *together constructively* on the sex *today*.

Mrs. G: You're right . . . we both made a lot of mistakes in the past! You know, deep down I've really felt sorry for Jack . . . I mean that he couldn't get turned on . . . and I've missed having sex too!

Doctor F: I think it's very important for both of you to communicate openly about your sexual feelings and needs ... You've both made the commitment to work this out. How about touching or kissing? Holding hands or giving each other back rubs for starters?

Mrs. G: We've started to do some of that again, but no real hugging or touching yet.

Jack G: Uh ... you know, it's always been hard for me, touching and all that ... hell, I still have a hard time telling Ilsa that I love her ... I never was one to tell anyone that I *loved* them.

Doctor F: Those are some therapy goals for us ... I would like you to figure out three or four times a week when it is convenient for both of you to spend 15 or 20 minutes talking and touching ... perhaps you can get some lotion and give each other a body massage ... you need to learn how to be intimate and loving without the booze ... uh, and forget about getting an erection or having intercourse ... How do these goals sound to both of you? For next week.

The patient's marital relationship was substantially improved at this point in the treatment process. Both Mr. and Mrs. G. wanted to improve their sexual relationship. They were also committed to undertaking time-limited sex therapy in order to modify Jack's erectile incompetence. Sex therapy was initiated within the context of ongoing intensive alcoholism psychotherapy. Basic sex education, communication and relationship skill building, and intimacy exercises were used by the therapist at this juncture in sex therapy. Several other sex therapy techniques specific to the treatment of impotence were employed later in treatment.

Sex therapy interventions can be essential to the successful intensive psychotherapy of many alcoholics. These treatment interventions are most appropriately initiated after the patient has been totally abstinent and committed to psychotherapy for several months. Individual psychotherapy for the patient's spouse and/or conjoint therapy may be indicated prior to beginning sex therapy and sex counseling. Communication and interpersonal skills training, basic sex education, intimacy development, and various sex therapy techniques need to be used to treat the sexually dysfunctional or deviant primary alcoholic. The psychotherapist may decide to refer some of these patients or couples to a sex therapist or sex therapy clinic for sexual counseling and/or sex therapy. Alcoholics and their spouses manifest a diversity of sexual problems. It is very important for the therapist and patient to deal with these issues as a part of the process of intensive alcoholism psychotherapy.

CONFRONTATION TECHNIQUES
IN INTENSIVE ALCOHOLISM PSYCHOTHERAPY

Confrontation strategies were discussed in Chapter Three. These interventions are used throughout the process of intensive alcoholism psychotherapy. The confrontation techniques that the psychotherapist employs during the middle stages of intensive alcoholism psychotherapy differ from those used early in treatment.

As discussed in Chapter Three, the therapist consistently utilizes supportive, controlled, alliance-building confrontations during the early stages of intensive alcoholism psychotherapy. Movement into the middle stages of therapy involves the counselor's progressive use of more direct, affective, and in-depth confrontation interventions. A working and productive therapeutic alliance provides the relationship framework for intensive and in-depth confrontation work. The therapist is able to implement high impact, affective confrontations without effecting a rupture in the therapeutic alliance at this stage in treatment. The patient is committed to treatment and experientially understands that the psychotherapist is an agent of constructive change. Thus, the patient does not flee from therapy or become enraged, agitated, or psychotic as a function of the therapist's confrontations.

The therapist's sense of concern, compassion, and love for the patient underlies his or her use of confrontation interventions. Therapist nonpossessive warmth, empathy, genuineness, and concreteness are also basic ingredients in rational and effective confrontation work. Early in the middle stages of intensive alcoholism psychotherapy, the therapist will need to consistently confront the patient relative to denial and defense mechanisms, "set ups" or excuses for drinking, and irresponsible and acting-out behaviors. These patients often fail to consciously recognize and comprehend their self-defeating patterns of behavior. The therapist needs to consistently point out these patterns of behavior through the use of direct confrontation strategies. It is also important for the therapist to consistently elucidate the aetiological affective components of the patient's inappropriate behaviors through interpretation and confrontation interventions. Each patient tends to block or scotomize from awareness particular areas of conflictive behavior and self-system pathology. The patient must be confronted about these realities and pathological issues over and over again.

Later in the middle stages of intensive alcoholism psychotherapy, effective confrontation often takes place regarding the therapist's systematic use of interpretations. Most primary alcoholics do not need intensive, high-impact confrontation work during the later stages of intensive alcoholism psychotherapy in order to comprehend and/or modify their various patterns of self-defeating behavior. Relapses or set-ups for relapse are exceptions to this generalization. In these situations, the psychotherapist needs to actively and directly confront the patient relative to (1) behaviors and processes associated with planning to drink, (2) the irrational nature of this process, (3) the consequences of further intoxication, (4) the need for intensified treatment, and (5) alternatives to further drinking and relapse.

The following therapy vignette was taken from the fifty-fourth session with Jack G. The patient was consciously struggling with the compulsion to resume drinking at this point in psychotherapy. Yet, he attempted to deny the intensity and magnitude of his desire to resume drinking.

> *Jack G:* Things are a lot better . . . why in the hell would I want to start drinking now? It just doesn't make sense, but then again, maybe it does.

> *Doctor F:* I'm concerned about your going to the VFW lounge two or three times a week . . . even though you haven't been drinking.

Jack G: Well, er ... I usually have a couple of tonic waters with lime and watch the others get drunk ... ha ... uh, Ilsa isn't drinking much either and even the sex problem is better ... hell, I don't want to blow it!

Doctor F: Do you think it's a little bit crazy to set in a bar all evening watching other people drink or get drunk?? Especially, if you can't drink ... I mean if you are an alcoholic or have decided to stop drinking.

Jack G: I get your point ... maybe it is a little bit strange.

Doctor F: Strange? Horseshit! It looks like a set up to drink to me.

Jack G: A set up? Er, I don't think so ... at least I haven't been thinking about drinking ... I'm not, like they say, planning a drink.

Doctor F: So you haven't been thinking about drinking?

Jack G: No! Besides, I haven't had a drink in almost a year ... ha, ha. That's the best I've done for over thirty years. You know, when I think about it, I can't believe I've been sober that long ... Uh, it's almost unreal.

Doctor F: And a part of your recovery has involved staying out of the bars and night clubs ... until the last two or three weeks ... that's a change, Jack.

Jack G: You're kinda right ... but everything is so much better. I feel like a new person! Like I said, I don't want to blow it.

Doctor F: That's often one of the dilemmas of alcoholism and recovery ... setting yourself up to drink when things are really starting to work out ... Uh, getting drunk when you've got every reason to stay sober and keep growing.

Jack G: We've talked about that before and I've heard it at AA ... Uh, the idea that alcoholics can't stand prosperity ... I don't know?

Doctor F: Yes. That's the self-defeating or masochistic part of you ... it's difficult to change and tricky.

It was very difficult for Jack to accept that he was, in fact, setting himself up to resume drinking by spending an inordinate amount of time in bars and drinking environments. The therapist attempted to consistently and rather forcefully confront the patient with these realities in this therapy segment. Many primary alcoholics become very susceptible to regression when they begin to evidence radical constructive life-style changes.

The psychotherapist needs to consistently confront the alcoholic patient about various ineffective and self-defeating behaviors, attitudes, and thoughts throughout the middle stages of intensive alcoholism psychotherapy. These confrontation interventions tend to be more direct, affective, and high-impact oriented than the confrontations that are used early in therapy. Consistent confrontation interventions are basic to the process of successful intensive alcoholism psychotherapy.

MAINTAINING AN ADDICTION FOCUS
IN INTENSIVE ALCOHOLISM PSYCHOTHERAPY

As delineated in Chapter Three, it is essential for the psychotherapist to maintain an addiction focus throughout the course of intensive alcoholism psychotherapy. This therapeutic procedure tends to be utilized rather spontaneously by many therapists during the early stages of alcoholism treatment. The patient's alcohol addiction and drinking behaviors are primary areas of therapeutic focus at this time.

It can be all too easy for the therapist and patient to fail to maintain an addiction focus as the psychotherapeutic process moves into the middle and later treatment stages. The failure to maintain an ever-present addiction focus tends to occur most frequently in cases where the patient has established total abstinence very early in treatment, remained abstinent, and often evidenced many other significant treatment gains. It is surprisingly easy for the therapist and patient to "forget," repress, and deny the basis for the patient's involvement in therapy. There is a good deal of clinical wisdom in the adage "a primary alcoholic is always only one drink away from a drunk." After several months of total abstinence and global constructive behavioral change, it can be relatively easy for the therapeutic dyad to unconsciously and collectively deny the patient's alcoholism vis-à-vis the failure to maintain an addiction focus in treatment. This unconscious therapeutic conspiracy can contribute to relapse.

The clinician also needs to avoid the utilization of an overdetermined addiction focus during the middle stages of intensive alcoholism psychotherapy. Traditionally, the psychotherapy of alcoholism has been limited to an addiction focus! Many psychotherapists focus their interventions primarily in the areas of the alcoholic's drinking and drinking behaviors. Effective intensive alcoholism treatment encompasses the therapeutic amelioration of both the alcoholism per se and the behaviors, affects, cognitions, and interpersonal style that maintain and support the addiction process. Effective therapeutic interventions transcend the addiction focus. Yet, a balanced, systematic, and ongoing addiction focus is always central to successful intensive alcoholism psychotherapy. The therapist's inability to help the patient understand and resolve conflicts and pathologies that are secondary or tertiary to the alcoholism can also facilitate relapse. Most alcoholics consistently resist the real emotional work that is required to resolve these sources of characterological conflict. Thus, the therapist needs to explore and interpret the patient's maneuvers that are designed to either (1) avoid a healthy ongoing therapeutic addiction focus, or (2) remain fixated in the realm of addiction focus.

The next therapy vignette was taken from the fifty-seventh interview with Jack G. He had been consciously and unconsciously struggling with the compulsion to drink for several weeks. He also actively resisted the therapist's attempts to maintain an addiction focus.

>   *Doctor F:* There is some magic about being totally sober one year . . . You've been sober longer than that . . . Uh, like you said.

>   *Jack G:* Yeah, and it doesn't bother me much any more . . . I mean that I'm not drinking . . . that I can't drink. We're think-

ing about going back to Germany this summer for a vacation ... guess we'll stay for six weeks or so.

Doctor F: To visit Ilsa's parents? Sounds like fun!

Jack G: Yeah. We'll be able to visit a lot of her relatives and, uh ... er, take our time ... Ho, Ho. There's some big beer drinkers in her family ... that German beer is strong stuff!

Doctor F: So you've done some thinking about the "drinking aspects" of vacationing with Ilsa's relatives in Germany? Would it be hard for you not to drink over there?

Jack G: It's up to me ... Uh, I don't think they would put any pressure on me to drink ... You know, like I've said before, maybe a beer or two wouldn't hurt? After all this time, I've wondered ... but I don't need it and I don't ever want to be like I was before I started seeing you.

Doctor F: You've been wondering if you could have a drink or two and stop for several weeks ... You consciously realize that you're thinking about drinking. How many times did you attempt to control your drinking before you entered therapy?

Jack G: Hell, ten thousand!! Ha, Ha ... but that was before ... Uh, I mean I've been sober for over a year ... I haven't been sober like this for over 30 years!

Doctor F: Are you ready for an extended vacation in Germany?

Jack G: I can handle the drinking part of it, if that's what your gettin' at ... I don't want to change the subject, but did I mention that I'm thinkin' about gettin' a part time job?

Doctor F: No, but let's come back to that later ... You feel like you're ready to be in a heavy drinking environment for an extended period of time ... Do Ilsa's parents and family know that you're a recovering alcoholic? Will they expect you to drink with them or have a few beers?

Jack G: We still haven't told them ... Uh, it's none of their business and they sure as hell can't force me to drink with them.

The patient had been totally abstinent for over one year at this point in therapy. Nonetheless, he continued to fantasize about drinking and consciously believed he could control his drinking. The therapist continued to focus upon these issues in this therapy vignette. It is very difficult for most primary alcoholics to accept the reality of not being able to return to controlled drinking. The patient needs to accept the reality of not being able to return to controlled drinking at all levels of conscious awareness. In essence, the patient must completely surrender to the reality of his or her alcohol addiction.

The intensive psychotherapy of alcoholism is aimed at resolving the patient's alcohol addiction and various other living problems. Therefore, the psychotherapist needs to maintain an ever-present addiction focus throughout the course of treatment. Therapists need to avoid the use of an overdetermined addiction focus in therapy. The addiction focus is only one component of the successful treatment process. However, failure to maintain an addiction focus during the middle and later stages of intensive alcoholism psychotherapy can be tantamount to enabling the patient to resume drinking.

RELAPSE IN INTENSIVE ALCOHOLISM PSYCHOTHERAPY

Relapse or massive regression (Forrest, 1978, 1984) may occur at any time during the process of intensive alcoholism psychotherapy. However, in the clinical experience of the author, relapse seems most likely to occur between the third and sixth and tenth and thirteenth months of treatment. This bimodal relapse distribution pertains to the psychotherapy of primary alcoholic patients who are motivated to recover and committed to the psychotherapeutic process. Alcoholics who are not motivated or in various other ways not "ready" for treatment tend to experience several relapses very early in therapy and usually terminate the psychotherapy relationship prematurely.

It is highly unrealistic for the psychotherapist to expect the primary alcoholic to enter therapy and simply never drink again as well as change adaptively in many other areas of living. Most of these patients do experience a massive regression or several relapses while in treatment. Relapse is not tantamount to treatment failure! It is important for the therapist to bear in mind that most of these individuals have been chronically intoxicated for many years. Many have not received adequate prior treatments. Some have never been in psychotherapy before. A few have received a plethora of alcoholism treatments, and yet they have remained intoxicated and grossly dysfunctional. Quite simply, it is always very difficult for the primary alcoholic to overcome and resolve his or her alcohol addiction and addictive character structure.

An alcohol-facilitated massive regression within the context of intensive alcoholism psychotherapy can actually be a therapeutic and learning experience for both patient and therapist. The therapist may be able to deter a relapse on some occasions by actively interpreting and confronting the patient's unconscious or preconscious processes that are operating to reinforce further drinking. The therapist needs to help the patient reexamine his or her program of recovery. Most patients stop "working" or modify their program of recovery a few weeks prior to relapsing.

Alcoholism counselors and therapists sometimes tend to feel "let down" and angry when their patients experience a relapse. These feelings and affects are understandable but irrational and therapeutically psychonoxious. These countertransference dynamics can result in the therapist's parataxic movement away from the patient after a relapse. The psychotherapist needs to make every effort to be actively involved in the patient's attempts to recover and continue in treatment at these junctures. Juxtaposed to these issues, the therapist should avoid overdetermined attempts to rescue patients from a massive regression. The therapist's overdetermined use of rescuing transactions (Forrest, 1979b) early in therapy can precipitate relapses and acting out during the middle and later stages of intensive alcoholism psychotherapy.

As touched upon earlier, most alcoholics have attempted to stop drinking, control drinking, and change various other behaviors hundreds of times on their own or with help. These efforts have failed or resulted in brief success. Drinking alcoholics seem to be unable to learn from their prior experiences. The insight and rational living that usually accompanies extended sobriety and involvement in intensive alcoholism psychotherapy enables many alcoholics to think more clearly, use better judgment and reasoning in decision making, and learn from prior experience. These individuals develop the capacity to learn about self as a function of relapse while in therapy. Relapse can also be a basic ingredient in the process of accepting self as an alcoholic.

Relapse in therapy helps some primary alcoholics face the unreality of fantasies about returning to social drinking. Most relapses are not limited to a few drinks. A drinking relapse usually results in a massive regression into other pathologic behaviors, affects, family and marital interactions, and living conflicts. Intoxication precipitates an acute exacerbation of the alcoholic's maladaptive behaviors and global adjustment style. The therapeutic exploration, integration, and resolution of these realities following relapse can be essential to recovery.

The therapist and patient also need to fully comprehend the potentially catastrophic consequences of relapse. Whenever the primary alcoholic returns to drinking, he or she has actualized a very destructive and possibly life-threatening choice. These patients jeopardize their physical and emotional well-being when they relapse. Serious legal, familial, marital, vocational, and living problems are often caused by relapse. For these reasons, the psychotherapist must make every effort to circumvent the relapse process and actively intervene in the event of relapse. Some patients need to be hospitalized or legally committed to an inpatient alcoholism treatment facility by the therapist, following relapse. In general, these direct and forceful therapeutic interventions may need to be implemented to help the patient explore and actualize nondrinking alternatives to situational stress. It is also very important for the therapist not to expect the patient to continue drinking. One of the alcoholic's destructive self-fulfilling prophecies involves the unconscious expectancy to remain intoxicated. This irrational and self-defeating belief system needs to be explored, disputed, and resolved by the therapist and patient. Indeed, it is important for the psychotherapist to consistently verbalize his or her confidence in the patient's basic capacity for growth and recovery.

There are unlimited sources of learning and growth potential that are associated with relapse. Relapse sometimes occurs in the most productive and effective of psychotherapy relationships. When relapse does occur within the context of intensive alcoholism psychotherapy, it is important for the therapist to (1) actively reinforce the patient's commitment to treatment, (2) point out to the patient that relapse does not mean that the patient has failed or that therapy is ineffective or "not working," (3) remain *self-aware* of these same realities, (4) systematically explore the global antecedents to the relapse or massive regression, (5) elucidate the therapist-patient relationship dynamics that were operational immediately prior to the relapse, (6) explore alternatives to drinking and relapse for possible similar future situations that could precipitate relapse, and (7) consider implementing short-term ancillary therapeutic support alternatives (intensified AA involvement, Antabuse, etc.). The therapist should also actively intervene to help the patient after he or she avoids treatment and remains intoxicated for several days. Many of these patients become grossly irrational and destructive following a few hours of drinking. A few are able to spontaneously stop drinking after a few hours or a few days of acute intoxication. Obviously, a great deal of therapist skill, experience, and acumen are required to effectively manage the diverse forms of relapse. Each patient manifests a relatively unique pattern and style of relapse.

It is helpful for the therapist to view relapse or massive regression as a process. The relapse phenomenon involves antecedent, process, and outcome variables that are relatively specific to each patient, therapist, and psychotherapy relationship. Relapse during the middle and later stages of intensive alcoholism psychotherapy is destructive and can threaten the therapeutic alliance. However, relapse can also be a paradoxically creative, learning, and growth-oriented experience that strengthens the psychotherapy relationship.

The following therapy vignette was taken from the sixty-third therapy session with Jack G. He had experienced a three-day massive regression prior to this session. This was Jack's first relapse since entering intensive psychotherapy.

Jack G: Yeah, uh, I've been running around like a blind dog in a meathouse for the last six weeks. Shit!

Doctor F: A blind dog in a meathouse?

Jack G: Er, I mean nervous and just running around. We've been talking about it in here, but I guess I didn't really understand how upset I was feeling ... Uh, that I was really wanting to take that first drink.

Doctor F: We have been trying to deal with that ... you had stopped making meetings for three weeks and weren't working your program of recovery.

Jack G: A damned set-up ... you know I was only able to drink for three days before all this happened to me ... uh, and I don't really know what happened on Saturday night ... I guess Ilsa took me to the emergency room after she found me walking around in a daze ... uh, beat to shit.

Doctor F: You do look bad ... are you physically OK?

Jack G: Yeah, I'm OK ... Got 18 stitches in my head and I'm sore as hell ... all over, but I'm gonna be alright ... You know, I only had three beers on Thursday night and I stopped ... but then I started drinking beer again on Friday afternoon when I mowed the lawn.

Doctor F: So you were able to control your drinking on Thursday but you got drunk on Friday and Saturday ... er, the control didn't last.

Jack G: You're right. You know, I had been thinking about drinking for a few weeks ... like you've said, maybe I was planning a drunk ... but I really thought I would be able to control it this time.

Doctor F: You convinced yourself that you could control your drinking after staying sober for so long.

Jack G: Yeah, but I couldn't ... ha, ha ... so I controlled my drinking for one night and look what it got me, beat to shit and a four hundred dollar hospital bill!! That's crazy ... really nuts!

Doctor F: I agree . . . you can't control your drinking and it's crazy for you to keep trying. Let's back up . . . uh, what were you doing . . . uh, what were you thinking about on Thursday when you started drinking?

Jack G: Nothing really. We went down to the VFW about nine on Thursday night and I just ordered a beer . . . and then I had two more later that night and stopped.

Doctor F: So things had been going fine on Thursday before you decided to have a few beers? No arguments with Ilsa or other major upsets?

Jack G: Not really. She wasn't even upset when I ordered that first beer . . . said it was my decision. Hell, she drank a couple of beers with me . . . Uh, come to think of it, we did get into it that afternoon about going to Germany and visiting her family . . . they're a bunch of damned drunks too!

Doctor F: The vacation and family issues have been sources of anxiety and stress for you . . .

Jack G: Kinda . . . but they were excuses . . . I really thought I could control my drinking. You know, I wanted to drink . . . hell, like you said, I stopped working my program of recovery. And, uh . . . I felt like I was on a "dry drunk" for a month or two.

Doctor F: Let's change gears. Have you been thinking about drinking since Saturday? Do you still have the urge to drink?

Jack G: No! Maybe I needed this last drunk . . . it might sound crazy, but I feel like I've really accepted that I can't drink . . . er, that I'm an alcoholic. We've been through that a thousand times but I feel like it took this drunk to really accept all that.

Doctor F: Uh huh . . . that makes sense.

Jack G: I even went to a meeting on Sunday afternoon- . . . that was tough after a year of sobriety! It was embarrassing, but I talked to my sponsor and I've started walking again . . . shit, I'm *afraid* to keep drinking!

The patient had struggled with the compulsion to drink for several weeks. He had also terminated many of the adaptive behavioral and life-style changes that maintained both his sobriety and improved mental health. His attempted social drinking was short-lived. The patient relapsed into alcoholic drinking and apparently was violently assaulted by three men some two days after reinitiating drinking. It was clearly apparent in this therapy vignette that Jack did realize and understand many of these issues. His insight was improved as a function of relapse, and he responded very favorably to this painful experience.

Relapse always occurs as a process. Whenever relapse takes place in therapy, the psychotherapist and patient need to explore fully (1) the various antecedents that led to the relapse, (2) how these factors facilitated relapse, (3) the relapse process, (4) immediate and long-term consequences of the relapse, (5) present and future alternatives to relapse, and (6) patient and therapist-oriented self-learning dimensions associated with the relapse. Relapse or massive regression can take place at any point in the process of intensive alcoholism psychotherapy. Relapse is always a painful and sometimes devastating experience for the primary alcoholic. Relapse can also be a productive and creative learning experience for the alcoholic during the middle stages of intensive alcoholism psychotherapy. Primary alcoholics are rarely, if ever, able to return to controlled or social drinking. Relapse may help the patient accept and integrate the concrete realities associated with being a primary alcoholic.

SUMMARY

The fundamental dimensions of the middle stages of intensive alcoholism psychotherapy were elucidated in this chapter. Facilitating patient insight and self-awareness are basic goals of treatment. Primary alcoholics deny, avoid, and repress self-oriented insight and awareness through intoxication and the overdetermined use of the avoidance defense system. Thus, therapeutically induced self-awareness tends to precipitate feelings of anxiety and trepidation. Interpretation is used by the psychotherapist to potentiate patient insight and self-awareness. The interpretative process helps resolve the patient's pathologic behaviors, cognitions, affects, and interpersonal style that stem from (1) profound early-life narcissistic injury and chronic interpersonal conflicts, (2) chronic affective disturbance, (3) characterological armoring, (4) identity and sexual disturbance, and (5) a self-defeating or sadomasochistic character style. The therapist also needs to maintain a consistent focus upon the patient's feelings and affect during the middle stages of treatment.

Resistance, transference, and countertransference dynamisms become operational during the middle stages of intensive alcoholism psychotherapy. Relapse, "forgetting" therapy sessions, being late for sessions, and late payments for treatment are examples of resistance. These patients begin to act out transference conflicts at this point in therapy by responding to the therapist as a parental introject or image. The patient's impulse control problems, authority conflicts, and narcissistic pathology emerge vis-à-vis resistance and transference phenomenon. Therapist countertransference distortions are frequently manifestations of overdetermined "rescuing" during the early stages of intensive alcoholism psychotherapy (Forrest, 1979b, 1984).

The psychotherapist needs to consistently explore, elucidate, and interpret the patient's various resistance and transference distortions. Extensive clinical experience, self-analysis, personal therapy, and ongoing psychotherapy supervision can be effective deterrents to therapist countertransference. Therapists cannot control their alcoholic patients.

The therapist shifts the content and focus of treatment to the here-and-now as the therapeutic process evolves into the middle and later stages. Eventually, the basic grist of treatment becomes centered in the here-and-now. The clinician must help the primary alcoholic (1) consciously understand and accept the conflicts and pathology of his or her past, (2) integrate the various relationships and roles of past-oriented problems and inappropriate behaviors with present problems and conflicts, and (3) behave, think, and feel appropriately and adaptively in the present. The patient is freed from the neurotic bondage of the past. It is also important for the therapist to avoid lengthy segments of therapy that are focused around previous drinking episodes and alcohol-facilitated

debauches. Drunk-a-logs rarely contribute to the success of intensive alcoholism psychotherapy.

A diversity of cognitive-behavioral strategies of alcoholism treatment can be efficaciously used in combination with extended,
intensive alcoholism psychotherapy. Cognitive-behavioral treatment strategies are based upon the principles of applied social
learning theory and utilized according to the relatively unique
needs of the patient. Thus, some patients receive relaxation training,
systematic desensitization, or self-hypnosis training while others
may receive assertion training, Antabuse maintenance, or behavioral
contracting. Multimodal treatment interventions (Lazarus, 1981)
are well-suited to the needs of most alcoholics and chemically
dependent patients. The specific methods, uses, and formats for
applying several cognitive-behavioral treatments were discussed
in this chapter. These treatments usually need to be employed as
therapeutic adjuncts during the middle stages of intensive alcoholism psychotherapy.

Most alcoholics manifest sexual problems and conflicts. Many
experience sexual dysfunction. Alcoholics also manifest identity
pathology and tend to feel inadequately masculine or feminine
(Wilsnack, 1973, 1984; Forrest, 1983a, 1983c). Alcoholism causes
various sexual dysfunctions and identity problems, and can facilitate deviant sexual acting out. It is inappropriate for the therapist
to begin sexual counseling and/or sex therapy with these patients
during the early stages of treatment. Sex therapy interventions are
appropriately initiated after the primary alcoholic has (1) entered
the middle or later stages of intensive alcoholism psychotherapy,
(2) established several months of total abstinence, (3) established a
working commitment to the therapeutic relationship, (4) actively
maintained a holistic program of recovery for several months,
and (5) significantly resolved the underlying symptom structure
(personal, marital and familial) that has caused and maintained
their sexual problems. Alcoholics need basic sex education. The
actual sex therapy techniques that the therapist uses will depend
upon the individual patient's sexual dysfunction or pattern of
conflicted sexual responding. Effective sex counseling and/or sex
therapy can be one component of the process of intensive alcoholism psychotherapy. The spouse of the alcoholic is also frequently

sexually conflicted and sexually dysfunctional. Therapists may use a number of different treatment formats to help these couples.

Confrontation techniques are used throughout the course of intensive alcoholism psychotherapy. The therapist uses more direct, affective, and high-impact confrontations during the middle stages of therapy. A working and productive therapeutic alliance enables the therapist to utilize affective and intense confrontations without causing a rupture in the therapy relationship at this stage of treatment. The therapist's sense of concern, love, and the central facilitative therapeutic ingredients always undergird the use of confrontation interventions.

The therapist's addiction focus needs to be maintained during the middle stages of intensive alcoholism psychotherapy. It can be easy to omit the addiction focus later in the treatment process if the patient has been totally abstinent and globally successful in the resolution of other conflicts. This unconscious therapeutic conspiracy can contribute to relapse. The therapist also needs to avoid the utilization of an overdetermined addiction focus. Traditionally, the psychotherapy of alcoholism has been limited to a basic addiction focus.

Relapse or massive regression tends to occur most frequently between the third and sixth and tenth and thirteenth months of intensive alcoholism psychotherapy with highly motivated patients. Relapse is always a potentially devastating and destructive event for the patient. However, relapse can also facilitate various sources of positive learning and therapeutic gain for primary alcoholics. Relapse occurs as a process. Relapse does not perfunctorily mean that the patient has failed or that treatment is not "working." Therapists need to realistically understand that relapse does take place in intensive alcoholism psychotherapy. Several specific therapist interventions that are used to circumvent or therapeutically manage relapse were discussed.

The "lion's share" of therapeutic work is accomplished during the middle stages of intensive alcoholism psychotherapy. This work can only be accomplished after the foundations of the treatment process have been established and worked through during the early stages of therapy. The various therapist techniques and strategies that were discussed throughout this chapter are essential to the process of helping primary alcoholics (1) maintain sobriety, and (2) actualize adaptive global behavioral, affective, characterological and personality, cognitive, and life-style changes. Indeed, the primary psychodynamic and psychotherapeutic process components of intensive alcoholism psychotherapy were explored in this chapter.

Chapter V

LATER STAGES OF
INTENSIVE ALCOHOLISM PSYCHOTHERAPY

INTRODUCTION

The later stages of intensive alcoholism psychotherapy include the eleventh through eighteenth months of treatment. A few primary alcoholics may require two or more years of ongoing therapeutic treatment in order to achieve lasting sobriety and recovery. However, it is generally realistic for therapists to expect that eighty percent of primary alcoholics can be successfully treated in eighteen months of intensive alcoholism psychotherapy.

Many patients do not require weekly therapy sessions during the later stages of intensive alcoholism psychotherapy. These individuals can be treated very effectively within the context of two sessions each month. The decision to see a patient twice a month during the later stages of treatment is based upon global progress during the early and middle stages of intensive alcoholism psychotherapy. Abstinence, global behavioral change and personality growth, vocational, marital, and family stability, cognitive control, and affective stability are patient-related factors that the therapist must evaluate in the process of deciding whether the patient should (1) continue in weekly intensive therapy, or (2) begin a less intensive therapy regimen. The patient also needs to be actively involved in the therapeutic decision-making process relative to frequency of treatment contacts during the later stages of therapy.

In general, the later stages of intensive alcoholism psychotherapy involve a consistent working through and reworking through of material that was elicited during earlier stages of therapy. However, many patients are confronted with the difficult tasks of making major life decisions, coping with personal and familial traumas and crises, and dealing with other significant life stressors during the later stages of the psychotherapeutic process. Thus, the process of daily living becomes an increasingly important source of grist for therapy later in treatment. A therapeutically-induced corrective emotional experience occurs as the patient learns how to cope with various daily living problems in the absence of intoxication and with the strengths that accompany several months of rational thinking and rational living.

The later stages of intensive alcoholism psychotherapy are often exciting, creative, rewarding, and filled with humor and fun for both patient and therapist. At this juncture in the therapeutic process, it is possible for the therapist and patient to objectively evaluate the patient's overall progress in treatment and daily living. Most patients develop the capacity to see the humor as well as the tragedy in their previous alcohol-facilitated behaviors and life-styles. It is exciting, stimulating, and deeply rewarding for the patient and therapist to experience the process of successful intensive therapy. The final stage of treatment can also be very productive in a creative sense. Many patients are able to view themselves, their relationships, and the world from a more realistic and more creative perspective. Some patients develop new hobbies, life goals, careers, or avocations.

It is important to point out that the final weeks and months of intensive therapy are also a time when a great deal of therapeutic work is taking place. Significant therapeutic breakthroughs can occur during this phase of treatment. Many of the concrete, as well as more esoteric, vicissitudes of alcoholism recovery emerge during the later stages of therapy. The recovering primary alcoholic becomes increasingly fully-functioning, develops the capacity for intimacy, and becomes more loving. Many of these individuals become socially concerned and actually involved in community and social issues.

This chapter addresses (1) synthesis and working through in intensive alcoholism psychotherapy, (2) identity consolidation and resolution of the projective identification mechanism, (3) intensive affective work, (4) dream interpretation, and (5) treatment termination. These therapeutic processes constitute the basic focus of the later stages of intensive alcoholism psychotherapy. Ancillary dimensions of the final stages of therapy are also discussed.

SYNTHESIS AND WORKING THROUGH
IN INTENSIVE ALCOHOLISM PSYCHOTHERAPY

The working-through process is superficially initiated during the early stages of therapy. This important dimension of intensive alcoholism psychotherapy intensifies and becomes progressively more affective and cognitive as the psychotherapy process moves into the middle stages of treatment. Indeed, the lion's share of the working-through process is usually accomplished during the middle stages of intensive alcoholism psychotherapy. However, the working through that occurs later in therapy is usually essential to the resolution of many of the patients' chronic neurotic conflicts. The working-through dimensions of intensive alcoholism psychotherapy constitute a process. Recognizing, accepting, attempting to modify, and eventually working through or resolving a conflict or set of conflicts at one point in the therapeutic process enables the patient to move on and change other sources of conflict later in treatment. It is as if the patient unlocks several doors early in therapy, only to find that each of these unlocked doors leads to several other doors that need to be unlocked if recovery is to become a reality. Indeed, therapy is analagous to a journey of painful and ultimately pleasant self-discovery.

The working through that takes place during the later stages of intensive alcoholism psychotherapy tends to be less affective and more intellectual, symbolic, and creative than the working through that occurs earlier in the therapy process. However, this very important therapeutic work cannot take place in the absence of significant working through and resolution of various neurotic conflicts during the early and middle stages of treatment. Later in therapy, the working-through process builds upon the self-insights, self-awareness, feeling resolution, and learning that has occurred earlier in treatment. The patient's avoidance defense system (Forrest, 1983c) has been significantly modified by this time. It is no longer necessary for the patient to prototaxically and reflexively utilize overdetermined denial, distortion, projection, and repression defenses in the service of the ego. Therefore, it is simply easier for the patient to consciously recognize, accept, and attempt to resolve various ineffective or pathologic aspects of the self later in treatment.

Integrated self-learning begins to take place later in therapy. The working-through process facilitates integrated, experiential self-learning. This form of learning refers to the patient's progressive ability to integrate cognitive and affective learning processes to the extent that healthy and consistent behavioral change is effected. Integrated self-learning occurs when the primary alcoholic is able to consistently think, emote, and behave rationally. Integrated learning has not taken place if the patient continues to "understand" that his or her thoughts, impulses, and affects are irrational or uncontrollable, but persists in behaving, thinking, and emoting ineffectively and irrationally. It is not enough for the patient to simply understand the irrational and maladaptive dimensions of his or her adjustment style on a cognitive level. Integrated learning brings all of the human components of the learning process together to effect healthy global adjustment and characterological change.

The later stages in intensive alcoholism psychotherapy involve a great deal of synthesizing and reworking of material and content that has been partially resolved during the earlier stages of treatment. A synthesis of the patient's fragmented thoughts, beliefs, feelings, and other intrapersonal processes that have been elevated to conscious awareness earlier in treatment occurs during the later stages of therapy. Historic, as well as present, intrapersonal and interpersonal realities become integrated and synthesized. Therapeutic synthesis enables the patient to integrate former repressed, denied, ego-dystonic material. This material is no longer ego-alien. Synthesis occurs when thought processes that were once repressed, avoided, and ego-dystonic become conscious, integrated in the here-and-now, and ego-syntonic.

Psychotherapists need to actively help their alcoholic patients integrate, synthesize, and work through the global therapeutic content of the early and middle stages of treatment during the later stages of intensive alcoholism psychotherapy. This therapeutic task is accomplished through the therapist's use of active interpretations, consistent association and elucidation of the patient's past and present neurotic conflicts, reinforcement of rational alternatives and choices in the here-and-now, and consistently relating the patient's addictive symptom structure to the therapeutic material that has been explored and partially resolved earlier in therapy. The therapist points out the various adaptive changes and sources of gain that the patient has actualized throughout the course of treatment while continuing to focus upon areas where the patient needs to do more work. In many therapeutic situations, it is easy for the counselor to point out to the patient how he or she formerly thought, emoted, or perceived relative to a certain issue, person, or life situation. The patient is usually able to see the distortion and errors in his or her earlier patterns of thinking, feeling, perceiving, and behaving. These moments in therapy can be anxiety-producing and threatening for the patient. However, the therapist's use of humor and wit in these situations can ease the relative pain of self-discovery and enhance the patient's ability to synthesize ego-dystonic material.

It is important for the therapist to continue to relate the patient's historic sources of narcissistic injury with daily living struggles and neurotic conflicts that actually take place during the later stages of psychotherapy. The therapist must also continue to interpret and analyze the patient's self-defeating behaviors and thoughts. At this juncture in the psychotherapeutic process, the primary alcoholic is usually able to recognize and modify patterns of self-inflicted narcissistic injury. Most patients develop the ability to identify potential objects and sources of narcissistic injury that are external or tangential to the self. An important therapist task involves helping the patient develop this capacity and to point out the narcissistically pathologic dimensions of the patient's object relationships. Thus, the psychotherapist helps the patient recognize and modify (1) historic and present patterns of self-inflicted narcissistic injury, and (2) historic and present patterns that involve allowing significant others to inflict narcissistic injury upon the self. These therapeutic strategies enable the patient to synthesize a consistent and balanced self-concept. Patterns of gross narcissistic fluctuation and shifting are extinguished and neutralized by these interventions. The patient develops a healthy and balanced sense of self-esteem and self-worth during the later stages of therapy.

The therapist's continued support and encouragement are important ingredients in the later stages of intensive alcoholism psychotherapy. It is beneficial to consistently point out to the patient that effective and optimal living involves more than abstinence. Indeed, sobriety alone is never enough! The therapist conveys an attitude that stimulates a desire for continued adaptive growth, change, integration, and learning.

Therapeutically-induced self working through and self-synthesizing can be processes that the patient can use in order to grow and deal with major life crises for the remainder of life. Self-therapy or self-analysis is a tool for rational living that many alcoholics develop during the later stages of treatment. In essence, the therapist teaches the patient a plethora of self-therapy techniques that can be used to cope with later life traumas and various neurotic quid pro quo oriented roles and behaviors. These self-therapy techniques may involve communication skills, relaxation, dealing with life on a "one day at a time" basis, social awareness, living with rational guilt, saying no and being assertive, overcoming anger and resentment, and knowing when to reinitiate psychotherapeutic treatment.

The next therapy vignette was taken from the eighty-third session with Jack G. At this point in therapy, Jack was continuing to resolve and synthesize his early-life experiences involving profound narcissistic need and entitlement deprivation.

Doctor F: You're able to accept how she hurt you and you can deal with those feelings . . . without pushing them down.

Jack G: That's right and, er . . . uh . . . you know, I've been able to understand how all that stuff that happened to me when I was a kid was a big part of my drinking and living problems. Boy, I sure didn't want to face all that a few months ago . . . uh, it really scared the shit out of me!

Doctor F: You used to get upset and even angry when we tried to talk about your mother and father . . . uh, your childhood and adolescent experiences.

Jack G: Well, I didn't think it would do any good to dig up the past, and it scared me. I know it's different, but it's kinda like seeing how Ilsa hurts me and how I get angry and try to hurt her . . . uh, I mean now and that's really how it's been for years.

Doctor F: Yes, the same basic issues of being hurt by someone you love and then retaliating apply to your marriage.

Jack G: I know it's crazy, but it's right ... I've treated Ilsa, my first wife, and every other woman I've really been involved with like my mother ... it's, er ... kinda like I want to hurt them because my mother hurt me ... I need to get even for what she did to me just because they're women, but there's more to it than that. I really want them to love me and take care of me ... uh, like a mother I guess ... both at the same time! Does this make any sense to you? ... er, do you know what I'm trying to say?

Doctor F: Uh, huh ... I do understand what you're saying ... it makes sense, but now that you've developed an awareness of these things, you're in a position to change ... or not get caught up in the same old battles and struggles.

Jack G: You know, that's been happening for the last six months ... and making it took that last drinking episode to ... Ilsa, or any other woman for that matter, is not my mother ... I don't have to be angry at them any more, and like we discussed a few hundred times ... Ha, ha, my mother and dad had a lot of problems ... but, I've really changed in that area too ... When I began counseling, I never wanted to see my parents again and like I mentioned a couple of weeks ago, now I'm going to California to see her ... and I'm a little bit nervous about it, but she's old and sick ... it's been fifty years since I've seen her!

Doctor F: We talked about that last session ... do you feel that seeing your mother again will help you work through these issues with you and Ilsa? ... uh, with yourself or with other women?

Jack G: Uh ... I've thought a lot about that in the last few weeks ... I don't really know ... I know that I don't feel the hatred that I used to and, uh ... I guess I feel sorry for her.

Doctor F: Seeing her is not going to be easy ... it will be upsetting I'm sure ...

Jack G: I know it, but I know that I can handle it ... I'll cry and all that, but I need to do it ... eh ... only it will help me deal with myself and Ilsa better ... I don't really know about that at this point ... another thing I wonder about is how she's going to handle seeing me ... uh, I don't want her to get all upset or feel guilty ... you know what I mean?

Doctor F: Yes ... and didn't you say that she is seriously ill?

Jack G: I guess she's been sick for years, or at least that's what Sis said. You know, I think I just want to see her because she *is* my mother ... it's ironic, because when I was drunk and before therapy, I didn't ever want to see her for the same reason ... uh, because she was my mother but she wasn't ... uh, she didn't want me, so why would I ever want her?? Those feelings or thoughts have changed!

The patient continued to struggle with various conflicts that were associated with his mother, early childhood, and narcissistic injury. As this therapy vignette demonstrates, Jack was able to cope with all of these matters much more rationally and adaptively during the later stages of therapy. He had developed a good deal of self-understanding and insight relative to his experience of chronic early-life narcissistic injury. Furthermore, he was able to work through and synthesize this process as it related to self-oriented neurotic conflicts, marital and male-female relations, and generalized patterns of interpersonal behavior.

The therapist and patient need to synthesize and work through the content of the early and middle stages of therapy during the later stages of intensive alcoholism psychotherapy. Synthesis refers to the final "putting together" process in therapy. The patient is able to rationally understand and recognize, accept, change or modify, and integrate the basic grist of the therapeutic process later in treatment. The psychotherapist facilitates this process through the continued use of interpretations, support, confrontations, cognitive examination and association of past and present dynamisms, and other creative intervention strategies. Most patients need to continue the working-through process during the later stages of intensive alcoholism psychotherapy process. Growth and recovery beyond sobriety (Forrest, 1983b) are facilitated by synthesis and working through later in treatment.

IDENTITY CONSOLIDATION AND RESOLUTION OF THE PROJECTIVE IDENTIFICATION MECHANISM IN INTENSIVE ALCOHOLISM PSYCHOTHERAPY

The ego-structure or self-system of the primary alcoholic is fragmented (Forrest, 1983c). Indeed, identity disturbance is a sine qua non of primary alcoholism. Identity consolidation is a basic goal in intensive alcoholism psychotherapy. The process of identity consolidation begins when the patient enters therapy. However, it is during the later middle stages and continuing through the final stages of therapy that identity consolidation becomes a focal issue in the treatment process. Most primary alcoholics are ready to consciously and rationally deal with identity pathology after six to eight months of intensive therapy. Neophyte counselors and therapists tend to focus on the alcoholic's identity conflicts much earlier in treatment. This therapeutic stance consistently results in patients fleeing from treatment or superficially dealing with these issues, and then recalcitrantly avoiding all identity-oriented therapeutic material.

Many primary alcoholics preconsciously and consciously fear decompensation. These patients verbalize to the psychotherapist a fear of "going crazy" or "losing my mind" early in therapy. The psychotherapist needs to supportively reassure these patients that they are not insane and, in fact, will not become psychotic. The therapist must also control the content of the therapeutic process and avoid premature, in-depth identity work early in treatment. It is important for the psychotherapist to remember that the therapeutic relationship per se is a major vehicle for identity consolidation. As the therapeutic alliance develops and strengthens, the patient experiences concomitant identity consolidation. Identity consolidation is fostered through modeling, emulation, identification, and incorporation at both behavioral and characterological levels.

Primary alcoholics experience chronic and intense feelings of anxiety. More specifically, the alcoholic's experience of intense anxiety is target specific in the sense of being interpersonally determined (Forrest, 1983c). However, interpersonally determined intense anxiety creates self-system fragmentation, or ego-deficit, during the early months and years of life. Interpersonal and intrapersonal anxiety is a deterrent to healthy ego development. Healthy consensual validation cannot consistently take place when one or both people in an intimate human encounter are acutely anxious. In this context, neither person in the interaction can experience healthy consensual validation.

A major task in the effective psychotherapy of alcoholism involves helping the patient extinguish various sources of interpersonal and intrapersonal anxiety, which cause identity defusion or self-system fragmentation. As the psychotherapeutic process moves through the early and middle stages, the patient begins to experience anxiety conflicts with the context of the therapeutic relationship. These affective conflicts neurotically parallel the patient's historic struggles and feeling disturbance in intense human relationships. However, a therapeutic resolution of the patient's intense anxiety is accomplished through the therapist's use of interpretation, in-depth exploration, confrontation, experiential learning, modeling, relaxation training, and other intervention strategies.

As the patient becomes globally less anxious, it is possible to begin to therapeutically modify depression, low self-esteem, rage and anger, paranoia, avoidance defenses, sadomasochism, and eventually self-system fragmentation. Later in therapy, most primary alcoholics begin to consciously and verbally struggle with the question, "Who am I?" The trust and depth of relationships that accompany several months of intensive alcoholism psychotherapy enable the patient to (1) develop a conscious awareness of identity pathology, (2) develop the emotional stability and ego-maturity that are needed to resolve these conflicts in therapy, and (3) eventually make the commitment to resolve these problems within the context of the psychotherapeutic relationship and remain committed to this task until a successful identity consolidation is effected.

The therapist consistently focuses upon the patient's basic sense of self and identity during the later stages of intensive alcoholism psychotherapy. Paradoxically, the early and middle stages of therapy have told the patient and therapist a great deal about the patient's identity. The identity pathology of the patient is elucidated and partially resolved early in therapy. Identity-oriented therapy content is more focused, more rational and cognitive, and less affective and distorted during the later stages of therapy. The therapist and patient rediscover and define the patient's identity early in treatment. The therapist and patient redefine, put together, and shape a relatively new patient identity later in the treatment process.

Male and female primary alcoholics tend to feel inadequately masculine and feminine (Wilsnack, 1984). Many of these individuals consciously struggle with intrusive homosexual thoughts and impulses. The gender-oriented sexual and identity conflicts of the alcoholic are grist for the middle and later stages of the therapeutic process. It is clinically important for the therapist to help the alcoholic establish a more adequately consolidated nuclear sense of self (Forrest, 1983a, 1983c) prior to beginning an intensive therapeutic focus in the areas of homosexuality, bisexuality, and gender identity. These issues are very threatening and anxiety-producing for most primary alcoholics. Therefore, the psychotherapist needs to supportively encourage the patient to simply share his or her questions, self-doubts, and long-term self-beliefs and perceptions that are associated with these issues. Many patients need to share and explore their adolescent homosexual experiences. Some act out homosexually or engage in other more deviant sexual behaviors only while intoxicated (Forrest, 1983a).

All of these areas must be fully explored and worked through by the patient in order to resolve basic identity pathology and facilitate healthy identity consolidation. Some patients need to be consistently reassured that they are adequately masculine or feminine. The meanings of homosexuality and bisexuality simply must be explained to many of these patients. The roles of drinking and chronic intoxication in the aetiology of self-system fragmentation and personality disorganization need to be discussed. Homosexual primary alcoholics often need extended therapeutic treatment for both alcohol addiction and diffuse identity and sexual conflicts. Most of these patients (Hatterer, 1970) are not appropriate candidates for psychotherapy that is aimed at modifying homosexuality.

It can be therapeutically efficacious to refer some of these patients to gay alcoholism treatment centers.

As discussed in Chapters Three and Four, a major therapist task in intensive alcoholism psychotherapy is that of significantly modifying the patient's avoidance defense system. Indeed, the primary alcoholic's character armor and rigidity must be modified if therapy is to be successful. A therapeutic resolution or significant modification of the patient's avoidance defense system (Forrest, 1983c) occurs during the middle stages of intensive alcoholism psychotherapy.

Projective identification is perhaps the most adaptive and yet pathologic component of the primary alcoholic's avoidance defense system. The projective identification defense mechanism is not one of the primary tripartite defenses that constitute the avoidance defense system. However, the projective identification process is an ultimate barrier to healthy and intimate human relating. Projective identification refers to the process of projecting self or self-system fragments upon significant others in order to facilitate identification. Thus, the primary alcoholic is essentially able to accept, interact, and identify only with people or objects that he or she perceives as extensions of self. The patient's narcissistic self-fixation is projected upon significant others and becomes the basis for interpersonal reinforcement of further pathological narcissism.

Many recovering alcoholics that become involved in the psychotherapy and treatment of alcoholism initially believe that non-alcoholic therapists cannot successfully work with this clinical population. Alcoholics Anonymous members also tend to believe this. Obviously, this position is clinically incorrect and irrational. The irrational belief system that supports the adage "only an alcoholic can treat other alcoholics" is based upon pathological projective identification! There are adaptive dimensions that are associated with the recovering alcoholism counselor's projective identification process. The therapist-patient basic common denominator of having alcoholism or a serious drinking problem can facilitate patient identification and motivation to enter treatment. However, every alcoholic is a unique and different person! The alcoholic patient can only be a very limited extension of the recovering alcoholic therapist or counselor.

Paranoia and paranoid dynamics are associated with the projective identification mechanism. Rigid thinking, compartmentalization, ego-splitting, and a "black-white" worldly view also relate to the projective identification process. The patient becomes suspicious, defensive, guarded, and perhaps floridly paranoid when he or she is unable to projectively identify with significant others or a valued object. Thus, the projective identification mechanism contributes to the maintenance of paranoid ideation, which further reinforces self-system fragmentation or ego-defusion.

Projective identification interferes with healthy identity consolidation on several levels. This defense mechanism facilitates the development of a regressive and static interpersonal fixation. The primary alcoholic can only establish object attachments that are self-extensions until the projective identification mechanism is resolved. Therefore, the patient's global intrapersonal as well as interpersonal levels of adjustment remain neurotically fixated in the absence of a therapeutic modification of this mechanism. The patient's interpersonal network or support system will be limited to people who rigidly maintain the same neurotic beliefs, attitudes, values, and life-style adjustments. Obviously, projective identification contributes to the problem of self-other differentiation. The patient is unable to consistently and adequately differentiate a nuclear sense of self until the projective defense mechanism is significantly resolved. Internal feelings of inadequacy, selflessness, dependence, inferiority, depression, and low self-worth are also reinforced by the projective identification process. Many of these patients verbalize that they feel like "vapor" or "mist." They do not have a consistent and firm sense of self. They feel as though they are somehow dissolving, evaporating, and floating.

The patient's projective identification is a paradoxically adaptive dimension of effective intensive alcoholism psychotherapy early in the treatment process. These patients tend to overidentify with their therapists. Indeed, primary alcoholics often decide to terminate or persist in therapy within the initial one to three therapy hours. If the patient consciously and preconsciously perceives the therapist as a self-extension, he or she will usually make an active commitment to the treatment relationship. This situation can be paradoxically adaptive. Projective identification can contribute to the development of a working therapeutic alliance. These issues may be directly associated with therapist-patient success or failure in alcoholism psychotherapy.

The psychotherapist needs to (1) understand the primary alcoholic's projective identification defense dynamics, and (2) systematically attempt to help the patient change this process throughout the course of intensive therapy. Early in therapy, the therapist allows the transference relationship and projective identification to occur without interpreting, confronting, or systematically exploring these processes. The therapeutic relationship building that takes place early in therapy provides the therapist and patient with an in-depth relationship framework that will endure the work of consolidating the patient's identity and resolving the projective identification mechanism during the middle and later stages of intensive alcoholism psychotherapy.

The therapist helps the primary alcoholic resolve or significantly modify the projective identification process during the later stages of intensive alcoholism psychotherapy by (1) consistently focusing upon the *patient's* feelings, beliefs, attitudes, cognitions, and self-process, (2) differentiating between the patient's, therapist's, and significant others' self-processes, (3) explaining, exploring, interpreting, and focusing upon the patient's style of projective identification and relating these matters to identity consolidation, and (4) exploring, interpreting, and clarifying the relationships between projective identification, identity consolidation, paranoia, self-other differentiation, and various identity-oriented issues. The psychotherapist must redundantly go over these issues with the patient. These therapeutic techniques enable the patient to think rationally for himself or herself, actualize more effective decision making, terminate paranoid thinking, initiate and maintain more healthy interpersonal relationships, express emotions appropriately, develop a positive sense of self-worth, feel whole, and simply consolidate a nuclear sense of self.

The following therapy vignette is from the eighty-seventh session with Jack G. The patient was resolving several basic identity-oriented issues at this point in therapy. It is important to point out that Jack was confronted with the task of resolving various additional identity conflicts associated with career, retirement, and the aging process. Projective identification dynamics are also explored in this vignette.

Doctor F: I think the real issue is how *you* feel about retiring.

Jack G: How I feel about it, or what I decide is the issue- . . . it's up to me and I have to make the decision . . . uh, ha, ha . . . that's been the hard part . . . I mean I'm getting a lot better at making up my own mind, but I still tend to let Ilsa or Frank . . . whoever, decide for me.

Doctor F: It's hard to decide for yourself . . . hard to think for yourself.

Jack G: That's for damn sure! Plus, you know there's always someone to tell you how to do everything and I'm one of those people that's just learning how to think for myself . . . and er, say *no!*

Doctor F: You worked on not feeling guilty or rejected when you say *no* or disagree with other people, er . . . but, there's more to it than that . . . can you see how you make yourself dependent and attached to these people when you always agree with them?

Jack G: Dependent? Uh, I'm not sure . . . I sure as hell let them run my life . . . control me when I do what they want to or think like them.

Doctor F: Uh huh . . . and that's part of making yourself overly dependent upon other people.

Jack G: It kinda makes sense . . . the more they tell me how to think or behave, the more I depend upon them to tell me how to think or live my life!! Say, that does make sense and, er, you know I do that to myself . . . I mean, I usually want to get advice or feedback from people who agree with me . . . You know, the ones that take my side! Uh, er . . . it can make me mad too.

Doctor F: Is that something that you've done for a long time?

Jack G: You mean kinda seek out people who would take my side?... er, I guess people who think like I do?

Doctor F: Yes.

Jack G: You know, I've thought about that from time to time over the last several weeks... I think the only people I've associated with for the last thirty years have been pretty much like me... I mean how they think, drinking... er, everything. Part of that probably happened because I was in the Army for so long and uh... some of it was probably ok, but I took it to the extreme.

Doctor F: So, you've pretty much identified with people that were just like you... uh, if they didn't think like you or whatever, you didn't get involved with them.

Jack G: That's right, and most of the people I associated with over the last ten or fifteen years were drunks!

Doctor F: Birds of a feather *do* flock together! Ha, Ha.

Jack G: There's a lot to that... er, I mean we really did think alike and we behaved alike... not just the drinking either. There was a lot of so-called peer pressure too.

Doctor F: And you're now able to see that that was unhealthy in a lot of ways?

Jack G: Yeah... you know, it's like the drinking... I had to decide for myself to stop drinking, and I've had to do it on my own... Now the retirement is up to me and I have to decide on that for myself... uh, it's all about the same even the things of trying to see other people's viewpoints or stopping avoiding people because they don't think like I do... uh, I'm working on these things and it's up to me to change.

Doctor F: It's sort of like learning how to really trust yourself and allowing yourself to trust in others at the same time... uh, uh... separating yourself and standing on your own feet without being anxious or afraid.

Jack G: Well, I'm getting there... slowly! Ha, ha. At least, I think so... and I have to recognize that the problem is not just with other people ... er, I can see that it's me. Not the Army or just the ole' drunks I used to hang around with ... my friends. ... There's a lot of security in knowing you're always right or your friends will always accept you ... take your side.

Doctor F: That all makes sense ... plus, like you said earlier, you make yourself angry or resentful by always having to depend upon others.

Jack G: You said it! But see, I needed that for a long time—Well, it made me feel right ... er, when other people agreed with me, it made me feel important ... uh, like a whole person.

Doctor F: How did you feel when you were out of your support system ... uh, so to speak?

Jack G: Nervous and sometimes scared shitless ... felt like I was fallin' apart sometimes ... but not always. You know, it may sound a little crazy, but I think I used to worry about being a "fag" or something because of some of these things.

Doctor F: Yes ... you were sure who you were ... uh, needed others to consistently tell you that you were ok ... maybe, that's part of it ... You needed them to tell you that you were a real man, not gay?

It is very apparent from this therapy vignette that Jack had developed the capacity to rationally understand, accept, and modify many of his chronic identity conflicts. The patient realized that symbiotic object attachments are intrapersonally and interpersonally determined. He was also beginning to modify his projective identification process. The patient's capacities for symbolic thinking and creative self-analysis were greatly expanded. He was beginning to consciously and internally understand how projective identification, symbiotic object attachments, basic self-security operations, and identity are interdependent processes.

A significant ego-synthesis or identity consolidation occurs in the primary alcoholic during the later stages of intensive alcoholism psychotherapy. The therapeutic relationship is a major vehicle for identity consolidation. The psychotherapist and patient openly explore the grist of early treatment stages. Internal feelings, self-perceptions, and self-beliefs that the patient manifests in the realm of identity need to be redundantly discussed, interpreted, and worked through by the therapeutic dyad. Therapists need to consistently focus upon the patient's sexual sense of self during the later stages of intensive alcoholism psychotherapy. The projective identification mechanism, paranoia, identity consolidation, ego-defusion, and self-security operations constitute basic therapeutic grist for the therapist and patient later in the psychotherapy process. A therapeutic resolution of the primary alcoholic's projective identification mechanism results in the subsequent modification of several other nuclear neurotic processes.

INTENSIVE AFFECTIVE WORK
IN INTENSIVE ALCOHOLISM PSYCHOTHERAPY

Later in the middle stages of intensive alcoholism psychotherapy, the therapist begins to consistently focus upon the patient's feelings and affect. The later stages of treatment involve focused and intensive affective work. Primary alcoholics experience a great deal of difficulty in the realm of managing feelings and affects. Many of these individuals will flee from treatment if the psychotherapist attempts to prematurely explore highly emotional, feeling content.

Alcoholics fear their emotions and feelings. They avoid and repress feelings. Many alcoholics are unable to correctly label their various emotions. The prototaxic, early-life affective world of the primary alcoholic has been chaotic, catastrophically anxiety-producing, and sometimes life-threatening. The psychotherapist's sensitive understanding of these realities is essential to the implementation of appropriately timed and focused affective work. The therapist initiates an intensified focus upon the patient's feelings during the later middle stages of intensive alcoholism psychotherapy. This process involves the therapist's use of interpretation, direct questioning about feelings, exploration of historic feelings and style of affect management, permission giving (in the sense of telling the patient it is simply OK or appropriate to express feelings), catharsis, labeling feelings, and consistent exploration and association of present life situations and feelings with early-life experiences and feelings. The therapist also needs to help the patient resolve affective conflicts that have actively reinforced and maintained the addiction process.

Primary alcoholics are able to openly explore and express their various repressed feelings and emotions later in the psychotherapeutic relationship. The security and basic trust that develops within the explicit context of several months of therapeutic interaction facilitates affective expression and resolution. Affective work in intensive alcoholism psychotherapy occurs as a process. The goal of helping the patient express, understand, and resolve affective conflicts and emotions is most effectively accomplished through an ongoing, consistent therapeutic focus on affective content. These patients do not resolve their essential affective pathology following two or three hours of intense, cathartic work. The psychotherapist needs to systematically and consistently help the patient express feelings, discuss feelings, and simply emote for several hours. Primary alcoholics must learn new and more rational patterns of emoting. They also need to unlearn or extinguish ineffective or inappropriate patterns of expressing emotions.

Many alcoholics irrationally believe that any open display of feelings and emotion is indicative of weakness, loss of control, or instability. Some male alcoholics associate crying and emoting with femininity. The therapist explores these irrational beliefs and then uses confrontation, interpretation, support, and disputing techniques to effect a therapeutic modification or resolution of the distorted belief system that supports the patient's affective pathology. Many patients learn to express their various feeling conflicts by practicing this pattern of behavior with the therapist. The therapist consistently helps the patient differentiate between feelings of hurt, anger, anxiety, guilt, and depression. In general, male alcoholics tend to respond to hurt or narcissistic injuries by behaving in an angry, anxious, impulsive manner. Often they do not recognize depression as depression, or hurt as hurt. Women alcoholics tend to get stuck in their feelings of hurt, depression, and guilt. They are unable to recognize feelings of anger, rage, and anxiety. The psychotherapist identifies these various feelings and affects as they occur in the psychotherapeutic relationship. The therapist then teaches the patient to properly label, recognize, experience, and modify these emotions.

Feelings and emotions are more spontaneously and rationally expressed as the patient develops the capacity to be increasingly open to his or her own experience during the later stages of intensive alcoholism psychotherapy. Feelings and the management of feelings constitute an integral part of the life process. Thus, as the patient becomes increasingly able to express feelings, show feelings, and stop repressing feelings, he or she also becomes more fully human. Many of these patients are unable to laugh, smile, or express humor early in therapy. Effective intensive alcoholism psychotherapy restores the patient's capacity to experience and express feelings of joy and humor.

The next therapy vignette is from the eighty-eighth session with Jack G. This session involved a good deal of therapeutic feeling or affective content. Jack had experienced a great deal of difficulty expressing feelings throughout his life. He also continued to have a difficult time focusing upon his emotions and feelings with the therapist.

Doctor F: So she really does want you to retire.

Jack G: Yeah . . . that's right. I've been thinking about it for several months . . . uh, you know I retired about fifteen years ago when I got out of the Army.

Doctor F: That's right, so you know how it feels to retire . . . but, uh . . . that was different.

Jack G: It was different, but at least I had to go through a few months of not really knowing what I was going to do . . . er . . . and retiring from the Army was bad. You know, I was drinkin' a lot then and I remember saying to myself . . . ha, ha . . . one hell of a lot of times as a matter of fact . . . ha . . . what now, Jack? Hell, I didn't know what I was going to do!

Doctor F: But you weren't retiring for *life*.

Jack G: You're right . . . uh, I knew that I wasn't really retiring and hell, I didn't want to retire . . . ha, ha, maybe for a few weeks, but not forever!

Doctor F: That's what's different about your situation now ... If you decide to retire now, it will probably be for life?

Jack G: If I quit now, it's for good ... uh, I don't want to be looking for a new job and hell ... uh, at my age, I probably couldn't get another job.

Doctor F: It would be more difficult to find another job at your age ... er, you're right. So you really have to be *ready* to retire this time.

Jack G: That's why it seems hard ... uh, uh ... we're ready financially ... hell, I've got over a hundred thousand dollars in CDs, uh, we've owned the house for years and I get a good retirement ... got my CHAMPUS and we shop at the commissary store ... what more could we ask for?

Doctor F: So you've tried to consider all the angles ... uh, I mean all aspects of retiring ... but, it's still hard for you to make the decision to retire?

Jack G: Yeah, it's hard.

Doctor F: What kinds of feelings and thoughts do you really have about retiring?

Jack G: A lot of different feelings ... but they're my feelings or thoughts and at least I've decided to make up my own mind ... it will be *my* decision.

Doctor F: So deciding for yourself is one issue and the feelings you have about retiring are another thing.

Jack G: That's exactly right. My feelings about retiring are really upsetting ... ha, ha ... I guess you know that by now. Uh, and it scares the hell out of me ... I guess I'm really afraid to retire ... and, er ... I've been waking up at night thinking about it ... what am I going to do? Should I keep on working? Uh, maybe I could take some classes at Pikes Peak (a community college).

Doctor F: So you've recognized that you're afraid to retire ... fear.

Jack G: Yeah, and it makes me nervous . . . uh, anxious, to use your term . . . ha, ha . . . but I'm sure as hell not nervous . . . or anxious like I used to be . . . uh, retirement can mean that it's the end of the line . . . er, er . . . your life's about over.

Doctor F: End of the trail? There are a lot of ways to view retirement . . . perhaps how you view retirement is related to your feelings of anxiety and fear?

Jack G: Well, I know that retirement doesn't have to mean it's all over . . . there's a lot left to do now that I'm sober and Ilsa and I are getting along better. If retirement is the end of the line, then I'd be lookin' at dying and I'm not ready to go . . . er, maybe that's another reason why it's hard to retire . . . uh, people think that you're ready to kick the bucket.

Doctor F: Uh, huh . . . the fear of dying and the fear of retirement can be related . . . I guess that's up to you . . . how you see retirement. It doesn't make sense to make yourself anxious or afraid by fearing retirement or death . . . but I'm glad that you can understand and explore your different feelings about these issues.

Jack G: Yeah, at least I know how I'm feeling now and I can talk about it . . . hell, a year or two ago, I would have been scared shitless . . . er, but I would have kept it to myself and if I'd still been drinkin', I'd have used it for an excuse . . . uh, it's always been hard for me to face my feelings or tell anybody else how I was feeling . . . ha, ha . . . I didn't even know how I was feeling then!

The patient was afraid to retire. He was also quite anxious about various life issues after retirement. However, he had developed the capacities to better understand his feelings, label feelings appropriately and, most importantly, share feelings more openly with the therapist and significant others. When the patient began intensive alcoholism psychotherapy, he repressed his feelings and avoided affective interactions. He was unable to rationally control these repressed affects when they were released. Indeed, the primary alcoholic manifests a bipolar style of affective management. Successful therapeutic treatment enabled

Jack to better integrate his various feelings and emotions.

The later middle and later stages of intensive alcoholism psychotherapy involve a consistent and in-depth exploration of the patient's feelings. Therapists need to actively help their alcoholic patients express feelings, discuss feelings, label feelings, and simply emote within the context of the therapeutic encounter. Most alcoholics harbor a plethora of irrational beliefs surrounding their emotions and feelings. These irrational belief systems need to be openly discussed and disputed by the therapist. The therapist also helps the patient express feelings of humor. Alcoholics can never be whole persons in the absence of developing a capacity for healthy emotional living. Therefore, helping the patient become a rationally emotional human being is one primary goal of intensive alcoholism psychotherapy.

DREAM INTERPRETATION
IN INTENSIVE ALCOHOLISM PSYCHOTHERAPY

Freud (1908) referred to the dream as "the royal road to the unconscious." He was also quick to point out that the scientific understanding of dreams has made little progress over many thousands of years. According to Freud (1908), dreams serve as a safety valve for the brain or emotions. Dreams possess the power to heal and relieve. The periodically regressive and even psychotic dream content of "normal" people enables them to behave and think rationally during waking hours. Freud (1908) hypothesized that ideas or content in dreams and psychoses have in common the characteristic of being fulfillments of wishes. Dreams are intricate measures of mental disorder. Dreams also make possible the distinction between primary and secondary processes in mental functioning. Stekel (1943) "found the dream to be an infallible mirror of the sick mind."

More recent (Hall, 1966) scientific investigations of dream processes indicate that there are two kinds of sleep: REM and NREM. These sleep patterns are differentiated by heart rate and breathing, relaxation of different muscle groups, and penile erection. An adult has four or five separate REM periods during a night of "normal" sleep. When a person is awakened during a REM sleep pattern, he is more likely to (1) have been dreaming, and (2) report dream content than when awakened during a NREM period. NREM dream reports (Hall, 1966) are more plausible, less bizarre, less affective, less visual, and more contemporary in content than REM dream reports. The "average person remembers a dream about every third morning" (Hall, 1966). There are significant individual differences in dream recall, and a few people have never remembered a dream. The biological function of dreams is to guard sleep. There is a need for REM sleep, and REM sleep deprivation can occur.

Hall (1966) reports that "when long dream series were analyzed by means of standardized scales, the result that astonished us the most was the great amount of thematic consistency that prevailed in each series. Each person dreamed about the same sort of thing from year to year even when there were radical changes in his waking life." This may be a reflection of the unchanging character of the unconscious. Indeed, Freud (1908) indicated that the unconscious is timeless and fully formed by the age of six.

Dreaming is a normal form of behavior. A dream is "a succession of images, predominantly visual in quality, which are experienced during sleep" (Hall, 1966). A dream is also a hallucination. Dreams take place in a brief period of time. Psychological processes, external realities, and bodily states produce dreams. The actual images of a dream are projections of the mind or thought processes. Dreams are creative expressions of the self. The dream also presents a very candid and accurate representation of a person's self-concept and areas of conflict.

Psychotherapists and mental health workers tend not to utilize the technique of dream interpretation and dream work in their treatment efforts with alcoholics and substance abusers. Behaviorally-oriented clinicians are not trained or experienced in therapeutic dream work. In fact, most therapists have not received training or supervision in dream interpretation. Only the psychoanalytically-oriented psychotherapists have received training and supervision in this realm. Hence, most therapists who work with alcoholics do not realize that dream work can contribute to the efficacy of the psychotherapeutic process.

It is clinically inappropriate to initiate any form of dream work during the early stages of intensive alcoholism psychotherapy. A few patients spontaneously report their dreams to the therapist during the early hours of therapy. The therapist needs to listen to these reports without making interpretations or initiating a basic therapeutic focus in the area of dream material. It is appropriate to tell the patient that dream work will comprise an important segment of the later stages of therapy. Some patients are ready to do dream work during the later middle stages of intensive alcoholism psychotherapy. The essential therapeutic precursors to initiating the process of dream interpretation and dream work in intensive alcoholism psychotherapy are (1) a working and productive therapeutic alliance, (2) a minimum of six months of total abstinence, (3) patient capacity for creative and symbolic thinking, and (4) global improvement of the patient's basic adjustment style.

Primary alcoholics tend to respond to premature dream work in intensive alcoholism psychotherapy by (1) using the dream content focus in the service of their addiction, (2) perceiving the therapist and dream exploration process as ridiculous, or (3) becoming agitated and terrified by the exploration and interpretation of their dream material. Patients who experience agitation vis-à-vis premature dream work usually flee from the treatment relationship. Alcoholic patients unconsciously wish to defeat the therapist and themselves during the early stages of therapy. The sadomasochistic characterological makeup (Forrest, 1983c) of the primary alcoholic is such that the patient primitively wishes to prove that he or she is worthless, incapable of recovery, and that the therapist's attempts to help are impotent. Consciously and verbally, the patient appears to want to recover from his or her addiction. Unconsciously, the patient wishes to defeat self, the therapist, and the therapeutic relationship early in the treatment process.

The psychotherapist initiates the process of active dream work during the later stages of intensive alcoholism psychotherapy. Dream exploration and interpretation are components of the overall treatment process. Dream work does *not* constitute the major focus or strategy of treatment. The therapist begins the process of dream work by suggesting that the bright, creative, and symbolic thinking patient begin to remember his or her dreams and report them in therapy. Dream work is of limited therapeutic benefit in the psychotherapeutic treatment of brain damaged, noncreative, cognitively limited primary alcoholics. It is helpful for some patients to write down the content of their dreams upon rising in the morning or during the course of waking in the night. It can also be very beneficial for the therapist to recall later in therapy dream content that the patient has spontaneously reported during the earlier stages of treatment.

The exploration and interpretation of a single dream can provide various therapeutic insights for the patient and therapist. However, it is always therapeutically efficacious to explore and interpret a series of dreams. The psychotherapist first explores the patient's associations and meanings that are associated with dream content. Therapists need to guard against premature, active interpretations of the patient's dream content. Indeed, active, premature, and in-depth interpretations are potentially psychonoxious for the patient.

A first step in the process of exploring and interpreting a dream series involves establishing a focus upon the manifest content of each dream. Over the course of several weeks or months of dream work, this technique is applied to the entire dream series. The identification of manifest content in a series of dreams elicits repetitive themes that are closely associated with the patient's basic pathology, life conflicts, defense mechanisms, thought processes, and interpersonal style. Repetitive dream themes reveal the patient's present and historic adjustment style. The therapist and patient need to systematically explore and integrate the manifest content of each dream and the dream series with the present and historic grist of the psychotherapeutic process. Dream content can help the therapist identify conflicts and issues that the patient has not sufficiently resolved. Dream content can also be an indicator or barometer of patient growth and change in therapy. Dreams can be indicators of conflict resolution and characterological change. The patient learns self-awareness, symbolic thinking, and conflict resolution techniques vis à vis the process of dream work.

A second technique in dream exploration and interpretation involves focusing upon the basic affects that are associated with the manifest dream content. The content of a dream or series of dreams consistently precipitates such feelings as anxiety, depression, fear or panic, humor, amusement, and astonishment in the patient. The psychotherapist needs to help the patient focus upon his or her feelings that were (1) associated with the explicit dream and dream content when it occurred, and (2) feelings and emotions that the dream and dream content evoke within the therapeutic encounter. The affective dimensions and manifest content of the dream are then associated with the patient's present and historic adjustment dynamisms. It is important for the therapist to actively explore, interpret, analyze, and reconstruct the patient's various affective reactions to the dream content. Patients also need to be given the opportunity to freely and openly share their various cognitive and affective responses to dreams that are reported and explored in therapy.

The third basic technique in dream interpretation in intensive alcoholism psychotherapy encompasses the exploration of latent or covert content and affects in each dream and dream series. Latent dream content and latent dream affects are usually confusing to the patient. The psychotherapist needs to help the patient explore the real life meanings and emotions that are associated with dream content that seems to be bizarre, incomprehensible, and confusing. The therapist's understanding of the patient's personality, character structure, life conflicts, personal symbols, and universal symbols makes the interpretation of latent dream content and affects possible. Each patient manifests a good deal of personal symbolism in his or her dream content. The psychotherapist develops an understanding of the patient's personal symbols through the process of intensive therapy. An exploration of a series of the patient's dreams over a period of several months also helps the therapist understand the covert meanings and feelings that are associated with dream content.

Another fundamental strategy of dream exploration and interpretation involves focusing upon the manifest and latent content and affects of a dream or dream series as they relate to the therapist-patient relationship. The patient's real feelings and thoughts about the therapist are often revealed through dream material. More specifically, feelings of anger, disagreement, authority conflicts, sexual impulses, and generalized transference conflicts are expressed in dreams. Therapists also express many of their preconscious and unconscious feelings and thoughts about patients through *their* dreams about patients. Thus, the clinician has access to two sensitive barometers of the therapeutic relationship: the patient's dreams and those of the therapist! Many patients express feelings and thoughts about the therapist in their dreams that they are unable to verbally share in the therapeutic relationship. The therapist enables the patient to consciously recognize and eventually share these feelings and cognitions in the therapeutic encounter via the process of dream interpretations.

The dream interpretation and exploration process also elucidates the patient's various sexual conflicts and impulses, anagogic and katagogic trends, religious and spiritual dynamics, feelings about death, and characterological bipolarity. Dream content can also be associated with the patient's future. The patient's historic and present neurotic conflicts are expressed vis-à-vis historic and present dream content. Future dreams reflect future neurotic conflicts in the absence of a successful psychotherapy experience. Dream content also reflects healthy personality growth and change.

Dream work can be a very creative and therapeutically efficacious component of the later stages of intensive alcoholism psychotherapy. Psychotherapists that are interested in developing clinical skills in this area should be encouraged to read the works of Freud (1908), Stekel (1943), Gutheil (1951), and Hall (1966).

The next therapy vignette was taken from the sixty-first session with Jack G. This was approximately ten days before the patient experienced a massive regression (*see* Chapter Four, section on relapse). The manifest content and affects in this dream were congruous with the patient's unconscious compulsion to return to drinking. The content of this particular dream was also prognostic of relapse.

Jack G: And I haven't been sleeping worth a damn for the last couple of weeks . . . uh, it's hard to get to sleep, and I toss and turn a lot.

Doctor F: So you're having trouble sleeping?

Jack G: That's for sure . . . and I've been having some bad dreams again ... like the ones I mentioned when I started in counseling ... hell, I've had some of those same dreams since I was a kid.

Doctor F: The anxiety dreams?

Jack G: Yeah, I can remember those dreams ... er, they're about the same but these damned dreams I've been having the last couple of nights are about drinking ... ha, ha ... I've been dreaming about getting drunk!

Doctor F: So you remember the specific content of these recent upsetting dreams quite well ... uh, you're drinking and actually getting drunk in your dreams?

Jack G: Right! And, er ... it's kinda scary to think about it now ... I mean, I don't want to drink and I don't *think* I'm planning to get drunk ... er, but we've been talking about it in here and you've also pointed out that I might be setting myself up.

Doctor F: You have said that you aren't consciously thinking about drinking ... not planning to drink.

Jack G: I haven't been, but these dreams sure are making me think about drinking ... er, in a way ... do you know what I mean?

Doctor F: Perhaps your dreams are telling you something? A part of you still wants to drink ... and the dreams about drinking do force you to *consciously* face your thoughts and feelings about drinking.

Jack G: That's hard for me to accept ... uh, hard to believe in a way, but it kinda does make sense.

Doctor F: You haven't told me the exact content of these dreams ... They're upsetting, but what actually happens in the dreams?

Jack G: Well, a couple of nights ago I dreamed that I was at the VFW with Ilsa and three or four other couples and there I was drinking ... drunk ... we were all drinking and laughing, having a party ... except I was shit-faced drunk in the dream

...I remember that and I was trying to play like I was sober . . . like I didn't want the rest of them to know that I was snockered.

Doctor F: And you were trying to hide the drinking in your dream . . . er, you were drunk but you didn't want the others to know this.

Jack G: Yeah . . . ha, ha . . . it was real, alright!

Doctor F: You seemed to be having a lot of uncomfortable feelings in the dream?

Jack G: I sure was! Mostly anxiety . . . I mean I didn't want Ilsa or the others to know that I was drunk, and I felt drunk in the dream . . . like I was afraid they would find out, but I was really anxious and when I woke up the next morning, I was still nervous as hell . . . it made me nervous for two or three days and guilty too . . . that sounds crazy but I felt guilty . . . like I had been drinking, but I hadn't.

Doctor F: So the feelings that you had in the dream and even after you woke up were very real . . . the feelings that you would have if you actually were drinking?

Jack G: That's right . . . uh, I mean it was real . . . the feelings and everything . . . that's what's so damned scary about those dreams! . . . It's like I went on a real drunk and I felt like I had been on a drunk for two or three days after the last dream . . . like I was on a "dry" drunk.

Doctor F: What does all this mean to you? Uh, what are these dreams and your feelings in the dream . . . er, or after the dream telling you?

Jack G: I'm not sure . . . maybe, like we've discussed, I'm dreaming about drinking because I do want to drink . . . er, but I don't want to go through all that hell again!

Doctor F: Uh, huh . . . so the dreams represent a struggle against drinking . . . er, unconscious . . . I think the dreams and your feelings that are associated with the dreams are also healthy reminders of what would probably happen with you if you decided to start drinking again . . . like the healthy part of you telling you what you don't need to learn from experience again.

The patient had been unconsciously and preconsciously struggling with the urge to return to drinking for two or three weeks when this therapy vignette was taped. However, he continued to consciously and verbally deny that he was experiencing internal dissonance over this matter. He did return to drinking some two weeks after this session. The manifest dream content and affect in this vignette clearly shows how Jack was struggling with the impulse to drink. Unfortunately, the therapist's attempts to explore and interpret this dream material did not result in the circumvention of a relapse. The content of the patient's dreams also reflected resistance, avoidance defenses, and a lack of ego-integrated acceptance of being alcoholic.

Dream work can add many therapeutically efficacious and creative dimensions to the later stages of intensive alcoholism psychotherapy. Bright, sensitive, creative, and symbolic thinking primary alcoholics respond favorably to therapeutic dream exploration and interpretation. The therapist needs to have extensive psychotherapeutic experience and didactic and clinical training in the explicit realm of dream work in order to use this treatment technique successfully. Techniques of dream interpretation include (1) focusing upon a dream series, (2) exploring the manifest content of each dream, (3) exploring the basic affects in each dream, (4) analyzing latent content and affects in the dream, (5) relating dream material to the psychotherapeutic relationship, and (6) focusing upon sexual content, personal and universal symbols, death content, bipolarity, and spirituality. It is important for the psychotherapist to utilize active interpretations in these content areas, but patients also need to be given the opportunity to fully explore their own interpretations and emotions that are associated with a dream or dream series.

TERMINATION IN INTENSIVE ALCOHOLISM PSYCHOTHERAPY

Many decades have passed since Freud addressed the question of when to terminate psychoanalytic treatment. The different "schools" of counseling and psychotherapy do not agree upon the optional length of treatment or even the required frequency of treatments for the various psychiatric disorders. In general, most psychotherapeutic treatment formats have become less intensive and shorter in duration over the past thirty years. The theory and practice of modern psychotherapy is also generally cognitive behavioral in orientation (Pattison, 1984). The behaviorally-oriented therapists advocate short-term treatment interventions for alcohol abuse and addiction, but they have often failed to delineate the precise techniques and methodologies for termination. Most textbooks that discuss the various theories of psychotherapy (Patterson, 1966; Truax and Carkhuff, 1967; Strupp, 1973; Yalom, 1975; Corsini, 1979) do not adequately address the matter of treatment termination.

The termination stages of intensive alcoholism psychotherapy are crucially important components of the therapeutic process. Indeed, the therapist's management of the termination stages of therapy with primary alcoholics is as important, if not more important, than managing the other stages of treatment. The therapist and patient need to jointly construct a flexible psychotherapy termination schedule. Premature termination can result in relapse and/or less than optional treatment results. A unilateral decision upon the part of the therapist or the patient to terminate treatment can likewise result in regression and a globally poor therapeutic outcome.

It is usually inappropriate for the therapist and patient to consider treatment termination prior to the patient's establishment of at least six to eight months of total abstinence. It is also essential for the patient to have developed and consistently practiced his or her program of recovery (Forrest, 1983b) for several months before the termination phase of therapy is initiated. I have found that most primary alcoholics respond very favorably to a psychotherapy termination format that involves a progressive and systematically increased time extension between sessions design. Most patients are ready to begin the termination stages of intensive alcoholism psychotherapy after twelve to sixteen months of treatment. It is important for the therapist to focus upon the patient's feelings and thoughts about beginning the termination phase of therapy for several sessions prior to the actual initiation of this process. The psychotherapist also needs to openly share his thoughts and feelings with the patient relative to the patient's readiness for termination and beginning this phase of the treatment process.

When the therapist and patient mutually agree that it is appropriate to begin the termination phase of intensive alcoholism psychotherapy, the patient is scheduled for sessions on an every-other-week or once-a-month basis. As indicated in Chapter Four, this treatment restructuring technique is appropriately initiated with some primary alcoholics following only six to eight months of treatment. At any rate, the decision to reduce treatment sessions to every other week, once a month, or perhaps once every three weeks is always a first step in the psychotherapy termination process. The therapist needs to explore the patient's adjustment to this new treatment format. The patient also needs to be actively reassured and told by the therapist before this modified treatment format is initiated that (1) the therapist is confident in his or her ability to successfully cope with this change in treatment format and termination, and (2) he or she can simply call for a therapy appointment between the newly scheduled sessions if this becomes necessary. It is very important for the therapist to make himself or herself readily available to the patient during the initial few weeks of the termination process.

In reality, relatively few patients call the therapist or need to make additional appointments between the newly scheduled sessions. It is important for the patient to know that he or she can return to weekly therapy if this is needed. A few of these patients do become somewhat overly dependent upon the psychotherapist via the process of several months of therapy. These individuals tend to call the therapist for various reasons and schedule "extra" sessions during the initial month or two of the termination process. The therapist and patient need to openly explore and resolve these issues as a function of the termination process.

Following the successful establishment of a treatment format that involves every-other-week sessions, the patient begins a monthly or once-every-six-weeks treatment regimen. This second treatment format modification is initiated after eight to ten every-other-week sessions. The patient is then seen in monthly or once-every-six-weeks sessions for another three to four months. I have then found it efficacious to see the patient in three subsequent follow-up sessions at six month intervals. Again, the patient is consistently told by the therapist at each of these treatment format change junctures that he or she can schedule additional treatment sessions as needed.

The psychotherapist needs to consistently and supportively inform the patient of his or her accessibility during the various stages of the termination phase of intensive alcoholism psychotherapy. Many of these patients tend to feel that a return to weekly or every-other-week therapy later in the termination process is regressive and indicative of a lack of "real" treatment progress. This is not usually the case, and the psychotherapist needs to further explore these feelings, beliefs, and issues with the patient. It is also wise for the therapist to bear in mind that a few patients will experience a major life crisis or trauma during the termination stages of therapy. Such an event may appropriately result in the patient's need for continued intensive therapy or short-term support.

It is important for the therapist to inform the patient during the final termination sessions and follow-up sessions that his or her door is always open. In other words, the therapist encourages the patient to remain open-minded to the alternative of returning to therapy if this is needed in the future. All human beings need some form of therapy from time to time. It is unrealistic for the patient to believe that he or she will never again experience significant emotional problems. Likewise, it may be equally unrealistic to expect that most of these individuals will never drink alcohol again. Treatment reengagement several months or even several years after terminating intensive alcoholism psychotherapy can be a deterrent to irrational living and relapse.

Scheduling the patient for follow-up sessions at six, twelve, and eighteen month intervals after treatment termination serves several therapeutic purposes. These contacts are therapeutic booster sessions for most patients. The therapist can reinforce earlier therapeutic gains and give the patient further encouragement to remain abstinent. Follow-up contacts provide the therapist with important longitudinal research data about patients, growth, and recovery after psychotherapeutic treatment and relapse. Most importantly, follow-up sessions sometimes enable the therapist to actively intervene in cases where the patient has resumed drinking or experienced various other life conflicts that dictate further psychotherapeutic treatment. Follow-up contacts also provide the patient and the therapist with a sense of ongoing human relatedness, contact, purpose, and achievement.

It is wise for the therapist to actively reinforce the patient's continued involvement in Alcoholics Anonymous during the termination stages of intensive alcoholism psychotherapy. Many patients feel a need to continue their AA attendance at least once a week or once a month after completing therapy. This decision is both healthy and appropriate. An ongoing commitment to AA helps the patient (1) maintain sobriety, (2) maintain a healthy and functional nonalcohol-oriented support system, and (3) continue to grow, change, and recover beyond simple sobriety.

The termination stages of intensive alcoholism psychotherapy tend to be emotionally stressful for the patient and therapist. Most primary alcoholics are quite ambivalent about terminating therapy. Therapists also experience conflicted and sometimes neurotic feelings about "letting go" of their patients. It must be remembered that the successful intensive psychotherapy relationship is a "corrective emotional experience" that modifies, resolves, and corrects the patient's personality and character structure, which have been pathologically shaped by earlier experiences in living with parents and significant others. Many of these patients have never before experienced a consistently intimate, supportive, loving, and healthy human relationship. Therefore, patients also fear "letting go" of their therapists. The various psychodynamic components that are associated with terminating the therapist-patient relationship need to be explored, faced, and resolved during the termination stages of intensive therapy. The complexities of terminating an extended psychotherapy relationship are in many ways as recondite and involved as those involved in terminating a parenting and/or marital relationship. The therapist and patient need to take the time that is necessary to face and resolve these complexities.

The termination stages of intensive alcoholism psychotherapy involve a mutually focused (therapist-patient) exploration of (1) personal and joint meanings and relevance of the psychotherapy relationship, (2) feelings that are associated with the psychotherapy relationship, (3) reliving past therapeutic experiences, (4) mutual grief and loss feelings that are associated with psychotherapy termination, and (5) restructuring of the present and future therapist-patient relationship. Intense feelings of grief, loss, and separation anxiety sometimes accompany the process of psychotherapy termination. The therapist helps the patient understand, accept, and resolve these termination-oriented cognitions and affects. Therapists also need to recognize and accept their own feelings of grief and loss that are determined by the termination process. Termination is a basic part of all human living and life itself. Termination is but another beginning! We must all learn how to accept the realities of thousands of terminations in our lives as challenging beginnings!

The final therapy vignette in this chapter was taken from the 104th session with Jack G. The patient had been in therapy for over two years at this point. He was being seen every six weeks as a part of the termination phase of treatment.

Jack G: Yeah, I guess I'm getting used to coming in every month . . . uh, six weeks.

Doctor F: It seems like a long time between our sessions now . . . almost like two or three months?

Jack G: Right! I would have never believed that I'd miss my therapy sessions . . . ha, ha . . . at least not two years ago. When we were meeting every week, it would seem like all I got done was to come to therapy.

Doctor F: And the two years really have passed quickly.

Jack G: That's for sure. Actually, the weeks between our sessions now seem to go by fast . . . kinda like when we changed to meeting every other week a few months ago.

Doctor F: How do you really feel about our termination schedule? Uh, what kind of *feelings* do you have about terminating period?

Jack G: The schedule is a good one ... like we've discussed, if I need to come in more often ... uh, if something comes up, I can always call you or come in for a session ... the *feelings* about ending therapy are another thing! Uh, I mean I want to terminate, but I guess I'm kinda afraid to stop therapy ... er, it's not easy.

Doctor F: The feelings about termination are the hard part ... at this point, it's important to remember that we're going to actually terminate in a few months ... and after that, I'll want you to come in every five or six months for follow-up.

Jack G: Yeah, I kinda feel good about terminating ... I know that it's down the pike, but it'll be here before we know it ... uh, maybe that's where the fear comes in ... I mean knowing that it will be here before we know it ... I think I'm beyond my dependency on you and therapy, but I know I'll miss these hours ... it's hard for me to tell you, Doc, but I really appreciate all you've done for me ... I look up to you and respect you for all you've *made* me do ... ha, ha ... it's been tough too!

Doctor F: Well, you're not entirely alone!! Ha, ha ... I will miss you too, Jack ... we've gotten to know each other well and ... uh ... we have a mutual respect for each other ... you have done the work to get better and I, for one, admire you for it.

Jack G: We've been through a lot together ... ha, ha ... at least it's gotten better the last several months ... er, and easier too ... I really look forward to therapy and that's why I'm going to miss coming in ... I guess I'll really miss you ... uh, it's like you're a special friend that I can depend on.

Doctor F: We both have a lot of feelings about terminating, and, er ... like I said, the *feelings* are the hard part of terminating a successful therapy relationship ... for the therapist and the client.

Jack G: I spent all of my life avoiding people and being afraid of my feelings ... uh, really afraid of life and people until I began to get sober and understand these things in therapy . . . You might say that therapy taught me to over-come these things and you know . . . uh, I think our relation-ship made that all possible.

Doctor F: Therapy enabled you to change a lot of your self-defeating behaviors and beliefs . . . Your, er . . . relationships with yourself and others have changed too.

Jack G: It might sound a little bit crazy, but the idea of stopping therapy might unconsciously mean . . . er, to me I mean, that I'm going to go back to my old self . . . uh, getting drunk would be just one part of that fear.

Doctor F: That does make sense . . . it's not crazy and that's part of the fear of terminating our relationship . . . but you need to tell yourself that you are not going to regress or stop growing because you stop therapy . . . actually, your therapy termination is a beginning.

Jack G: Yeah, uh . . . ha, ha . . . it is a beginning, but I have trouble handling new situations and new beginnings . . . ha, ha . . . I'm glad we're taking our time and talking about these things . . . quitting therapy isn't easy!

Doctor F: It's not easy and that's exactly why we need to look at these issues and hopefully deal with them . . . that's another part of why it's so important for you to stay active with AA and work your recovery program.

Jack G: Well, uh . . . I'm still getting to a meeting every week and working out . . . taking care of myself and I'm not going to give up my program of recovery . . . I guess that I'm going to need to replace the therapy part of program with something else.

The final months of intensive alcoholism psychotherapy in-volve resolving various issues that are related to the process of treatment termination. This therapy vignette demonstrates how the psychotherapist helps the primary alcoholic explore and re-solve intense feelings and emotions that are associated with the termination phase of therapy. The patient was ambivalent about terminating therapy. However, he was in the process of successfully working through these termination-related conflicting feelings and cognitions. The therapist was also able to openly share some of his personal feelings about the patient, their professional relationship, and the termination process.

The termination phase of intensive alcoholism psychotherapy is usually two to six months in length. This phase of therapy is a crucially important component of the overall psychotherapeutic process. Follow-up sessions with the patient are scheduled at six-month intervals. Alcoholism is a multivariantly determined disorder (Forrest, 1983c). Interpersonal factors play a significant role in the aetiology of primary alcoholism. According to this model (Forrest, 1983c), people can and do make people alcoholically sick or disturbed. People also can and do help people recover from alcoholism. The psychotherapeutic relationship per se is the major curative agent in intensive alcoholism psychotherapy. This is why termination is such an important and strategically difficult part of the treatment process.

Patients need to be totally abstinent, committed to the psychotherapy relationship, and actively working a program of recovery for at least six to eight months before the termination phase of treatment is initiated. A structured treatment termination format works well with this clinical population. The psychotherapist needs to consistently help the patient explore and work-through feelings that are associated with the therapist, the therapeutic relationship, and termination. These patients should also be encouraged to reenter therapy, if needed, subsequent to termination.

ANCILLARY CONSIDERATIONS
IN INTENSIVE ALCOHOLISM PSYCHOTHERAPY

The psychotherapist continues to maintain an addiction focus during the later stages of intensive alcoholism psychotherapy. This aspect of therapy is less intensive and less focused later in treatment. However, the therapist consistently explores the patient's feelings about sobriety and recovery, and thoughts and impulses concerning drinking.

It is also important for the therapist to continue to point out and confront the patient's various scotomizations during the later stages of intensive therapy. Indeed, confrontation interventions need to be utilized by the therapist throughout the course of treatment. It is usually far easier for the patient to internalize the therapist's confrontations later in treatment. Confrontation interventions tend to be less disturbing and less affective at this juncture in the psychotherapeutic process. Primary alcoholics respond more appropriately to the therapist's confrontations later in treatment.

A few of these patients relapse during the later stages of therapy or shortly after termination. These individuals simply need to be encouraged to reenter therapy on an intensive (weekly or twice weekly) basis for two to four additional months. As discussed in earlier chapters, relapse does not mean that psychotherapy, the patient, or the therapist failed. Some of these patients are recalcitrant and require more extended, extensive professional care. It is very important for the clinician to actively reinforce the message "it is OK" to reenter therapy (after termination) during the termination stages of intensive alcoholism psychotherapy.

Intensive alcoholism psychotherapy is a challenging, difficult, rewarding, and creative experience for the patient and therapist. This particular treatment modality is relatively time-consuming and requires a good deal of patient and therapist commitment to the treatment process. Treatment success during the early therapy hours helps motivate many primary alcoholics to make the commitment to remain engaged in intensive, long-term alcoholism psychotherapy. Most patients are able to evidence significant therapeutic gains as a function of (1) establishing a working and productive therapeutic alliance, (2) completing the genetic reconstruction phase of therapy, (3) developing practical social and coping skills, and (4) developing more rewarding and healthy interpersonal attachments. These patients also simply function better psychologically, interpersonally, and socially as a result of being sober. The psychotherapist's cognitive-behavioral interventions later in the treatment process teach the patient lifelong coping skills.

The therapeutic process can be very exciting, stimulating, and creative for the therapist, as well as the patient. Therapists should be sensitive to the unique treatment needs of each patient. Provocative therapy techniques (Farrelly, 1964, 1983) can frequently be utilized with these patients later in the treatment process. It is exciting and creative for the therapist to simply share the human experience of growth and change with alcoholic patients in psychotherapy. Most of these patients are eventually able to feel very positive about their psychotherapy experiences with the therapist. Therapists and patients grow as a function of their psychotherapy experiences. Psychotherapy can constructively change self-perceptions, beliefs, attitudes, feelings, and behaviors. Psychotherapy can also be "for better or worse" (Truax and Carkhuff, 1967; Forrest, 1978) for patients and therapists.

SUMMARY

The later stages of intensive alcoholism psychotherapy encompass the eleventh through eighteenth month of treatment. The final weeks and months of therapy are exciting, challenging, and often facilitate many ambivalent feelings in the patient.

A great deal of working through takes place during the later stages of intensive alcoholism psychotherapy. This phase of the working-through process is more cognitive-symbolic and rationally affective than earlier phases. Integrated self-learning begins to take place later in therapy. Integrated self-learning takes place when the primary alcoholic is able to consistently think, emote, and behave rationally. Therapists need to help their alcoholic patients integrate, synthesize, and work through the basic therapeutic grist of the early and middle stages of treatment during the final stages of intensive alcoholism psychotherapy.

The therapist can actively teach the patient several self-therapy techniques during the final stages of therapy. Most of these patients develop the capacity to accurately explore and interpret their own affects, self-dialogue, and daily living problems. Growth and recovery beyond basic sobriety are facilitated by synthesis, working through, and self-analysis during the later stages of therapy. Synthesis, working through, and self-analysis processes need to be consistently associated with the matters of narcissistic injury and narcissistic pathology (Forrest, 1983c).

Identity consolidation occurs during the later stages of intensive alcoholism psychotherapy. The earlier stages of therapy begin to foster the patient's capacity to extinguish interpersonal and intrapersonal sources of anxiety that have historically caused identity defusion and self-system fragmentation. The trust and depth of relationship that accompanies several months of intensive alcoholism psychotherapy enables the patient to (1) develop a conscious awareness of identity pathology, (2) develop the emotional stability and ego-strength that are prerequisite to resolving these conflicts in therapy, and (3) remained committed to the therapeutic work of effecting a successful identity consolidation. The patient's sexual acting out, sexual avoidance, and homosexual and bisexual conflicts need to be fully explored and resolved during the later stages of psychotherapy.

The projective identification process is elucidated and resolved later in treatment. Actually, projective identification constitutes one component of the primary alcoholic's avoidance defense system. The therapeutic management of the alcoholic's projective identification mechanism and paranoid ideation were discussed in this chapter. The primary alcoholic can only establish object attachments that are neurotic self-extensions prior to the therapeutic resolution of the projective identification mechanism. The therapeutic relationship as such is a major vehicle for constructive identity consolidation.

The later stages of intensive alcoholism psychotherapy involve focused and intensive affective work. Alcoholics fear their emotions and feelings. Most of these patients are not psychologically "ready" to begin intensive affective work until the later part of the middle stages of therapy. The therapist consistently helps the patient identify feelings and differentiate between feelings of hurt, anger, anxiety, depression, and guilt. Effective alcoholism therapy enables the alcoholic to experience and express the entire continuum of human emotions.

Dreams are intricate measures of emotional adjustment. Dreams are also creative expressions of the self. The roles of dream interpretation and dream work in intensive alcoholism psychotherapy were explored in this chapter. Many therapists and mental health workers do not utilize dream interpretation and dream work in their treatment relationships. The psychotherapist explores and interprets the manifest content of each dream in a dream series. Repetitive dream themes reveal the patient's present and historic adjustment conflicts. The therapist also explores (1) affects that are associated with manifest dream content, (2) affects that the dream content evokes within the therapeutic encounter, (3) latent dream content and latent affects associated with dream content, (4) dream content that is related to the therapist-patient relationship, and (5) sexual, bipolar, and spiritual dream themes. Dream work is therapeutically most productive when the patient is bright, creative, and a symbolic thinker.

Termination is perhaps the most important process in intensive alcoholism psychotherapy. Termination is a process that is initiated after (1) the patient has maintained at least six to eight months of continuous abstinence and (2) actively maintained a comprehensive program of recovery for several months. A structured therapy termination model was discussed. The therapist needs to help the patient express and resolve various ambivalent feelings that are associated with therapy termination. A few follow-up therapy assessment sessions should be scheduled at six-month intervals following termination. The psychotherapist needs to encourage the patient to return to therapy if additional treatment is indicated. Therapists also need to consciously understand their feelings and cognitions that are associated with termination. Termination is but another paradoxical beginning in life.

Finally, the therapist continues to maintain an addiction focus during the final stages of intensive alcoholism psychotherapy. The therapist also continues his or her confrontation interventions with the patient. The process of intensive alcoholism psychotherapy can be exciting, difficult, stimulating, creative, challenging, and rewarding for both the patient and therapist. Therapists, as well as alcoholic patients, grow as a function of the psychotherapeutic process.

Chapter VI

THE VICISSITUDES OF ALCOHOLISM RECOVERY

INTRODUCTION

Many behavioral scientists and psychotherapists continue to believe that very few, if any, chronic alcoholics are able to stop drinking and actualize adaptive personality and behavioral changes. In general, therapists and the public accept the belief "once a drunk, always a drunk." Most people simply expect alcoholics to continue their patterns of pathological consumption and pathological behavior. Approximately one-third of psychotherapists in private practice (Bratter, 1979, 1984) refuse to treat alcoholics and addicts. Alcoholics are perceived as "weak-willed," "evil," "morally degenerate," and "crazy" by many people. Unfortunately, a sizeable segment of our population tends to believe that alcoholics do not "deserve" medical and professional treatment.

The simple fact is that alcoholics can and do recover. There are several hundred thousand primary alcoholics in the United States that have stopped drinking and, in essence, recovered. Many of these individuals prefer to call themselves "recovering" alcoholics. In spite of these semantic differences, the alcoholisms can be successfully treated. Perhaps the greatest single deterrent to successful alcoholism treatment is the alcoholic's refusal to seek out treatment! As will be discussed later in this chapter, once the alcoholic enters some form of treatment, his or her chances for recovery are greatly improved. There appear to be no radical treatment outcome differences between such alcoholism treatment modalities as individual, group, AA, conjoint, family, and Antabuse therapy (Emrick, 1974, 1975, 1980). When untreated, chronic alcoholism is a fatal disease or disorder. Spontaneous remission rates for the alcoholisms are low (Zimberg, 1982). In the clinical experience of the author, the spontaneous remission rate for primary alcoholism is less than ten percent.

Psychotherapists and other behavioral scientists are beginning to realize that chemically-dependent patients can be successfully treated. This awareness and realization, in part, stems from the growing collective realization that a plethora of health and social problems are caused or facilitated by alcoholism and alcohol abuse. In essence, society is more aware of the tragic consequences of drinking and driving, alcohol-related suicides and homocides, teenage alcohol and drug abuse, alcohol use and general health, and the monetary cost of alcoholism and alcohol abuse that is shared by every person. The American collective has demanded that alcoholics be treated and rehabilitated during the past decade. These social and economic realities have resulted in the establishment of hundreds of military and community alcohol and drug rehabilitation programs, training, education and certification programs for addiction counselors, drunk driving programs, and thousands of patient referrals to these programs and facilities. Billions of federal and state dollars have been used to develop alcohol and drug treatment, education, and prevention programs.

Clinicians and the lay community have been educated about alcoholism recovery and addiction through the public exposure of former First Lady Betty Ford, Billy Carter, Wilbur Mills, and a long list of movie stars, politicians, and public figures. These recovering alcoholics have openly discussed their addiction histories, personal lives, and recoveries on national television shows, radio talk shows, and in newspaper articles. Personal disclosures by prominent recovering alcoholics have no doubt played important roles in our collective understanding and acceptance of alcohol addiction as a major health problem. These disclosures have also enabled other addicts to seek out treatment and validated the reality of addiction recovery.

Unfortunately, many therapists, as well as the general public, perceive alcoholism recovery as simply abstinence from alcohol. As discussed throughout this text, alcoholism recovery entails a great deal more than sobriety. Intensive alcoholism psychotherapy is a viable treatment modality for facilitating holistic recovery, sobriety, cognitive changes, behavioral changes, affective changes, social and interpersonal changes, and global constructive life-style changes. Intensive alcoholism psychotherapy is an alternative to chronic alcoholism and/or sobriety without emotional health, well-being, and serenity.

This chapter addresses (1) the question of alcoholism treatment efficacy in general and (2) the vicissitudes of alcoholism recovery beyond abstinence. Alcoholism treatment outcome data are presented. The pragmatic and esoteric vicissitudes of alcoholism recovery that can result from effective intensive alcoholism psychotherapy are also delineated.

GENERAL ALCOHOLISM TREATMENT EFFECTIVENESS

The assessment of alcoholism treatment outcome effectiveness is very difficult. Treatment-evaluation research is subject to many thorny methodological problems. Researchers and clinicians in the alcoholism field (Armor, Polich, and Stambul, 1978) cannot agree upon the definitions of "alcoholic," "problem drinker," and "alcohol abuser." Behavioral scientists have employed a diversity of alcoholism treatment outcome assessment criteria in effectiveness studies. Some alcoholism counselors and treatment personnel believe that the only valid measure of treatment outcome is abstinence versus continued drinking. These clinicians assume that the achievement of abstinence will result in the amelioration of the alcoholic's various conflicts. However, empirical data (Gerard, et al., 1962) indicate that a sizeable segment of abstinent alcoholics are overtly disturbed. The controlled drinking issue has created a great deal of heated controversy in the alcoholism field for more than three decades. Research data (Davies, 1962; Pattison, 1966; Sobell and Sobell, 1973; Sobell and Sobell, 1976) have long indicated that a few treated alcoholics are able to return to controlled or "normal" drinking and also maintain stability in other areas of living. Recently, the Sobell and Sobell data (1973) has received severe criticism by alcoholism researchers. It has been suggested that treatments that attempt to return alcoholics to controlled or social drinking may, in fact, be extremely iatrogenic and life-threatening (Forrest, 1983c).

Methodological flaws in alcoholism treatment outcome research include definitions and semantics, sample size, lack of control groups or inadequate controls, sample bias, contamination of treatments, patient selection, therapist and treatment variables, and inadequate follow-up assessments. In spite of these research weaknesses, the available alcoholism treatment outcome data does indicate significant improvement rates. Emrick (1974, 1975, 1979) has conducted extensive reviews of the alcoholism treatment outcome research data and concluded that treatment of any kind generally improves patient functioning. An evaluation of 265 evaluation-outcome studies of psychologically-oriented alcoholism treatments (Emrick, 1974) indicated nearly a 70 percent improvement rate. One-half of the alcoholics who improved as a result of treatment achieved varying periods of abstinence. Reports of alcoholism treatment success (Armor, Polich and Stambul, 1978) range from 30 to 75 percent, depending upon the type of treatment and outcome criteria employed in the investigation. Hill and Blane (1967) concluded that alcoholism treatment effectiveness was generally less than 50 percent.

There is little empirical evidence of the efficacy of traditional individual psychotherapy as an alcoholism treatment. An investigation of the success of intensive psychoanalytically-oriented individual psychotherapy of alcoholics (Moore and Ramseur, 1960) indicated a 30 percent improvement rate after three and one-half years of treatment. Hayman (1956) also investigated the success of psychiatrists who treated alcoholics with analytically-oriented individual therapy. Over one-half of these psychiatrists reported no treatment successes.

The effectiveness of group therapy in alcoholism treatment is also questionable. Some investigations (Ends and Page, 1959; Forrest, 1978) report favorable changes in psychological test results and abstinence rates following group treatment in hospital and residential treatment settings. Family therapy (Wegscheider, 1981) is believed to be the "treatment of choice" for alcoholism by many clinicians. However, there are very few empirical studies of the effectiveness of family therapy in alcoholism treatment. The use of tranquilizers, phenothiazines, lithium, and LSD are of little therapeutic value in the treatment of alcoholism.

Disulfiram, or Antabuse treatment, appears to produce over 50 percent success or improvement rates (Wallerstein, 1956, 1957; Forrest, 1984). Researchers (Armor, Polich, and Stambul, 1978) have suggested that Antabuse treatment may be "equal in efficacy to more costly and time-consuming psychotherapeutic methods with some clients." However, the indiscriminate use of Antabuse with all alcoholic patients in an alcoholism treatment facility is clearly contraindicated. Antabuse cannot be utilized in the treatment of alcoholics manifesting cardiovascular disease, cirrhosis, and various other serious medical problems.

Behavioral therapists have reported 80 to 90 percent success/abstinence rates in the treatment of alcoholism with aversion therapy (Anant, 1967; Wellman and Evans, 1978). However, it has also been reported that 40 to 60 percent of alcoholics who are treated with aversion therapy return to excessive drinking following six to twelve months of abstinence. It is important to point out that there are several different aversion therapy models that are used to treat alcoholics. The covert desensitization, imagery, and verbal and emetic chemical models of aversion therapy for alcoholism are clearly superior to electric shock. Lovibond and Caddy (1970) reported a 77 percent success rate using an operant-conditioning alcoholism treatment program that punished heavy drinking rather than moderate drinking. Sobell and Sobell (1972, 1973) reported 80 percent and 75 percent success rates twelve months after treatment for their total abstinence and controlled-drinking treatment groups. The control groups in these investigations evidenced only 33 percent and 26 percent improvement rates. As touched upon earlier, the Sobell and Sobell data have been severely criticized, and apparently there were several serious methodological flaws in their studies.

Industrial alcoholism treatment programs consistently report very high success rates. Pfeffer and Berger (1957) reported a success rate of 92 percent with alcoholics treated in group therapy on a voluntary basis within an industrial alcoholism program. Another industrial alcoholism group treatment program (Forrest, 1980) reported nearly a 95 percent success rate. Cowen and Nittman (1984) suggest that industrial alcoholism treatment programs consistently produce success rates in the range of 80 to 95 percent. Most of the alcoholism treatment outcome effectiveness literature is based upon male samples. Some clinicians (Wallgreen and Barry, 1970) report that alcoholism develops more rapidly and severely in women. Researchers report contradictory findings relative to this issue and sex as a prognostic variable in alcoholism treatment (Armor, Polich, and Stambul, 1978). Research does suggest (Davis, 1966) that sobriety in women alcoholics is associated with voluntary commitment, dependency, and marital difficulty, while sobriety in male alcoholics is correlated with number of previous treatments/admissions, effect of alcoholism on the family, divorce, and fear of marital rejection. Abstinence in male alcoholics has also been found to correlate with full-time employment after treatment, short-term (one week) abstinence prior to beginning treatment, previous history of active AA involvement, deceased mother, or infrequent (less than monthly) contact with the mother if she is alive.

A psychopathic or sociopathic personality makeup is the most consistent indicator of poor alcoholism treatment prognosis for males and females (Ritson, 1971; Forrest, 1983c). Alcoholics who are the most psychologically and socially competent benefit the most from psychotherapeutic treatment. Pattison (1983, 1984) has suggested that improvement rates are associated with the degree of "fit" between the patient's treatment needs and the modalities, goals, and methods of the actual rehabilitation program.

In a comprehensive study involving nearly 30,000 patients that were treated at over forty alcoholism treatment centers throughout the United States (Armor, Polich, and Stambul, 1978), it was found "at 18 months, about 67 percent of the treated clients are in remission, compared with only 53 percent of those making a single contact with the treatment center. Among clients with high amounts of treatment (one month of inpatient care and about 15 outpatient visits), the remission rate climbs to 73 percent, but among those with low amounts, the remission rate is only slightly better than for untreated alcoholics." (p. 117) Long-term abstinence correlated positively with amount of treatment in this study. Interestingly, these researchers (Armor, Polich, and Stambul, 1978) found that alcoholism remission rates depend not only upon the presence or amount of treatment, but "also on the nature of the client's other treatment. The highest remission rates appear among those client groups that received *only* ATC treatment or AA treatment . . . if a client received other additional treatment (not from the ATC or from AA), his chances are much poorer and his prognosis does not improve notably, even if he receives high amounts of ATC treatment." (p. 119) It was also found that AA raises the remission rate from 55 to 71 percent for clients receiving little or no ATC treatment. Furthermore, regardless of the amount of ATC treatment, regular AA participants were about 20 percent more likely to be long-term abstainers than non-AA participants.

The Armor, Polich, and Stambul (1978) study also manifests methodological flaws. Nonetheless, this sophisticated investigation does report a relative improvement rate of approximately 70 percent for treated alcoholic males. Very importantly, these researchers also found very few differences among remission rates for various alcoholism treatment modalities. They indicate that "remission is prevalent even for clients with the worst possible prognosis," and "there appears to be a substantial spontaneous remission rate (50%)."

It is significant that the Alcoholics Anonymous *Big Book* (1939) indicates that one-half of the alcoholics who actively commit themselves to the AA program recover or begin to get better very quickly. Another 25 percent eventually begin "to recover or get better." It is suggested in the *Big Book* that some alcoholics (the other 25%) seem to be constitutionally incapable of recovery. These nonempirically-determined recovery or improvement rates are quite congruous with the general alcoholism treatment outcome data that are reported in the behavioral science literature (Emrick, 1983).

In summary, it is well established that many, if not most, alcoholics can recover or improve as a result of participating in a diversity of alcoholism "treatments." Perhaps the greatest single obstacle to alcoholism recovery is simply the alcoholic's refusal to enter some form of therapy or rehabilitation. In the author's experience, it is realistic to expect intensive alcoholism psychotherapy to result in a 75 to 85 percent remission rate. Furthermore, intensive alcoholism psychotherapy facilitates global adaptive changes beyond basic abstinence. A discussion of the adaptive, concrete, and esoteric changes that intensive alcoholism psychotherapy helps facilitate is included in the final sections of this chapter.

THE VICISSITUDES OF
ALCOHOLISM RECOVERY BEYOND ABSTINENCE

As delineated in the previous section of this chapter, the alcoholism research treatment data clearly indicate that various treatment modalities help many alcoholics establish abstinence or significantly reduce their levels of alcohol consumption. In the clinical experience of the author, total abstinence is the basic prerequisite to other significant adaptive cognitive, behavioral, affective, and interpersonal changes in the psychotherapy of primary alcoholics and many secondary and reactive alcoholics. Abstinence, in combination with intensive alcoholism psychotherapy and a holistic program of recovery, unlocks the door to the vicissitudes of recovery that are discussed in this chapter.

RESPONSIBLE LIVING AND RATIONAL THINKING

Effective intensive alcoholism psychotherapy helps the primary alcoholic develop the capacity for globally responsible living. These patients begin to pay their bills on time, follow through on personal commitments, tell the truth, and accept personal responsibility for mistakes and errors. They stop lying, acting out, stealing, and "conning" or pathologically manipulating other people. Successful psychotherapeutic treatment extinguishes patterns of spouse abuse, child abuse, and sexual abuse. The psychotherapist teaches the primary alcoholic patterns of responsible living. Glasser (1965) has defined responsibility as "the ability to fulfill one's needs, and to do so in a way that does not deprive others of the ability to fulfill their needs. A responsible person also does that which gives him a feeling of self-worth and a feeling that he is worthwhile to others." (p. 15) Glasser (1965) has suggested that people do not act irresponsibly because they are "mentally ill." People are "ill" or psychologically disturbed because they behave irresponsibly!

The drinking alcoholic is basically incapable of responsible living. With effective treatment and recovery, the alcoholic gains the capacity to work and live responsibly. It is important to note that recovery facilitates the capacity for *consistent* responsible living. In other words, the recovering alcoholic behaves responsibly in all areas of life. The recovering person accepts responsibility as a worker or employee, parent, spouse, and friend. According to Glasser (1965), "when a responsible man says that he will perform a job for us, he will try to accomplish what was asked, both for us and so that he may gain a measure of self-worth for himself. An irresponsible person may or may not do what he says depending upon how he feels, the effort he has to make, and what is in it for him. He gains neither our respect nor his own, and in time, he will suffer or cause others to suffer." (p. 13)

The chronically or acutely intoxicated primary alcoholic is incapable of rational thinking. Alcohol and other mood-altering chemicals impair judgment, reasoning, and the thought process. Recovery enables the alcoholic to think, feel, and behave rationally. Drinking alcoholics and addicts blame others for their various difficulties and irresponsible behaviors. Their thinking is distorted, projective, and parataxic. The intoxicated alcoholic is incapable of consistently exercising good judgment and rationally assessing choices and alternatives. Indeed, the cognitive style of the drinking alcoholic precludes rational thinking.

Rational thinking involves (1) accurate assessment and realization of situational and life alternatives, (2) utilization of effective problem solving skills, (3) affective and cognitive mediation, and (4) thinking through situations rather than behaving impulsively and emotionally. The recovering primary alcoholic is able to simply think through situations. He or she is able to rationally assess the long-term and short-term consequences of different decisions, choices, and alternatives in any given situation. Intensive alcoholism psychotherapy helps the alcoholic comprehend the irrational components in his or her thought process or cognitive style. Effective treatment enables the patient to successfully change and/or dispute his or her various irrational beliefs and disturbing thoughts (Ellis, 1979).

The general cognitive and attitudinal sets of the drinking primary alcoholic are disturbed. Effective treatment facilitates cognitive and attitudinal shifts in the direction of flexibility. The patient's pattern of "all or none," "black and white," and prejudiced thinking changes. Cognitive rigidity, inflexibility, and armoring are significantly ameliorated by intensive alcoholism psychotherapy.

RESTORATION OF THE SELF

Alcoholism recovery results in a restoration of the self or self-system (Sullivan, 1953). In fact, many primary alcoholics develop an adequately consolidated nuclear sense of self through effective intensive alcoholism psychotherapy and recovery. These individuals actually develop a healthy self vis à vis the treatment process, rather than restore the self to a previous level of healthy and adaptive functioning. They were never able to function adequately prior to treatment.

The self-system of the recovering alcoholic is first and foremost adequately consolidated. This means that the alcoholic establishes a basic and stable nuclear identity as a result of therapeutic treatment and recovery. The ego-structure of the recovering person is no longer pathologically fragmented, structurally weak and inadequate, and affectively overdetermined. The ego-boundaries are much more adequately defined. There is a synthesis of good and bad ego-introjects, and the recovering person's intrapersonal processes are no longer governed by the "splitting" mechanism (Kernberg, 1975, 1980).

The internal world of the recovering primary alcoholic is not a chronic cauldron of anxiety and stress (Yost and Mines, 1984). Healthy, recovering alcoholics are able to consistently experience self in the absence of anxiety and internal discord. Serenity is an important hallmark of alcoholism recovery. The recovering alcoholic is open to the experience of his or her various emotions and feelings. Affects are no longer repressed, denied, or suppressed. These persons no longer appear to be behaviorally anxious, stressed, and tense. Their anachronistic self-process is significantly modified by effective intensive alcoholism psychotherapy.

Recovery and the restoration of the self also involve enhanced self-esteem and a more positive sense of self-worth. The recovering person no longer feels inadequate, inferior, and worthless. The self-system of the recovering person is better integrated. Therefore, these individuals do not vascillate radically with regard to basic feelings of self-esteem and self-worth. The basic narcissism of the recovering primary alcoholic is adaptively consistent and stabilized. Drinking primary alcoholics are self-centered, grandiose, narcissistic, and outright megalomaniacs one moment and depressive and preoccupied with feelings of inferiority, worthlessness, and inadequacy a few minutes or hours later.

Successful psychotherapeutic treatment of the alcoholic results in a holistic restoration of the self. A functional and healthy interpersonal recovery is essential to the restoration of the self. Interpersonal recovery synergizes intrapersonal recovery. Many of these patients are in need of direct medical care prior to the initiation of intensive alcoholism psychotherapy and/or other psychological treatments. Thus, the physical restoration of the self can be an integral component of the recovery process. A holistic restoration of the self involves various intrapersonal, interpersonal, physical, and spiritual subsystems.

Alcoholism recovery is a birth or rebirth (Forrest, 1978) of the self. The alcoholic self literally and symbolically dies as the recovery process unfolds. Old behaviors, pathologic thoughts, beliefs and attitudes, disturbed relationships, and destructive feelings and impulses are terminated. The alcoholic self is in many respects antithetical to the recovering self. Many recovering alcoholics spontaneously verbalize to their therapists that they feel as though they have been "reborn." This experience of feeling "reborn" is not a specific religious or spiritual conversion. The recovering person simply feels different, new, and whole. A new and often radically different self emerges through the recovery process.

Recovery also enables the alcoholic to establish a personal sense of dignity, respect, and integrity. Alcoholics systematically lose their self-respect, dignity, and integrity as a result of their various inappropriate and alcohol-facilitated behaviors. The restored and healthy self has a basic sense of integrity, respect, and dignity. In the absence of a basic sense of self-respect, dignity, and integrity, the self-system never can be fully restored.

A restoration of the alcoholic family member's self can help facilitate self-integration and self-restoration in the nonaddicted spouse, children, and others. Recovery always potentiates and synergizes self-restoration in those closest to the alcoholic.

BECOMING A FULLY FUNCTIONING PERSON

The recovering or recovered primary alcoholic is no longer an emotional cripple. Intoxicated alcoholics can never achieve their optional potential as human beings. Sobriety, therapy, and recovery simply enable the alcoholic to become more fully human. The initial weeks and months of the recovery process are emotionally stressful and difficult for many alcoholics. In fact, these individuals often feel that sobriety makes them less functional for several months. Yet, sobriety and recovery initiate a process of health and well-being for the vast majority of primary alcoholics. As the alcoholic completes the middle stages of intensive alcoholism psychotherapy, he or she begins to consistently internalize the experience of living without rigidity, defense, and distortion. These individuals are no longer afraid of their cognitive and emotional reactions to various life experiences.

Fully functioning people (Forrest, 1983b) are (1) open to experience, (2) live fully each moment and each day, (3) trust their own judgment and choices, and are less dependent upon external sources of approval and/or disapproval. Successful psychotherapeutic treatment helps many primary alcoholics develop these traits to varying degrees. It may take several years of recovery for some alcoholics to actualize these traits. An *optimal* goal of therapy is to help the patient become more fully functioning. It is important to point out that as the alcoholic begins to recover and becomes more fully functioning, he or she very often facilitates positive growth and change in family members and significant others. The recovery process is interpersonally and intrapersonally synergistic in nature.

As touched upon several times in this text, whenever the primary alcoholic has a spouse and/or family, these individuals also need to be actively encouraged to enter psychotherapy or some form of treatment. Psychotherapeutic treatment and a program of recovery can enable family members to become more open to their experience, less rigid, less defensive and armored, live life more fully, and trust their choices. In order to become fully functioning, the alcoholic and other family members need to experience a sense of basic security. Effective intensive alcoholism psychotherapy and various other treatments can help the alcoholic and individual family members achieve a sense of basic security that fosters the capacity to be fully functioning.

BECOMING INTIMATE AND RELATIONSHIP ORIENTED

Alcohol addiction is an intimacy disturbance (Forrest, 1983c). The drinking primary alcoholic is incapable of behaving and living intimately. Healthy intimacy cannot take place between intoxicated people. Drinking alcoholics lack the capacity to be intimate with self. Likewise, alcoholics cannot be genuinely relationship oriented when they are drinking and intoxicated. Many drinking alcoholics appear to be relationship oriented, gregarious, and "people oriented." In reality, these individuals are only able to maintain superficial, distorted, and alcohol-facilitated relationships. Drinking alcoholics avoid genuinely intimate relationships. These persons fear intimacy and in-depth human relationships.

Healthy intimacy involves relationship depth, emotional depth and expression, and openness or authenticity. Intimacy begins with the capacity to communicate openly and honestly with another human being. Expressing feelings, sharing experiences, empathy, honesty, and transparency or self-disclosure (Jourard, 1964; Forrest, 1970; Hountras and Forrest, 1970) are some of the other basic ingredients in intimate human relationships and encounters.

Intimacy may or may not include sexuality and sexual relationships (Forrest, 1983a). Sexually active or promiscuous primary alcoholics are unable to be intimate and loving within the context of their sexual relationships. Healthy intimacy with self and another human being is a basic precursor to genuine and healthy sexual intimacy. There is no intimacy or love in alcohol-facilitated sexual acting-out experiences. The alcoholic's sexual acting-out escapades and debauches are neurotic attempts to be intimate and relationship oriented. Many drinking alcoholics are also afraid of sexual involvement and sexual intimacy with their spouses. These couples avoid all forms of sexual intimacy for months and years. The capacity for intimacy is also a precursor to healthy loving and sexuality.

Psychotherapy is an intimate relationship. The depth of relationship that develops in ongoing intensive alcoholism psychotherapy helps the alcoholic learn to be intimate and relationship oriented. Recovery involves learning how to be comfortable with self and significant others. The therapeutic relationship also teaches the alcoholic basic interpersonal, social, and intimacy skills. The psychotherapist and patient must maintain eye contact, and they listen and talk to each other in a multiplicity of intimate ways. The interactions and communications that take place in intensive psychotherapy are very intimate. Yet, the psychotherapeutic relationship should never involve sexual or physical intimacy between the therapist and patient. Sexual acting out between the therapist and alcoholic patient exacerbates and reinforces the patient's intimacy and relationship conflicts.

Therapy helps the patient develop the capacity for self-intimacy. Successful psychotherapy facilitates the processes of self-discovery and self-awareness. Recovery involves healthy self-intimacy. The intoxicated alcoholic cannot be intimate with himself or herself. These patients need to become intimate with self and at least one other human being while totally abstinent in order to become adaptively relationship oriented. The intimacy of the therapeutic relationship eventually generalizes and the patient becomes relationship oriented and intimate outside of the therapeutic context. Psychotherapy is a form of experiential learning and teaching that facilitates self and relationship intimacy.

The recovered or recovering primary alcoholic simply develops the capacities for intimate and relationship-oriented living. These individuals can openly share their feelings, thoughts, and beliefs with significant others. They no longer fear intimacy and intimate human encounters. Their general social and interpersonal skills improve. They can tolerate and live with themselves without fear and anxiety. They also learn how to accept themselves as complete human beings. Their relationships with other people are no longer disturbed and parataxic. Quite importantly, they very often de-

velop new relationships with other well-adjusted and healthy
people.

DEVELOPING THE CAPACITY TO LOVE AND WORK EFFECTIVELY

The drinking primary alcoholic experiences a plethora of problems in his or her attempts to love and work. In fact, Father Joseph
C. Martin has stressed the point that drinking alcoholics are
incapable of loving. Most of these individuals attempt to love and
work effectively. However, the intoxicated alcoholic's attempts to
love and work are always distorted and relatively ineffectual.

Intoxicated alcoholics are first and foremost incapable of loving
themselves. The self-love of the drinking alcoholic is distorted
and narcissistic. Healthy self-love is a basic prerequisite to loving
others in a healthy manner. Internal feelings of worthlessness,
inferiority, anger, depression, anxiety, guilt, and confusion make
it impossible for the primary alcoholic to manifest a healthy love
of self and significant others. It is very difficult for the drinking
alcoholic to simply like self, let alone love self and others! Alcoholics are perpetually at war with themselves. They continually fight
an internal battle with self over such matters as liking, disliking,
loving, and hating self and others.

Recovering alcoholics discover or rediscover the true meaning
of love. Love is the feeling of affection, caring, and attraction for
another human being. First and foremost, love is giving of self.
Love involves the capacity to place the loved person above or on
an equal level with self. Love is selfless giving and caring. Love
also encompasses the capacity to be committed to contributing to
the healthy development and well-being of another person or
group of people. Compassion, empathy, honesty, responsibility,
and concern are dimensions of loving behavior.

Drinking alcoholics are unable to consistently work effectively.
Most drinking alcoholics experience a diversity of vocational,
career, and work problems. Their patterns of work are inefficient.
They sometimes are unable to work because of hangovers and
alcohol-facilitated physical illness. Some alcoholics have lost several jobs as a result of their drinking. Even the seemingly successful alcoholic physician *and* attorney *are* seriously impaired in their

careers and professions. The intoxicated person is unable to be efficient, responsible, and functional in any work environment. Drinking alcoholics always seem to find fault with the job, supervisor, or work associate. Many of these individuals seem to be preoccupied with figuring how to avoid work and job responsibilities. Their primary concern is often simply sneaking another drink in the work environment without being caught by a boss or supervisor.

Healthy adjustment is closely associated with a person's capacity to love and work effectively (Reich, 1961). Intensive alcoholism psychotherapy helps the recovering primary alcoholic learn how to love and work effectively. Most of these individuals can begin to experience and share feelings of affection, caring, and loving for other human beings after a few months of sobriety and therapy. They also become responsible and productive members of the work force. Developing the capacity to love and work is one of the most rewarding and exciting aspects of the recovery process. Alcoholics tend to be sensitive, perceptive, and emotional people. Psychotherapy enables them to cope with personal sensitivity and emotions in a rational and productive manner.

The patient's alcohol addiction often contributes to loving and working disturbances in other family members (Forrest, 1983b). The healthy synergism of alcoholism recovery frequently includes the restoration of the capacity to love and work productively in family members. Family members of the alcoholic become angry, enraged, depressed, and confused in their relationships and interactions. Recovery is a family process. Family members need to learn how to like and love themselves, the alcoholic, and each other. They also need to develop or regain the capacity to work productively and successfully.

BECOMING SOCIALLY AWARE AND SOCIALLY CONCERNED

The drinking alcoholic has a very limited and pathologic level of social awareness and social concern. Indeed, the social world of these individuals revolves around drinking and intoxication. Intoxicated alcoholics are not in touch with the various realities of social living. Their social concerns are fixated, regressive, and narcissistic. These persons are incapable of being genuinely and realistically concerned about their families, the local community or the world community. As indicated throughout this text, the alcoholic is only marginally concerned about his or her personal well-being. The intoxicated alcoholic is the center of his or her universe.

Effective intensive alcoholism psychotherapy facilitates a healthy development of social awareness and social concern in most primary alcoholics. Many of these patients become cognizant of their deep feelings about people and society after twelve to eighteen months of treatment and recovery. They develop a social consciousness. Social concern and social consciousness (Sullivan, 1953) form the basis for making creative, constructive contributions to society. The social concerns of many of these people eventually involve personal, active attempts to foster healthy community change. Jack G. expressed this sentiment when he said, "By God, I'm startin' to feel like I can make the world a little bit better or even safer place to live in."

Recovering alcoholics can be agents of adaptive social change within their families, work environments, and communities. Recently in this country, several recovering alcoholics have made significant social and political contributions at a national level. Many recovering people simply become involved in helping others understand the various social problems in our society that are associated with alcoholism and drug addiction. Some of these recovering individuals eventually obtain academic training and employment in the addictions field. Many play important roles in the treatment and recovery of other alcoholics and addicts through their deep commitments and involvements with the Alcoholics Anonymous community. The early stages of the alcoholic's recovery process are basically self-focused. Later in the treatment process, many recovering primary alcoholics are able to grow beyond the encapsulation of self-recovery and develop the capacity for facilitating various forms and levels of social change. For the alcoholic, sobriety, effective therapeutic treatment, recovery, and an evolving sense of social awareness and social concern are prerequisites to being an agent of healthy social change.

Family members of the primary alcoholic also become less socially aware and less socially concerned as the addiction process malignantly unfolds. The alcoholic family member's recovery often helps other family members develop more healthy levels of social awareness and social concern. The spouse and family of the drinking primary alcoholic are usually so emotionally preoccupied and upset with the drinker and their personal problems that they are unable to be socially aware and concerned. The recovery process fosters healthy social awareness and social concern in every family member. The spouse, children, and extended family members of the recovering alcoholic can also become agents of healthy social change.

DEVELOPING THE POTENTIAL FOR SELF-ACTUALIZED LIVING

Every recovering alcoholic manifests the potential for some form or degree of self-actualization. These individuals can potentially live life in a more self-actualized manner. Self-actualization represents the ultimate or *optimal* level of effective human functioning. Very few people become truly self-actualized. Self-actualization is the fullest, most complete differentiation and harmonious blending of all aspects of a person's total being. Creativity is a component in self-actualized living. The self-actualized person continually strives to become more fully developed, complete, creative, and integrated.

Many recovering alcoholics, and even a few psychotherapists, do not understand the meaning of the concept *self-actualization*. I suspect that most therapists would find it conceptually difficult to perceive or appreciate the self-actualization potential of any chronically intoxicated person. Indeed, it is impossible for the alcoholic to live a self-actualized life-style in the absence of recovery, sobriety, and effective intensive alcoholism psychotherapy. Maslow (1954) delineated fifteen characteristics that distinguish self-actualized people from the ordinary run of people. The basic characteristics of the self-actualized person are (1) being reality-oriented, (2) acceptance of self, others, and the material world, (3) spontaneity, (4) problem-centeredness rather than self-centeredness, (5) detachment and a need for privacy, (6) autonomy and independence, (7) appreciation of people and things in a fresh rather than stereotyped manner, (8) history of profound mystical or spiritual experiences, although not necessarily religious in nature, (9) identification with mankind, (10) intimate relationships with a few specially loved people that tend to be profound and deeply emotional rather than superficial, (11) democratic values and attitudes, (12) ability to distinguish means from ends, (13) sense of humor that is philosophical rather than hostile, (14) manifestation of a wealth of creativeness, and (15) resistance to conformity to the culture.

The self-actualizing dimensions of the primary alcoholic are not ubiquitously encountered by therapists and family members after a few weeks or months of effective treatment. To the contrary, most alcoholics begin to evidence a few of the basic characteristics of self-actualization following *several months* of total abstinence, involvement in intensive alcoholism psychotherapy, and consistently working a holistic program of recovery.

Recovery from alcohol addiction always encompasses becoming more reality oriented, more accepting of self and others, changing pathologic self-centered behaviors, initiating new relationships, and even resisting many social or cultural imperatives to conform. A profound mystical or spiritual experience is central to the recovery process of many alcoholic persons. As discussed earlier in this chapter, recovering persons also begin to appreciate people, develop a sense of social concern, become less hostile and angry, laugh and enjoy life, and are more democratic.

Family members of the drinking primary alcoholic are incapable of being self-actualized. Typically, the family members of the alcoholic are struggling to meet their basic survival needs. They feel insecure and trapped. They also feel unloved and have low self-esteem. The alcoholic's recovery can potentially help other family members become more self-actualized. However, in the clinical experience of the author (Forrest, 1983b), each family member needs to establish and work his or her personal program of recovery for several months in order to become more self-actualized. Alcoholism is a family disorder. The nondrinking or nonalcoholic family members in the alcoholic family system are also in need of intensive psychotherapeutic treatment.

The following therapy vignette was taken from a follow-up session with Jack G. This follow-up session occurred some twenty-one months after the patient had actually terminated treatment. He had continued to remain sober and was significantly improved.

Doctor F: I certainly appreciate your coming in for follow-up, Jack . . . Uh, as I mentioned on the phone, it's been over six months since our last follow-up session, and I wanted to know how you're doing.

Jack G: It's good to get back in . . . uh, I look forward to seeing you for these sessions . . . it seems like six months sure goes by fast, but I'm keepin' busy and things are goin' great . . .

Doctor F: So things have been going pretty well?

Jack G: Yeah . . . you know, we've really been enjoying life . . . er, and for me, that's different . . . I mean, I feel relaxed and don't have all that pressure I had three or four years· ago . . . and I don't even think about drinking. Ha, ha . . . that's still the same!

Doctor F: You haven't had to struggle with the drinking issue for a couple of years now.

Jack G: I'm really happy about that because it used to be one day at a time . . . like the AA slogan, but I'm too busy and enjoy life too much to be preoccupied about drinking or gettin' drunk . . . Hell, there's not enough time in the day now!

Doctor F: I was wondering, what have you actually been doing to enjoy yourself? Uh, what have you done these past six months?

Jack G: Mostly travel . . . uh, I finished the history class that I was taking at Pike's Peak Community College about five months ago . . . The class met every Tuesday and Thursday night, and by golly, I got a B . . . uh, just missed an A, but since then we bought a camper and we've been to Wyoming on one trip and Missouri on another . . . er, we were on the trip to Missouri for three weeks . . . visited some old Army friends that we hadn't seen for over ten years, and had a hell of a time!

Doctor F: So you've spent a lot of time traveling and

visiting and still taking a few classes at PPCC.

Jack G: Yep! Like I said, we're enjoying life . . . We did a lot of traveling when I was in the service, but I was always drunk or drinking . . . uh, to be truthful, I don't remember a lot of those trips and what I do remember is bad . . . Ilsa and I were always fighting then.

Doctor F: Both of you are able to enjoy your trips now, and . . . uh, you're able to remember what you saw or who you visited with now . . . ha, ha.

Jack G: Exactly . . . I've really come a long way in the last few years, Doc . . . it seems like I can understand myself so much better, and I know for sure that I'm a hell of a lot more aware of what's going on around me . . . before, it was like I was always in a fog or a daze or something.

Doctor F: Let's switch years for a bit . . . are you still walking or attending meetings?

Jack G: Ha, ha . . . I knew you'd be checking me out . . . as a matter of fact, I walked two miles before I came in . . . and I'm still getting my exercise four or five times every week, and I go to a meeting every week or so . . . a thing that I've gotten involved in since I was in the last time is 12-step work . . . uh, I have been making a 12-step call or two a week and taking a lot of phone calls from the central office (AA) . . . you know, I feel really good about getting involved with helping other alcoholics . . . guess I've really changed in that area too!

Doctor F: So you've been consistent with your recovery alternatives . . . uh, you're still really working your program of recovery.

Jack G: Uh, huh . . . actually, I've expanded my original program of recovery . . . I get a lot out of helping other people . . . uh, it's like I really know what they're going through . . . did I tell you that we've gotten more involved in the church too?

Doctor F: You didn't mention church . . . it sounds like you have gotten more involved with other people and life over the last several months.

Jack G: I've felt like a different person the last two or three years... like I've told you before, I got a second lease on life... Ha, ha... it's spiritual in a way or... er... I've felt blessed, so we are going to church almost every week.

Doctor F: Well, you are a different person in many respects ... your recovery has helped cause a lot of positive changes in you.

Jack G: Yeah, it's even hard for me to believe when I really think about it... I like me... uh, and I feel good about the changes and other people tell me the same things!

Doctor F: The changes are pretty damned obvious, Jack. Ha, ha... You should feel better!

Jack G: You know, it's just nice being able to look at yourself in the mirror each morning... I like me now, but I sure used to hate what I saw in the mirror every morning.

This therapy follow-up vignette demonstrates many of the positive gains that Jack G. had actualized during and after treatment. He remained totally abstinent following treatment termination. The patient no longer felt chronically anxious. He was not preoccupied with drinking. He had enrolled in college, enjoyed vacationing, and devoted a good deal of his time to the process of helping other alcoholics in their struggles to overcome alcoholism. This patient became involved with a church group and clearly felt more comfortable with other people. His self-esteem was greatly improved and he was no longer narcissistically fixated. He had also actively maintained his program of recovery for nearly two years after terminating intensive alcoholism psychotherapy.

SUMMARY

Primary alcoholics can stop drinking and actualize various other adaptive personality and behavioral changes. The alcoholisms (Pattison, 1984) are treatable disorders. A major deterrent to successful alcoholism treatment is the addicted person's refusal to enter therapy or some form of rehabilitation program. Several of the recent social factors that have simply made it easier for thousands of alcoholic persons to seek out professional alcoholism treatment were discussed.

The evaluation of alcoholism treatments and treatment effectiveness is difficult. Semantic problems, design and methodological inadequacies, poor follow-up, treatment contamination, and sample bias are a few of the primary sources of weakness in alcoholism treatment effectiveness research (Emrick, 1983). In spite of these methodological problems, it has been consistently reported in the alcoholism treatment effectiveness literature (Emrick, 1974, 1975, 1983; Armor, Polich, and Stambul, 1978) that approximately 70 percent of alcoholics entering treatment evidence significant positive gains. Furthermore, various alcoholism treatments seem to produce consistently favorable outcomes. Behavioral treatments and industrial treatment programs report 80 to 90 percent success rates. In sum, it is well-established that most alcoholics can improve or recover as a result of participation in a diversity of alcoholism "treatments." Intensive alcoholism psychotherapy systematically results in a 75 to 85 percent recovery rate.

Abstinence is the cornerstone of alcoholism recovery. However, a fundamental goal of intensive alcoholism psychotherapy is always recovery beyond abstinence. Too many recovering or recovered alcoholics are sober but globally conflicted and miserable. Optimal recovery from primary alcoholism includes developing the capacities for (1) responsible living and rational thinking, (2) restoration of the self, (3) becoming a fully-functioning person, (4) becoming intimate and relationship oriented, (5) developing the capacity to love and work effectively, (6) becoming socially aware and socially concerned, and (7) developing the potential for self-actualized living. The parameters of each of these dimensions of optimal recovery were elucidated.

The recovery process is synergistic. Recovering alcoholics often facilitate healthy and adaptive changes in other family members and significant others (Ackerman, 1983). Indeed, the recovering alcoholic's presence can exert a ubiquitously adaptive impact on significant others. The follow-up therapy vignette that was included in this chapter demonstrates this reality.

Intensive alcoholism psychotherapy is a difficult, challenging, and rewarding process for both patient and psychotherapist. Many therapists do not feel comfortable with alcoholics and other addicts. Intensive alcoholism psychotherapy is a very effective treatment modality when utilized by psychotherapists who (1) feel comfortable with alcoholics and basically like these individuals, (2) are compassionate, (3) are empathic, (4) are genuine, (5) are capable of utilizing confrontation and active therapeutic interventions rationally and responsibly, (6) are not chemically dependent or substance abusers, (7) are persistent and consistent, (8) can tolerate intimacy, nurturance, and dependency, (9) are able to delay various therapeutic gratifications, (10) are insightful but simultaneously concrete, (11) are not narcissistically pathologic, (12) internally and cognitively comprehend the psychopathology of alcoholism, and (13) are basically secure, rational, and responsible human beings.

The personality structure and character style of the psychotherapist are crucially important variables in determining the success or failure of intensive alcoholism psychotherapy. A good therapeutic "fit" between therapist and patient is essential to successful and effective psychotherapeutic work with primary alcoholics. Therapists also need to be able to accept the precarious and tenuous nature of all therapeutic relationships (Fromm-Reichmann, 1950, 1959). Some primary alcoholics fail to recover in spite of the psychotherapist's almost superhuman efforts. It must be remembered that a few primary alcoholics seem to be recalcitrant to all forms of treatment.

BIBLIOGRAPHY

Ackerman, R. J.: *Children of Alcoholics: A Guidebook for Educators, Therapists and Parents*. Holmes Beach: Learning Publications, 1978.

Ackerman, R. J.: *Children of Alcoholics: A Guidebook for Educators, Therapists and Parents*. Holmes Beach: Learning Publications, Rev. 2nd Edit., 1983.

Adler, G., and Myerson, P. G. (Eds.): *Confrontation in Psychotherapy*. New York: Science House, 1973.

Alcoholics Anonymous. New York: Alcoholics Anonymous World Services, Inc., 1939.

Anant, S. S.: A note on the treatment of alcoholics by a verbal aversion technique. *Canadian Psych.*, 1967, *8*, pp. 19–22.

Armor, D. J., Polich, J. M., and Stambul, H. B.: *Alcoholism and Treatment*. New York: John Wiley & Sons, 1978.

Ayerst Laboratories. *Guidelines for Antabuse (Disulfiram) Users*. New York, 1981.

Bandura, A.: *Principles of Behavioral Modification*. New York: Holt, Reinhart and Winston, 1969.

Black, C.: Children of alcoholics: Dynamics and treatment. Lecture, Psychotherapy Associates, P.C. Ninth Annual Advanced Winter Workshop, *Treatment and Rehabilitation of the Alcoholic*, Colorado Springs, Colorado, Jan 31 to Feb 1, 1983.

Black, C.: *It Will Never Happen to Me*. Denver: M.A.C., 1981.

Blane, H. T.: Pleasures and Problems of College Drinking. Medical Foundation Conference on Stress-Related Problems Among College Students. Harvard University, Nov. 1982.

Blane, H. T.: *The Personality of the Alcoholic: Guises of Dependency*. New York: Harper and Row, 1968.

Blume, S. B.: Women and alcohol. In Bratter, T. E. and Forrest, G. G. (Eds.): *Current Management of Substance Abuse and Alcoholism*. New York: The Free Press, 1984.

Blum, E. M., and Blum, R. H.: *Alcoholism: Modern Psychological Approaches to Treatment*. San Francisco: Jossey-Bass, Inc., 1969.

Bratter, T. E.: Group treatment of addicts. In Bratter, T. E., and Forrest, G. G. (Eds.): *Current Management of Substance Abuse and Alcoholism*. New York: The Free Press, 1984.

Bratter, T. E.: The psychotherapist as a twelfth step worker in the treatment of alcoholism. *Family and Community Health, Vol 2, No. 2*, August, pp. 31–58, 1979.

Bratter, T. E.: The psychotherapist as a twelfth step worker in the treatment of alcoholism. In Davidson, S. V. (Ed.): *Alcoholism and Health*. Germantown: Aspen Systems Corporation, 1980.

Cadoret, R. J., Cain, C. A., and Grove, W.: Development of alcoholism in adoptees raised apart from alcoholic biologic parents. *Arch. Gen. Psychiat.*, 1980, *37*:561-563.

Cahill, C. A.: Safety of disulfiram. *New Engl. J. Med.*, *287*:935-936, 1972.

Cala, L. A., and Mastaglia, F. L.: Computerized Tomography in Chronic Alcoholics. *Alcoholism: Clin. and Exp. Res.*, 1981, *5*:283-303.

Cameron, N.: *Personality Development and Psychopathology: A Dynamic Approach*. Boston: Houghton Mifflin Co., 1963.

Corsini, R. J.: *Current Psychotherapies (Ed.)*. ITASCA: F. E. Peacock Publishers, Inc., 1979.

Cowen, R., and Nittman, M.: Industrial and EAP intervention models. Lecture, Psychotherapy Associates, P.C., Tenth Annual Advanced Winter Workshop, *Treatment and Rehabilitation of the Alcoholic*, Colorado Springs, Colorado, Feb. 8, 1984.

Dahlstrom, W. G., and Welsh, G. S.: *An MMPI Handbook*. Minneapolis: University of Minnesota Press, 1960.

Davies, D. L.: Normal Drinking in Recovered Alcohol Addicts. *Quat. J. Stud. Alc.*, 1962, *23*, pp. 94-104.

Davis, H. F.: *Variables Associated with Recovery in Male and Female Alcoholics Following Hospitalization*. Doctoral Dissertation, Texas Technological College, 1966.

Della-Giustina, V. E., and Forrest, G. G.: Depression and the dentist. *GA J. Dent.*, Aug., 1979, pp. 15-17.

Diagnostic and Statistical Manual of Mental Disorders. Second Edition (DSM-II), Washington, D.C., American Psychiatric Association, 1968.

Diagnostic and Statistical Manual of Mental Disorders. Third Edition (DSM-III), Washington, D.C., American Psychiatric Association, 1980.

Eckardt, M. J., and Feldman, D. J.: Biochemical correlates of alcohol abuse. In Seixas, F. A. (Ed.): *Currents in Alcoholism, Vol. III*. New York: Grune and Stratton, 1978.

Edwards, G.: The status of alcoholism as a disease. In Phillipson, K. V. (Ed.): *Modern Trends in Drug Dependence and Alcoholism*. New York: Appleton-Century-Crofts, 1970.

Ellis, A., and Harper, R.: *A Guide to Rational Living*. Englewood Cliffs: Prentice-Hall, Inc., 1961.

Ellis, A.: Rational-emotive therapy training. Lecture, Psychotherapy Associates, P.C. Fifth Annual Advanced Winter Workshop, *Treatment and Rehabilitation of the Alcoholic*, Colorado Springs, Colorado, Feb. 1, 1979.

Ellis, A: Rational-emotive therapy training. Lecture, Psychotherapy Associates, P.C. Seventh Annual Advanced Winter Workshop, *Treatment and Rehabilitation of the Alcoholic*, Colorado Springs, Colorado, Feb. 6, 1981.

Ellis, A.: Treatment of erectile dysfunctions. In Leiblum, S., and Pervin, L. (Eds.): *Principles and Practice of Sex Therapy*. New York: The Guilford Press, 1980.

Emrick, C. D.: A review of psychologically oriented treatment of alcoholism: I.

The use and interrelationships of outcome criteria and drinking behavior following treatment. *Quart. J. Stud. on Alc.*, 1974, *35*, 523–549.

Emrick, C. D.: A review of psychologically oriented treatment of alcoholism: II. The relative effectiveness of different treatment approaches and the relative effectiveness of treatment versus no treatment. *J. Stud. on Alc.*, 1975, *36*, 88–108.

Emrick, C. D.: Methodology in alcoholism research. Lecture, Psychotherapy Associates, P.C. Ninth Annual Advanced Winter Workshop, *Treatment and Rehabilitation of the Alcoholic*, Colorado Springs, Colorado, Feb. 1, 1983.

Emrick, C. D.: Perspectives in clinical research: Relative effectiveness of alcohol abuse treatment. *Family and Community Health, Vol. 2, No. 2*, August, pp. 71–88, 1979.

Emrick, C. D.: Perspectives in clinical research: Relative effectiveness of alcohol abuse treatment. In Davidson, S. V. (Ed.): *Alcoholism and Health*. Germantown: Aspen Systems Corporation, 1980.

Ends, E. J., and Page, C. W.: Group psychotherapy and concomitant psychological Change. *Psych. Mono.*, 1959, *73*, No. 480.

Fann, W. E., Karacan, I., Pokorny, A. O., and Williams, R. L.: *Phenomenology and Treatment of Alcoholism*. New York: SP Medical and Scientific Books, 1980.

Farrelly, F.: Provocative therapy training. Lecture, Psychotherapy Associates, P.C. Ninth Annual Advanced Winter Workshop, *Treatment and Rehabilitation of the Alcoholic*, Colorado Springs, Colorado, Jan. 31 to Feb. 1, 1983.

Farrelly, F.: *Provocative Therapy*. Palo Alto: Science and Behavior Books, Inc., 1964.

Fenichel, O.: *The Psychoanalytic Theory of Neurosis*. New York: W. W. Norton, 1945.

Fenna, O., Mix, L., Schaefer, O., and Gilbert, J. A.: Ethanol metabolism in various racial groups. *Can. Med. Assoc. J.*, 1971, *105*:472.

Forrest, G. G.: *Alcoholism and Human Sexuality*. Springfield: Thomas, 1983a.

Forrest, G. G.: Alcoholism and the reservation indian. Research and clinical paper compiled at the M.S.B.S. Research Project, Turtle Mountain Rehabilitation and Counseling Center, Belcourt, North Dakota, November 1976.

Forrest, G. G.: *Alcoholism, Narcissism, and Psychopathology*. Springfield: Thomas, 1983c.

Forrest, G. G.: Antabuse treatment. In Bratter, T. E., and Forrest, G. G.: *Current Management of Substance Abuse and Alcoholism*. New York: The Free Press, 1984b.

Forrest, G. G.: *Confrontation in Psychotherapy with Alcoholics*. Holmes Beach: Learning Publications, Inc., 1982.

Forrest, G. G.: *How to Cope with a Teenage Drinker: New Alternatives and Hope for Parents and Families*. New York: Atheneum, 1983b.

Forrest, G. G.: *How to Live with a Problem Drinker and Survive*. New York: Atheneum, 1980.

Forrest, G. G.: Motivating alcoholic patients for treatment. Lecture, Fourth Annual Colorado Summer School on Alcoholism, Glenwood Springs, Colorado, June 11, 1978b.

Forrest, G. G.: Negative and positive addictions. *Family and Community Health*, 2(1): 103–112, 1979a.

Forrest, G. G.: Psychodynamically-oriented treatment of alcoholism and substance abuse. In Bratter, T. E., and Forrest, G. G. (Eds.): *Current Management of Substance Abuse and Alcoholism*. New York: The Free Press, 1984.

Forrest, G. G.: Setting alcoholics up for therapeutic failure. *Family and Community Health*, 2(2):59–64, 1979b.

Forrest, G. G.: *The Diagnosis and Treatment of Alcoholism*. Rev. 2nd Ed. Springfield: Thomas, 1978.

Forrest, G. G.: *The Mountain Bell at Colorado Springs Industrial Alcoholism Treatment Program: A 12-month Follow-up Study*. Unpublished manuscript, Medical Department, Mountain Bell, Colorado Springs, CO, Fall 1980.

Forrest, G. G.: *Transparency as a Prognostic Variable in Psychotherapy*. Unpublished doctoral dissertation. University of North Dakota, Grand Forks, North Dakota, 1970.

Freud, S.: The future prospects of psychoanalytic therapy. In *Collected Papers*. London: Hogarth, Vol. II, 1953.

Freud, S.: *The Interpretation of Dreams*. New York: Avon Books, 1965 (Orig. pub. 1908).

Fromm-Reichmann, F.: *Principles of Intensive Psychotherapy*. Chicago: University of Chicago Press, 1950.

Fromm-Reichmann, F.: *Psychoanalysis and Psychotherapy*. Chicago: University of Chicago Press, 1959.

Gerard, O. L., Saenger, G., and Wile, R.: The abstinent alcoholic. *Arch. Gen. Psychiat.*, 1962, 6, pp. 83–95.

Gilberstadt, H., and Duker, J.: *A Handbook for Clinical and Actuarial MMPI Interpretation*. Philadelphia: Saunders, 1965.

Glasser, W.: *Positive Addiction*. New York: Harper and Row, 1976.

Glasser, W.: *Reality Therapy: A New Approach to Psychiatry*. New York: Harper and Row, 1965.

Goodwin, D. W.: The genetics of alcoholism. In Gottheil, E., et. al.: *Etiologic Aspects of Alcohol and Drug Abuse*. Springfield: Thomas, 1983.

Gottheil, E., Druley, K. A., Skoloda, T. E., and Waxman, H. M.: *Etiologic Aspects of Alcohol and Drug Abuse*. Springfield: Thomas, 1983.

Gutheil, E. A.: *The Handbook of Dream Analysis*. New York: Washington Square Press, 1951.

Hall, C. S.: *The Meaning of Dreams*. New York: McGraw-Hill Book Company, 1966.

Harris, T.: *I'm OK—You're OK: A Practical Guide to Transactional Analysis*. New York: Harper and Row, 1969.

Hatterer, L. J.: *Changing Homosexuality in the Male*. New York: McGraw-Hill Book Company, 1970.

Hayman, M.: Current attitudes to alcoholism of psychiatrists in southern california. *Am. J. of Psychiat.*, 1956, *112*, pp. 484–493.

Heath, D. B.: Sociocultural perspectives on addiction. In Gottheil, E. et. al. (Eds.): *Etiologic Aspects of Alcohol and Drug Abuse.* Springfield: Thomas, 1983.

Hill, M. I., and Blane, H. J.: Evaluation of psychotherapy with alcoholics: A critical review. *Quart. J. Stud. on Alc.,* 1967, *28,* pp. 76–104.

Horn, J. L., Wanberg, K., and Foster, F. M. *The Alcohol Use Inventory-AUI.* Center for Alcohol-Abuse Research and Evaluation. Denver, CO, 1974.

Hountras, P. T., and Forrest, G. G.: Personality characteristics and self-disclosure in a psychiatric outpatient population. *College of Education Record,* University of North Dakota, *55:*206–213, 1970.

Jellinek, E. M.: Heredity and alcohol: Science and society. *Quart. J. Stud. Alc.,* pp. 104–114, 1945.

Jellinek, E. M.: *The Disease Concept of Alcoholism.* New Haven: College and University Press, 1960.

Kernberg, O. F.: *Borderline Conditions and Pathological Narcissism.* New York: Jason Aronson, Inc., 1975.

Kernberg, O. F.: *Internal World and External Reality.* New York: Jason Aronson, Inc., 1980.

Kernberg, O. F.: *Object Relations Theory and Clinical Psychoanalysis.* New York: Jason Aronson, Inc., 1976.

Khantzian, E. J.: Psychopathological causes and consequences of drug dependence. In Gottheil, E., et al. (Eds.): *Etiologic Aspects of Alcohol and Drug Abuse.* Springfield: Thomas, 1983.

Knauert, A. P.: Differential diagnosis in the treatment of alcoholism. Lecture, Psychotherapy Associates, P.C. Sixth Annual Advanced Winter Workshop, *Treatment and Rehabilitation of the Alcoholic,* Colorado Springs, Colorado, Feb. 8, 1980.

Knauert, A. P.: The differential diagnosis of alcoholism. Lecture, Psychotherapy Associates, P.C. Eighth Annual Advanced Winter Workshop, *Treatment and Rehabilitation of the Alcoholic,* Colorado Springs, Colorado, Feb. 2, 1982.

Knauert, A. P.: The Treatment of Alcoholism in a Community Setting. *Family and Community Health, 2*(1):91–102, 1979.

Knauert, A. P.: Treatment techniques with unmotivated clients. Lecture, Psychotherapy Associates, P.C. Ninth Annual Advanced Winter Workshop, *Treatment and Rehabilitation of the Alcoholic,* Colorado Springs, Colorado, Feb. 3, 1983.

Knight, R. P.: Psychodynamics of chronic alcoholism. *J. Neru. Ment. Dis.,* 1937, *86:*538–548.

Lawson, G., Peterson, J. S., and Lawson, A.: *Alcoholism and the Family.* Rockville: Aspen Systems Corporation, 1983.

Lawson, G., Petrosa, R., and Peterson, J.: Diagnosis of alcoholism by recovering alcoholics and by nonalcoholics. *J. Stud. on Alc., Vol. 43,* No. 9, pp. 1033–1035, Sept., 1982.

Lazarus, A. A.: *The Practice of Multi-Modal Therapy.* New York: McGraw-Hill Book Company, 1981.

Liebson, I., and Bigelow, G. E.: Substance abuse as behavior. In Gottheil, E., et.

al. (Eds.): *Etiologic Aspects of Alcohol and Drug Abuse.* Springfield: Thomas, 1983.

Lovibond, S. H., and Caddy, G.: Discriminated aversive control in the moderation of alcoholics' drinking behavior. *Behavior Therapy*, 1970, NY1, pp. 437–444.

MacAndrew, C.: The differentiation of male alcoholic outpatients from nonalcoholic psychiatric outpatients by means of the MMPI. *Quart. J. Stud. Alc.*, 1965, 26:238–246.

Malatesta, V. J., Pollack, R. H., Crotty, T. D., and Peacock, L. J.: Acute alcohol intoxication and female orgasmic response. *J. Sex Research, Vol. 18*, No. 1, pp. 1–17, Feb, 1982.

Marcovitz, E.: On addiction. In Gottheil, et. al. (Eds.): *Etiologic Aspects of Alcohol and Drug Abuse.* Springfield: Thomas, 1983.

Martin, J. C.: Alcoholism and the family. Lecture, Psychotherapy Associates, P.C. Sixth Annual Advanced Winter Workshop, *Treatment and Rehabilitation of the Alcoholic*, Colorado Springs, Colorado, Feb. 4, 1980.

Martin, J. C.: *No Laughing Matter: Chalk Talks on Alcohol.* San Francisco: Harper and Row, 1982.

Maslow, A. H.: *Motivation and Personality.* New York: Harper and Row, 1954.

Masterson, J. F.: *The Narcissistic and Borderline Disorders: An Integrated Developmental Approach.* New York: Brunner/Mazel, 1981.

May, R.: Psychotherapy and the daimonic. In Mahrer, A., and Pearson, L. (Eds.): *Creative Developments in Psychotherapy.* New York: Aronson, 1973.

Mendelson, J. H., and Mello, N. K.: *The Diagnosis and Treatment of Alcoholism.* New York: McGraw-Hill, 1979.

Menninger, K.: *Man Against Himself.* New York: Harcourt, Brace and World, Inc., 1938.

Milt, H.: *Basic Handbook on Alcoholism.* New Jersey: Scientific Aids Publications, 1969.

Moore, R. A., and Ramseur, F.: Effects of psychotherapy in an open-ward hospital in patients with alcoholism. *Quart. J. Stud. on Alc.*, 1960, 21, pp. 233–252.

Morse, R. M., and Swenson, W. M.: Spouse response to a self-administered alcoholism screening test. *J. Stud. Alc.*, 1975, 36:400–405.

Paolino, T. J., and McGrady, B. S.: *The Alcoholic Marriage: Alternative Perspectives.* New York: Grune and Stratton, 1977.

Patterson, C. H.: *Theories of Counseling and Psychotherapy.* New York: Harper and Row, 1966.

Pattison, E. M.: A clinical systems approach to alcoholism treatment. Lecture, Psychotherapy Associates, P.C. Ninth Annual Advanced Winter Workshop, *Treatment and Rehabilitation of the Alcoholic*, Colorado Springs, CO, Jan. 31, 1983.

Pattison, E. M.: A critique of alcoholism treatment concepts: with special reference to abstinence. *Quart. J. Stud. on Alc.*, 1966, 27, pp. 49–71.

Pattison, E. M.: Differential treatment of alcoholism. In Fann, W. E., et. al.: *Phenomenology and Treatment of Alcoholism.* New York: SP Medical and Scientific Books, 1980.

Pattison, E. M.: Pitfalls and pratfalls of psychotherapy with alcoholics. Lecture, Psychotherapy Associates, P.C. Tenth Annual Advanced Winter Workshop, *Treatment and Rehabilitation of the Alcoholic*, Colorado Springs, CO, Feb. 6, 1984.

Pfeffer, A. Z., and Berger, S.: A follow-up study of treated alcoholics. *Quart. J. Stud. on Alc.*, 1957, *18*, pp. 624–648.

Rachman, S. J., and Hodgson, R. J.: *Obsessions and Compulsions*. New Jersey: Prentice-Hall, Inc., 1980.

Reich, W.: *Character Analysis*. New York: The Noonday Press, 1961.

Reik, T.: *Listening with the Third Ear*. New York: Pyramid Books, 1948.

Ritson, R.: Personality and prognosis in alcoholism. *British J. of Psychiat.*, 1971, *118*, pp. 79–82.

Rogers, C. R.: *Client-Centered Therapy*. Boston: Houghton Mifflin, 1952.

Ryback, R. S., Eckardt, M. J., and Paulter, C. P.: Biochemical and hematological correlates of alcoholism. *Res. Commun. Chem. Patrol. Pharmacol.*, 1980, *27*:533–550.

Salzman, L.: *The Obsessive Personality*. New York: Science House, 1968.

Schad-Somers, S. P.: *Sadomasochism: Etiology and Treatment*. New York: Human Sciences Press, Inc., 1982.

Schuckit, M. A., Goodwin, D. W., and Winokur, G.: A half-sibling study of alcoholism. *Am. J. Psychiatry*, *128*:1132–1136, 1972.

Schuckit, M. A.: Disulfiram (Antabuse) and the treatment of alcoholic men. In *Raleigh Hills Foundation Advances in Alcoholism*, *Vol. II*, No. 4, pp. 1–5, Apr., 1981.

Schuckit, M. A.: Gamma glutamyl transferase and the diagnosis of alcoholism. *Advances in Alcoholism*, Irvine, Raleigh Hills Foundation, 1981, *Vol. 2*, No. 5.

Selzer, M. L.: The Michigan Alcoholism Screening Test: The quest for a new diagnostic instrument. *Amer. J. Psychiat.*, 1971, *127*:89–94.

Sena, D. A.: Neuropsychological assessment of alcoholism: Special considerations, treatment planning, recovery and research. Lecture, Psychotherapy Associates, P.C. Tenth Annual Advanced Winter Workshop, *Treatment and Rehabilitation of the Alcoholic*, Colorado Springs, CO Feb. 8, 1984.

Shaw, S., Lue, S., and Lieber, C. S.: Biochemical test for the detection of alcoholism: Comparison of plasma alpha–amino–n–butyric acid with other available tests. *Alcoholism: Clin. and Exp. Res.*, 1978, *2*:3–7.

Shoemaker, L. D.: Alcohol, the brain and recent research. Lecture, Psychotherapy Associates, P.C. Eighth Annual Advanced Winter Workshop, *Treatment and Rehabilitation of the Alcoholic*, Colorado Springs, CO, Feb. 5, 1982.

Smith, J. J.: The effect of alcohol in the adrenal ascorbic acid and the cholesterol of the rat. *J. Clin. Endocrin*, *11*:792, 1951.

Smith, J. J.: The endocrine basis of hormonal therapy of alcoholism. *N.Y. State J. of Med*, *50*:1704–1706, 1711–1715, 1950.

Sobell, M. B., and Sobell, L. C.: Alcoholics treated by individualized behavior therapy: One-year treatment outcome. *Behavior Research and Therapy*, 1973, *11*, pp. 599–618.

Sobell, M. C., and Sobell, L. C.: *Individual Behavior Therapy for Alcoholics: Rationale, Procedures, Preliminary Results and Appendix.* California Mental Health Research Monograph, No. 13, Department of Mental Hygiene, Sacramento, CA, 1972.

Sobell, M. B., and Sobell, L. C.: Second year treatment outcome of alcoholics treated by individualized behavior therapy: Results. *Behavior Research and Therapy*, 1976, *14*, pp. 195–215.

Sobell, M. B., and Sobell, L. C.: Training responsible drinking with state hospital alcoholics. Paper presented at the American Psychological Association Annual Meeting. Chicago, Aug., 1975.

Solomon, R.: Stress and alcoholism: Positive coping alternatives. Lecture, Psychotherapy Associates, P.C. Ninth Annual Advanced Winter Workshop, *Treatment and Rehabilitation of the Alcoholic*, Colorado Springs, CO, Feb. 4, 1983.

Steiner, C.: *Games Alcoholics Play.* New York: Grove Press, 1971.

Stekel, W.: *The Interpretation of Dreams.* New York: Liverwright, 1943.

Strupp, H. H.: *Psychotherapy: Clinical, Research and Theoretical Issues.* New York: Jason Aronson, Inc., 1973.

Sullivan, H. S.: *The Interpersonal Theory of Psychiatry.* New York: W. W. Norton and Company, Inc., 1953.

Szasz, T. S.: *Ceremonial Chemistry.* New York: Doubleday, 1974.

Szasz, T. S.: *Schizophrenia: The Sacred Symbol of Psychiatry.* New York: Basic Books, Inc., 1976.

Szasz, T. S.: *The Myth of Mental Illness.* New York: Dell Publishing Co., 1961.

Tarter, R. E.: The causes of alcoholism: A biopsychological analysis. In Gottheil, E., et. al. (Eds.): *Etiologic Aspects of Alcohol and Drug Abuse.* Springfield: Thomas, 1983.

Truax, C. B., and Carkhuff, R. R.: *Toward Effective Counseling and Psychotherapy: Training and Practice.* Chicago: Aldine, 1967.

Wallerstein, R. S.: Comparative study of treatment methods for chronic alcoholism: The alcoholism research project at winter VA hospital. *Am. J. Psychiat.*, 1956, *113*, pp. 228–233.

Wallerstein, R. S.: *Hospital Treatment of Alcoholism: A Comparative Experimental Study.* Menninger Clinic Monograph Series No. 11. New York: Basic Books, Inc., 1957.

Wallgreen, H. and Barry, H.: *Actions of Alcohol. Vol. II.* Amsterdam: Elsevier, 1970.

Wegscheider, S.: *Another Chance: Hope and Health for the Alcoholic Family.* Palo Alto: Science and Behavior Books, Inc., 1981.

Wellman, L. E., and Evans, J. H.: Applied social learning theory. In Forrest, G. G.: *The Diagnosis and Treatment of Alcoholism.* Springfield: Thomas, 1978.

Williams, R. J.: *Nutrition and Alcoholism.* Norman: University of Oklahoma Press, 1951.

Wilsnack, S. C.: Femininity by the bottle. *Psychology Today*, pp. 39–43, Apr. 1973.

Wilsnack, S. C.: Women and alcohol. Lecture, Psychotherapy Associates, P.C.

Eighth Annual Advanced Winter Workshop, Treatment and Rehabilitation of the Alcoholic, Colorado Springs, CO, Feb. 2, 1982.

Wilsnack, S. C.: Women and alcohol: Research and treatment. Lecture, Psychotherapy Associates, P.C. Tenth Annual Advanced Winter Workshop, *Treatment and Rehabilitation of the Alcoholic*, Colorado Springs, CO, Feb. 8, 1984.

Winokur, G., Reik, T., Rimmer, J., et al.: Alcoholism: III. Diagnosis and familial psychiatric illness in 259 alcoholic programs. *Arch. Gen. Psychiat.*, 1970, 23:104–111.

Wolpe, J.: *The Practice of Behavior Therapy*. Englewood Cliffs: Prentice Hall, 1969.

Yalom, I. D.: *The Theory and Practice of Group Psychotherapy*. New York: Basic Books, Inc., 2nd Ed. 1975.

Yost, K., and Mines, R. E.: Stress and Alcoholism. In Bratter, T. E., and Forrest, G. G. (Eds.) *Current Management of Substance Abuse and Alcoholism*. New York: The Free Press, 1984.

Zimberg, S. *The Clinical Management of Alcoholism*. New York: Brunner/Mazel, Inc., 1982.

NAME INDEX

SUBJECT INDEX

A

Abstinence
  addiction focus and, 111–112
  as goal, 49
  dream interpretation and, 149
  in men, 173
  recovery and, 169, 170, 190
  reinforcement of, 51
  role of, 175
  termination and, 156
Acting out
  intimacy and, 180–181
  purpose of, 17–18
  resolution of, 77
  sexual pathology and, 103
Addiction
  reinforcement of
    affective conflicts in, 143
Addiction focus
  abstinence and, 111–112
  initiation of, 68–71
  maintenance of, 111–114, 123, 163, 166–167
  orientation of, 89
  transcendence of, 112
Adjustment
  work and, 183
Adolescence
  reconstruction of, 60–61
Adolescent(s)
  addiction of
    speed of, 4
    drinking style of, 21
    modeling for, 21
Affect
  focus on, 142
  pathology of
    modification of, 143
Affective disturbance

interpretation of, 76
AIN (see Alcoholic interpersonal network)
Al-Anon
  as psychotherapy component, 50
Alcohol (see also Ethanol)
  effect on brain, 7
  obsession with, 19
  psychological dependence on, 4–5
  withdrawal from
    symptoms of, 4
Alcohol abuse
  definition of (DSM–II), 35
Alcohol addiction
  definition of (DSM–II), 35
Alcoholic
  as social change agent, 184
  anxiety of, 13
  avoidance defense system of
    development of, 13–14
  behavioral traits of, 8
  characteristics of, 3–4, 17–18, 40, 93, 94
  cognitive set of
    disturbance in, 176–177
  dependency of, 15
  depression in, 31–32, 40
  early life experience of
    exploration of, 59–60
  family of
    pattern of, 20
    reactions of, 28
  misdiagnosis of, 30
  oral fixation of, 14–15
  parents of, 20–13
  sexual pathology of, 13, 102
  thought process of, 176
  work problems of, 182, 183
Alcoholic interpersonal network (AIN)
  description of, 21–22
Alcoholics Anonymous

ABOUT THE AUTHOR

Gary G. Forrest, Ed.D., Ph.D., is a clinical psychologist practicing in Colorado Springs, Colorado. He is Executive Director of Psychotherapy Associates, P.C., and the Institute for Addictive Behavioral Change. Involved in the treatment of alcoholics, substance abusers, and their families for over twenty-five years, Dr. Forrest's many books on addiction include *Alcoholism and Human Sexuality*, *Chemical Dependency and Antisocial Personality Disorder: Psychotherapy and Assessment Strategies*, and the forthcoming *Countertransference in Chemical Dependency Counseling*.